The New Joy of Photography

The New Joy of Photography

By the Editors of Eastman Kodak Company

Marianne Richards

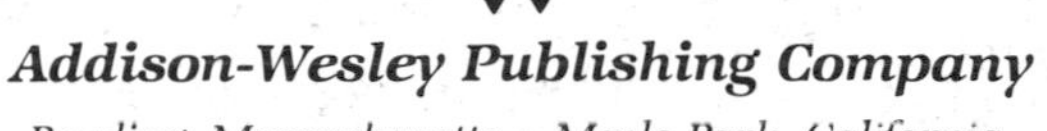

Addison-Wesley Publishing Company

Reading, Massachusetts • Menlo Park, California
Don Mills, Ontario • Wokingham, England • Amsterdam
Sydney • Singapore • Tokyo • Madrid • Bogotá
Santiago • San Juan

The New Joy of Photography Staff

Eastman Kodak Company

Martin L. Taylor	*Editor, Original and Revised Edition*
Keith A. Boas	*Editorial Supervisor*
Paul F. Mulroney	*Supervisor, Commercial Publications*
Jacklyn R. Salitan	*Project Coordinator*
Jeffrey J. Pollock	*Director, Joint Publishing Ventures*
Jean Leavy-Ells	*Editorial*
Charles W. Styles	*Production Supervisor*
Annette L. Dufek	*Production Coordinator*

Addison-Wesley Publishing Company

Cyrisse Jaffee	*Editor*
Doe Coover	*Editor-in-Chief*
Bernard Quint	*Designer, Original Edition*
Kenneth J. Wilson	*Designer, Revised Edition*
Donald Earnest	*Writer, Original Edition*
Russell Hart	*Writer, Revised Edition*
James Danzinger	*Writer, "The Personal Style of Annie Leibovitz"*
Theresa Burns	*Writer, "The Personal Style of Eliot Porter"*
Amy Bedik	*Photo Researcher*
Perry McIntosh	*Production Supervisor*
Barbara Wood	*Production/Operations Manager*
Ann DeLacey	*Manufacturing*

ISBN 0-201-11693-6 (hardcover)
0-201-11692-8 (paperback)
BCDEFGHIJ-KR-89876
Second printing, May 1986

Library of Congress Cataloging-in-Publication Data
Main entry under title:
The New joy of photography.

Updated ed. of: The joy of photography. c1979.
Bibliography: p.
Includes index.
1. Photography. I. Eastman Kodak Company.
II. Joy of photography.
TR146.N5 1985 770 85-11212
ISBN 0-201-11693-6
ISBN 0-201-11692-8 (pbk.)
Cover spectrum by J. Lanman, Photographer
Cover design by WGBH Design
Set in 10 point Zapf International by DEKR Corporation

Contents

Part I

The Vision

Part II

The Tools

Part III

The Image

Part IV

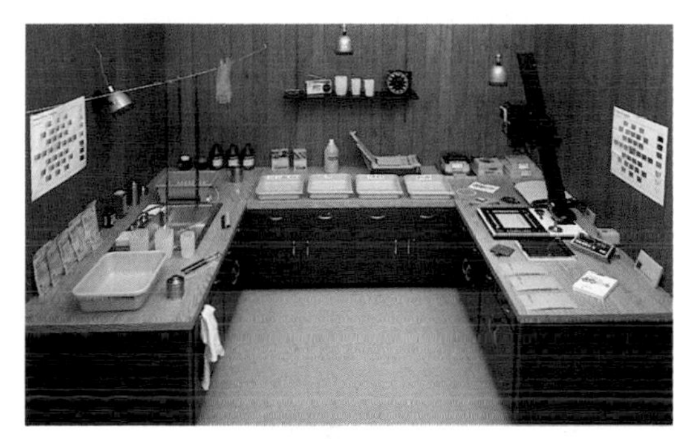

The Process

Part V

The Joy

The New Joy of Photography

Introduction

Taking pictures today is easier than ever. New technology in cameras and film has made fine picture-taking a possibility for nearly everyone. Yet photographers of all ages and of all levels of experience still share the aspiration of photographers from decades past: to learn to take better pictures. Even as we become accustomed to the ease of using fully automated cameras, we remain eager to improve our skills and develop new techniques for self-expression through photography.

With a steady hand, some imagination, and an eye for the distinctive, anyone can develop a personal style of photography. It matters less what kind of camera you use than how keen your interest and motivation are. Whether you take pictures to satisfy the artist within you or to preserve the memories of special people and times, ***The New Joy of Photography*** is designed to help you improve those results.

In Part I, "The Vision," we discuss the visual elements that create a photograph—line, shape, pattern, texture, and form—and some basic techniques of composition. We also examine the properties of light, for, like the painter's oils, light is the photographer's medium. Special portfolios by Harry Callahan, Annie Leibovitz, and Eliot Porter illustrate the very different and distinctive personal styles of three of today's greatest photographers.

In Part II, "The Tools," we present basic information on how to operate a camera and describe the wide array of equipment available to photographers: lenses, filters, flash attachments, tripods, and other accessories. In this section you'll learn especially how to use today's fully automatic cameras to their best advantage and how to solve some of the most common photographic problems.

Part III, "The Image," is designed to provide you with the tools and techniques for the specific kinds of pictures you take, whether they are pictures of people, landscapes, wildlife, sports, architecture, or still-life arrangements.

Part IV, "The Process," offers the latest information and step-by-step instructions for many darkroom procedures, for both black-and-white and color film, as well as tips on several imaginative darkroom techniques. And in Part V, "The Joy," you'll learn how to make the most of your pictures—how to care for them, how to mount and display them, and how to use them for a variety of purposes.

Since the first edition of ***The Joy of Photography*** was published in 1979, over one million copies have been used by photographers around the world. Our aim in that book, as it is in this one, was to instruct and inspire, to instill confidence in any photographer. We hope you will find useful the information and images that follow; and we hope that they will open your eyes to the exciting possibilities photography offers. Most of all, we hope that ***The New Joy of Photography*** will help you see and take better pictures.

Franco Fontana/The Image Bank

Part I

The Vision

The joy of photography is learning to see

. . . to reflect and respond

Taking photographs can be richly rewarding. Whether it captures a memorable moment or experiments with abstract concepts, a photograph allows you to express your personal vision of the world. And no matter the subject, technique, or composition, implicit in its visual impact is an emotional truth.

The process of taking a photograph is interactive, a source of challenge, discovery, and revelation. The final result maintains this momentum: The photograph communicates something about the photographer's perception and elicits a response—unexpected or deliberate—from the viewer. This sense of dialogue is in itself an inspiration. We derive great pleasure in photographs that cause us to pause and ponder or rush us headlong into the experiential moment.

As with any language, photography has a vocabulary that must be learned before you can fully express an idea. Just as a child learns to speak, you have to experiment with this vocabulary to master it. You can do this by viewing a wide range of photographs and by taking pictures frequently, re-assessing your expectations with your results.

The New Joy of Photography will help you become visually articulate, the first step toward achieving a personal vision in photography.

A photograph conveys mood. Below, the tranquility of a lazy summer day is suggested by a boy and his dog drifting in an inner tube, while the great swell of waves, at right, evinces the power and turbulence of natural forces.

Neil Montanus

Ray Atkeson

. . . to expect the unexpected

Arthur Twomey

To take effective pictures, you need to train yourself to see the world as the camera does. The camera doesn't have your powers of selective observation; it won't ignore cluttered backgrounds or foregrounds, or portray both a broad view and details in sharp focus at the same time. It can compensate for differences in the intensity of light only in a limited way. And even the most sensitive film doesn't have the extraordinary sensitivity of your eyes. Most important, while you see in three dimensions, your camera can create only a flat, two-dimensional image of a subject.

This section of the book is designed to help you "see" photographically. First we will identify the several basic elements that make up a photographic image—shapes, lines, patterns, and textures—and analyze how

The visual surprise of an unexpected angle is the key to many good pictures. By climbing down into a deep crevice in a rocky southwestern desert the photographer obtained this shot of a jagged fragment of vivid blue sky. The young man glimpsed on the overhanging ledge emphasizes the enormous size of the fissure.

Dr. Erich Salomon © Peter Hunter, The Hague

each affects our perception of a picture. Then we will discuss the means by which these elements can be orchestrated to express the mood or concept you want to communicate. Finally, because light is what creates the image your film records, we will consider its qualities—intensity, direction, color, and character—as well as its daily and seasonal changes.

The basic mechanics of photography are easy to learn and, with practice, will become second nature to you. Although a good part of this book is devoted to mechanics—because technical expertise is important—imaginative "seeing" is what separates the inspired photographer from the merely competent one. Developing an eye for good photographs begins with simple observation of the things around you: the way the light plays off a curtain, the shape of a rock, or a baby's yawn. Study the familiar and ordinary things you take for granted, and you will be surprised at what they reveal to you. Edward Steichen, one of photography's prime movers, took hundreds of pictures of a shadblow tree near his house in Connecticut over a fifteen-year period. "Each time I look at those pictures," he said, "I find something new there. Each time I get closer to what I want to say about that tree."

Beginning photographers especially need to remember that seemingly unremarkable subjects can make remarkable photographs. Most important is simply being alert and continually ready to respond to people, events, and places, as Erich Salomon was for his famous photograph, "Briand's Surprise" shown above.

The best photographers are alert as well as unflappable. Pioneer photojournalist Erich Salomon, who used an early miniature camera to get candid shots of Europe's top statesmen, was caught in the act when he tried to photograph the French premier with a group of his cabinet ministers at a banquet in 1931. Even as his presence was discovered, the photographer was quick enough to capture his subjects' good-natured reaction.

. . . to develop a personal style

Isaac Bashevis Singer

©Jill Krementz

© Jill Krementz

Kurt Vonnegut, Jr.

As you take more and more pictures, you will find yourself drawn to certain kinds of subject matter and approaches. Eventually, your photographs will become recognizably your own. The development of a distinctive personal style is necessarily a process of self-discovery.

The portraits of Kurt Vonnegut, Jr. and Isaac Bashevis Singer on these pages are the work of Jill Krementz. A photographer who considers herself as much a photojournalist as a portrait photographer, Krementz is well known for her relaxed, revealing photographs of writers. She almost always photographs people in their homes or other surroundings where they feel comfortable. The result of this approach is an appealing intimacy and immediacy that enhances our understanding of the artist.

Although Krementz's photographs often include objects that symbolize the writer's craft, such as books, manuscript, or typewriter, she also utilizes settings that reflect an artist's style or personality. In this informal portrait of Kurt Vonnegut, Jr. on a Central Park outing with his daughter, his attire—and mode of transportation—is suggestive of the whimsical feeling of his work. The picture's candid quality is in sharp contrast to the portrait of Isaac Bashevis Singer, whose intense gaze establishes a serious, formal tone and whose lowered head suggests both modesty and intellect. Both of these portraits are excellent examples of Krementz's distinctive vision and her photographic style, in which provocative portraits capture the essence of their subject.

Learning to trust your instincts and to experiment with new techniques and unusual perspectives is what creating a personal style of photography is all about. And when it all comes together—when the shutter clicks and you know it's right—that is the joy of photography.

Capture the decisive moment

While we see human and natural events as a continuum of time and space, the camera can preserve only an instant in those events. In that moment everything exists in a unique physical relationship to everything else, and moving things—people, animals, machines—are recorded at one precise stage of their continuous motion. But what is an essential limitation of still photography is also one of its greatest challenges: to make that instant convey the dynamic of motion and emotion inherent in the experience. A photograph of a high jumper or a child's eager wave taken a split second too early or too late will fail to express the essence of that tremendous effort. The disappointment of such missed shots is all too familiar to many of us.

In photographing a world constantly in flux you must also think about the relationships between its parts, moving and static. Just as you need to recognize the instant at which a subject in motion is most expressive, you should also be able to see when it relates to its surroundings in the most meaningful way. Perhaps the photographer who has most consistently managed to do both is Henri Cartier-Bresson. He has described his approach as one that seeks to identify the "decisive moment" in any scene of human endeavor: that fraction of a second in which all elements work together harmoniously to express the event in the best way. In the picture at far right, for example, he has frozen the futile efforts of a puddle jumper at the instant before his failure. In so doing he has evoked an almost physical sensation in us, an urge to see the action completed. But on another level, the shapes and tones in the image exist in a perfect and eternal balance.

Many of Cartier-Bresson's pictures address at the same time the emotional aspect of an event, such as in the picture at immediate right of a young boy impressed with the importance of his mission. We don't need to know the boy either to figure out what he is doing or to sense what he is feeling. This universal understanding makes the image both endearing and memorable. Even photographs that depict quieter subjects and attitudes—contemplative, peaceful, somber—have an implied rhythm, and thus their own "decisive moment."

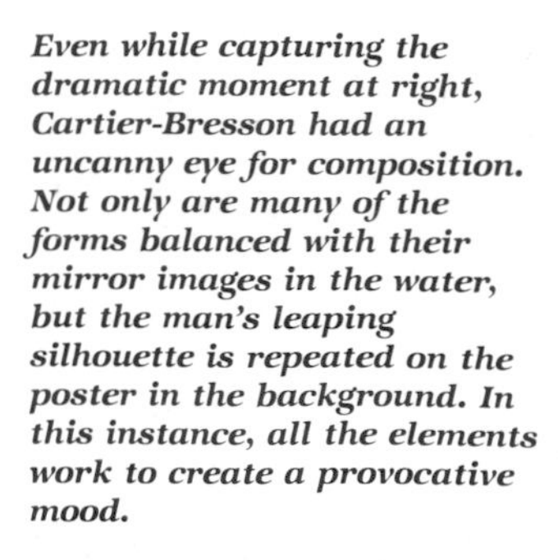

Even while capturing the dramatic moment at right, Cartier-Bresson had an uncanny eye for composition. Not only are many of the forms balanced with their mirror images in the water, but the man's leaping silhouette is repeated on the poster in the background. In this instance, all the elements work to create a provocative mood.

The "decisive moment" is not always one of intense, dynamic action. Rather, it may be a fleeting facial expression or a revealing interaction, as Henri Cartier-Bresson demonstrates in this shot of a self-satisfied young boy on a Sunday morning errand.

Henri Cartier-Bresson

Henri Cartier-Bresson

Record movement . . . freeze action

Robert Kretzer

The blurred streaks of color in this photo of a little girl swinging simulate our own experience of motion, which is as much a physical sensation as it is an observed thing. The picture was made by panning —following a moving subject with the camera, a technique that is explained on page 186.

Steven Carras

In this image, the dynamic grace of a ballerina is depicted at the peak of a leap. The vigorous movement of some subjects is best expressed by freezing them at such moments.

. . . and show the serenity of endless time

Paul J. Goldman

The dramatically lighted profiles of an elderly woman and her grandchild are evocative of the changing human seasons, the cycle of life. Both are gazing into the distance—the woman perhaps contemplating the past while the child peers toward the future.

A rowboat mirrored on a perfectly placid lake is a strikingly beautiful image, as well as a visual representation of the constancy and serenity of the natural world.

Janet Tait

Identify shapes

The basic outline of an object—whether the gnarled limbs of a silhouetted tree or the gentle curve of a leaf—usually has the greatest initial impact on a viewer. We recognize familiar forms in a picture before we pause to appreciate more subtle qualities, such as textures or patterns. The good photographer understands this and develops an instinctive eye for the juxtaposition of unusual or striking shapes.

A useful technique for dramatizing the shape of an object is to isolate your subject, moving close to crop it tightly, thus eliminating extraneous details. A change in camera angle can have the same effect. In either case, the result will often be a photograph that is striking in its simplicity. Keeping alert to likely sources for such shapes—in nature, urban settings, and still lifes—will help you perceive new opportunities for interesting photos.

In more complex compositions, shapes are basic building blocks. They can echo each other's form or be played against one another to create balance, patterns, or tension. Shapes can bring a touch of surprise or mystery to an image, as when a subject is portrayed from an unexpected angle or only a tantalizing segment of an unknown object is revealed.

Sometimes shapes will be obvious, as in the picture of trees on the facing page, but others will be hidden within a larger framework, as are the ornamental windows in the building facade to the right. Capturing the unconventional or unexpected image is often a photographer's delight.

Martin L. Taylor

In photographing shapes, sometimes a part is more powerful than the whole. In the composition of leaves above, no single leaf is shown in its entirety.

The rich monochromatic brown of the building façade at right concentrates our attention on the highlights and shadows that describe each window. When shapes such as these are repeated, a pattern emerges.

Jules Zalon/The Image Bank

Dick Durrance/Woodfin Camp

In this picture of trees, the strong, twisted contours of the trunks are effectively offset by the lacy filigree of the smaller branches. Look for such contrasting shapes and textures.

Notice lines of direction and distance

Lines are avenues for the eyes. They show direction and distance; they describe the edges of shapes and define boundaries. They can also convey the impression of action or force. Lines are very important in photography because they can lead the viewer's eye to the center of interest in your pictures.

Photographers often use lines to create a sense of depth in an otherwise flat, two-dimensional surface. This impression of depth is strongest when parallel lines recede toward a point on the horizon. These lines do more than create a sense of perspective. They lure the viewer toward that faraway point, and generally an object that appears at or near that juncture will be perceived as important. Sometimes, however, a variety of lines within an image will create interesting designs and optical patterns. In the photograph of the Brighton Beach boardwalk, opposite, the image succeeds not so much because it directs the eye toward the distance, but because, unexpectedly, it does not. The startling intersection of lines and angles—vertical, slanted, horizontal—contained in the planks, railing, and figure suggests a connected busyness underscoring the loneliness of the scene.

Lines also serve to define surfaces, both flat and irregular, as in the picture of the canyon at top right. Keep in mind that lines can be strong and hard-edged, or they can be gentle and delicately defined, as they are in the rows of heather at right.

In a composition with several elements, lines can direct our eyes from one form to another or provide a visual connection between objects that would otherwise seem unrelated. Lines can also define the direction of a force or action. In the picture of the tug-of-war on page 20, the strong diagonal stance of the participants intersects the straight horizontal of the rope, forming a visual arrow.

John Blaustein/Woodfin Camp

Because the light in the photograph above is soft and shadowless, the lines formed by the erosion of sedimentary rock are particularly important in describing the canyon's undulating surfaces.

Sébastien Marmounier

Standing out against the muted purple of a field of heather, the narrow, receding line of ochre-colored earth between rows creates a sense of depth in this image. The bright yellow wedge of the field behind the trees reinforces the perspective.

© N. Jay Jaffee

The soft sheen of the rain-varnished boardwalk in the photograph at left makes its lines stand out forcefully. The lone figure is an effective human counterpoint to its striking geometry.

Emphasize lines of action and force

In this picture of polo players, the photographer has suggested movement by using a slow shutter speed to blur it. Faster moving parts, such as the horses' feet, are more blurred and thus indicate the direction of movement. The powerful lines created by the horses' and riders' legs enhance the impression of forceful motion.

Michael O'Brien/Archive Pictures, Inc.

The repeated diagonal figures of the boys engaged in this tug-of-war, and the taut horizontality of the rope, give us a visceral sensation of the tremendous stress on the rope.

Jodi Cobb/Woodfin Camp

In the exuberant scene at right, the photographer has frozen motion to convey a sense of its direction. The dramatic gap in the line formed by the swinging rope and the boy's arm tells us that he is airborne, and his bent knee points the way.

Peter Miller/The Image Bank

Find rhythm in patterns

When similar shapes, lines, or colors are repeated at more or less regular intervals, they create patterns. An abundance of these patterns, both natural and man-made, surrounds us—cars in a parking lot, people lined up for a movie, a row of pine trees. You can use these repeating forms to imbue a photograph with a sense of orderliness and harmony that is as pleasing to the eye as a melodious refrain is to the ear.

At the same time, the rhythmic effect of pattern can convey deeper feelings about the subjects in a picture. The pattern formed by the oars of the racing shell at far right eloquently expresses the repetitive rhythm of rowing. In the orderly line of guardsmen above, we sense the discipline inherent in ceremonial precision.

Because patterns are strong visual forces that give harmony and unity to a picture, even the merest suggestion of a pattern can be eye-catching. This is especially true when the elements come together by chance, as in the motorcycle race pictured at lower right. The visual rhythm is more random here, but the arrangement of yellow jerseys imposes pattern on an otherwise cluttered scene.

On the other hand, in pronounced and almost perfect patterns, the eye is invariably drawn to any disruption in the rhythm of recurring forms. In the shot of the guardsmen, for example, the group leader stands out because of his slightly forward position and his open mouth. As with other visual elements, you can learn to use patterns by first isolating them and then experimenting with their many possibilities.

Gary Whelpley

Ozzie Sweet

Robert McManis

In the overhead shot of a rowing crew at right, the dominant pattern created by the oars is echoed by the splashes they have left behind and by the bright red oar tips and the crewmen's tops.

A straight-on frontal view of Canadian guardsmen stepping a precise slow march forms a striking pattern. Every element of their ceremonial regalia, from beaver helmets to brass buckles, is repeated down the line. By judiciously cropping the top and bottom of the picture, the photographer further emphasized the photo's horizontal design.

Shapes need not be all the same size or color to suggest a pattern. Backlighted by the low winter sun and all tacking at the same angle, these iceboats—and their faint reflections in the frozen lake surface—are just different enough in size and sail to create a sense of depth. The width of the lake itself is emphasized by the tiny sail in the background at center.

It is recurring bright yellow jerseys rather than the motorcyclists themselves that bring order to this chaotic shot of a dusty off-road race. The yellow stands out because it is the predominating hue, contrasted only by an occasional red or blue jersey.

Peter Gales

Recognize the texture of form

Texture adds a strong sense of realism to photographs because it appeals directly to our sense of touch. It tells us about the nature of a subject, whether it be the smooth surface of old paint interrupted by coarse cracks, or the fine hairs on a cat's head.

The same light that reveals the form of an object also conveys its texture, giving us a sense of its three-dimensionality. In imparting this impression of substance, texture helps us sense an object's weight and bulk, as well as its softness or hardness. And on a purely two-dimensional level, texture makes a photograph visually more active, stimulating the viewer's eye.

Strong light raking obliquely across an object accentuates its surface characteristics in sharper detail than any other source of illumination, and it is especially effective in black-and-white shots because they depend entirely on tonal changes to suggest texture and form. In color photographs, subtle shadings of surface hue are often more effectively portrayed by soft, even lighting.

Texture, although usually best shown in close-ups, can also be a strong feature of a more distant shot. In the photograph of neatly planted fields on pages 28 and 29, for example, distance makes individual plants blend into a soft, bushy texture.

N. Jay Jaffee

Although we normally think of a cat as soft and warm, the textural details displayed by strong sidelighting here give a surprising sense of sharp, bristly whiskers, ears, and fur. Yet the direct gaze of the cat retains our notion of feline allure; the contradiction of texture and expectations gives strength to the image.

In this close-up, soft light enhances the delicate curl and subdued colors of cracked and peeling paint. Although the actual subject of the photograph may not be immediately apparent, these textural qualities are impressive because they are shown in detail, leaving the larger (and perhaps less appealing) surface to the imagination.

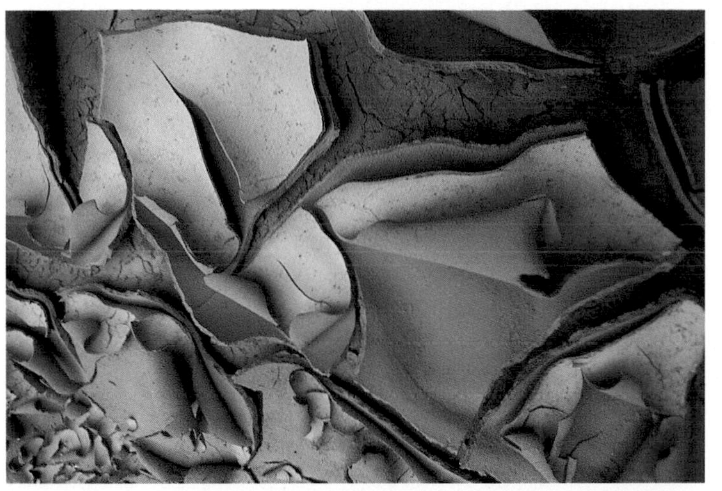

Ernest Braun/The Image Bank

Sebastien Marmounier

Textural differences add interest to the repeated fanlike form of the heather. The pattern and mirrored color scheme, made up of individual green and purple plants, make an appealing design that gives a sense of rounded fullness, punctuated by the bright orange of a single butterfly.

Marc Romanelli/The Image Bank

In this study of abandoned machinery, the warm, raking light of late afternoon augments an old gear's rusty hues and makes its pitted texture more pronounced.

Get a feeling for size and space

In addition to increasing the sense of distance between statue and temple, the wide-angle lens has exaggerated the size of the head, creating an unexpected disparity in scale between foreground and background. The fog and cool light add to the mystery.

Ansel Adams

In this unusual photograph by Ansel Adams, the combination of a downward-looking perspective and a flat, distant background tends to de-emphasize the scale of the rocky pinnacle. But by including a fragment of the adjacent sheer cliff, and silhouetting the climbers' figures against a hazy background, Adams has restored its massive proportions.

In daily life we rarely feel compelled to stop and judge the size of an object unless it is far away, unfamiliar, or seen from a puzzling perspective. But in a photographic composition, which presents a flat version of reality, one of the first things we look for is a guideline that helps us establish the size and proportion of the objects in a scene.

The enormous size of the rocky projection at left is clear only because we recognize the tiny figures as climbers and their scale is familiar to us. Any object of known size can have this effect, but human figures are particularly compelling when juxtaposed with massive natural or man-made shapes because we identify with their vulnerability.

On the other hand, size and space may be creatively distorted, as in the photograph at right of the remains of a temple. By choosing a low angle of view and getting as close as possible to the statue, the photographer has made the head predominate, reinforcing the scene's ethereal quality.

© Brian Blake/Photo Researchers, Inc.

Shape . . .
Line . . .
Pattern . . .
Texture . . .
Scale . . .
Form . . .

Many of the visual elements we have discussed are present in this subtle study of French farmland. The rectangular patchwork of planted fields forms a familiar pattern, but the shapes of the individual sections are given rounded contours by the gentle upward slope of the land. The intersection of the rows of plants by stronger horizontal lines gives the image a structure that strengthens its soft light and muted color scheme. And the light and long-distance perspective of the image combine to give the plants an unexpectedly soft, brushy texture.

Alain Courtois

Arrange and compose pictures

Ronnie Kennedy

A lighthouse and the sun against a darkening red sky are all the elements needed to convey the mood of an ocean sunset. At the same time, the long linear shape of the light tower contrasts nicely with the sun's roundness.

When isolated and highlighted, each of the visual elements—shape, line, pattern, and texture—can become the subject of an exceptional photograph. However, most photographs depend on many or all of these elements in varying proportions.

As a photographer, you want to use these elements knowledgeably to structure your picture in a meaningful way—one that conveys a mood or shares an insight with the viewer. This presents a problem: Unlike a painter, you cannot pick and choose freely, eliminating one object, shifting the position of another, or changing the color of a third. Still, you have a great deal more flexibility in creating the arrangement than you may think. You can move closer or farther away, shift to one side or another, raise or lower the camera, tilt it up or down, or turn it vertically or horizontally. And, as you'll see in Part II, you can change emphasis dramatically by choice of shutter speed, aperture, lens, film, filter, and lighting.

How you use these options to organize a picture will depend on what you want to say and the visual connections you want to make. There are no hard-and-fast rules for composition. But there are some general guidelines that a photographer should consider.

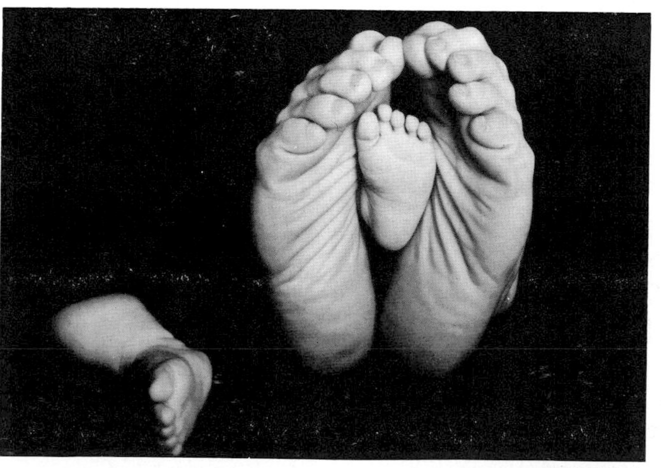

Craig Stewart

As a composition, the playful contrast of adult and infant feet at left owes its strong visual impact to the fact that the feet are isolated against a dark background. Had the photographer tried to simplify the image by photographing only the main grouping, the entire character of the picture would have been radically altered. Instead of imparting a playful quality, it would have become a cool, symmetrical puzzler that would leave the viewer wondering about the missing foot.

Ernst Haas

To compose the idyllic scene above, master color photographer Ernst Haas selected a vantage point that allowed him to emphasize its quiet, pastoral quality. He is able to keep all the elements small and in harmonious balance without sacrificing the unexpected visual delight of the two women who have paused to observe the scene.

Your goal is to create a photograph that will effectively convey your subject, theme, or idea. Composition is a deliberate effort. You need to analyze all of the elements in a scene, then arrange them for the effect that you want to achieve. Sometimes just one element will be sufficient to carry your idea. Simplification can produce powerful images, such as the lighthouse in sunset at left. Other times you may need several elements to tell your story. You may want a balanced, harmonious picture, or you may choose to convey a feeling of precariousness or stridency.

Often the main subject of your photograph will dominate and be supported by other elements and details. The viewer's eye is first drawn to your main image and then led around the frame. The dominance need not come from sheer physical size. In the Ernst Haas picture above, the two brightly clad women, while no larger than other shapes in the photograph, capture our interest because of their position and their colorful clothing.

. . . to create balance . . . and imbalance

It might seem that the most harmonious and appealing image would be symmetrical—the main subject in the center of a picture and other elements distributed around it evenly. But such compositions usually strike us as static because they lack two qualities that often elicit a viewer's interest—tension and movement. In a successful photograph, a more dynamic kind of balance often prevails: bright primary colors offset by more muted hues; dark masses contrasting with lighter-toned areas; or intricately detailed objects against spacious, empty surroundings, such as in the snow scene on the facing page.

There are no absolute rules about how to position different elements in the overall scene. Experimenting with both centered and off-center approaches will allow you the freedom to interpret a scene in different ways. By placing a prominent object to one side, for instance, you may evoke a very different mood or message than by having the main subject squarely in the center. You should take into consideration whether or not your intent is to narrate or describe a scene or, by including an unexpected element, to provide a different interpretation. You may reveal humor or pathos in an otherwise predictable picture.

Consider yourself a designer, and in designing your image remember that the format itself—horizontal, vertical or even square—can also change the impact. Subjects that you might reflexively shoot as horizontals, such as landscapes or everyday scenes, may be more exciting as verticals, and vice versa.

Try not to have a preconceived notion of how best to represent your subject. As you peer through the viewfinder, keep in mind how various elements—the subject, lighting, patterns and shapes—will interplay in the final result.

Glen San Lwin

Almost perfect symmetry is the most striking feature of the above shot of a barn with whimsically human features. In addition to the pleasing arrangement of windows and doors, accented by their bright color, the silhouette of the horses, standing slightly to the left, lends a touch of surprise to the placid mood.

Derek Doeffinger

This picture of a crane on a wharfpost has a daring simplicity. The placement of the bird and post close to the left-hand edge of the image leaves room for the sun and its golden wake, giving them an importance almost equal to the silhouette. Its asymmetry also lends a certain drama to an otherwise tranquil scene.

Shinzo Maeda/The Image Bank

In this Japanese snow scene, the sky occupies fully two-thirds of the image, and the normal tonal relationship between sky and earth is reversed. The reduction of foreground and minimal texture in the snow-covered hills flatten the image and enhance the delicate tracery of the plants and tree. In addition, the small tree starkly outlined against the white expanse of snow helps contain the larger landscape and makes the image more compelling.

Choose the best viewpoint

A simple change in your camera viewpoint can have a powerful effect on the mood and visual impact of your pictures. The same scene can appear radically different depending on whether you shoot it from above, below, or at eye level. Climb a few stairs or find an upper-story window for downward shots, or squat or even lie on the ground to angle your camera upward.

An eye-level angle, since it is the way we usually look at the world, conveys realism—the everyday appearance of a scene. When people or objects are photographed from below, however, they appear to tower over the viewer and are infused with power and dominance. Shot from above, the organization of elements in the picture becomes clearer, as in the crowd scene at lower right. This treatment can also diminish the scale of a subject.

In open landscapes, the moods evoked by shifts in angle can be dramatic. When a scene is shot from a low angle, the horizon in the picture moves downward, revealing an expanse of sky and emphasizing the spaciousness of the landscape. From a high angle, if you aim the camera down, the horizon appears near the top of the scene and the land seems to stretch away endlessly.

In deciding when to depart from a customary point of view, remember that both high and low angles are a way of including more of a subject than a straight-on, eye-level picture will permit. Sometimes this can be a very practical solution to photographing in limited space. Both high and low angles are also useful in simplifying a composition. By shooting upward, you can isolate a subject against the sky or a plain wall and eliminate foreground detail. By shooting downward, you may be able to eliminate a cluttered background.

Sébastien Marmounier

Lawrence Fried/The Image Bank

Herb Jones

This dreamy eye-level view of a fogbound lake is so compelling that it needs no embellishment.

The gargoyle framing this view of Paris from Notre Dame has two functions. As a reference point that helps locate and define the picture, its presence in the foreground provides depth and perspective. And as an expressive, if inanimate observer, it comments on the expansiveness of the view and makes us wonder about the centuries of change it may have witnessed.

An eye-level picture of a crowd usually can portray only a small portion of such a scene. But a high vantage point separates the figures and suggests its size, as in the photo at left of a gathering in Russia.

The low angle of view in the picture at right emphasizes the massiveness of the building's columns and gives the statue of George Washington a heroic scale in keeping with its subject.

Lou Jawitz/The Image Bank

. . . the most effective angles

City windows have long been the object of photographers' fascination. In this picture, an oblique side angle turns the window into a mirror, elegantly contained by the sweeping curve of its frame.

© N. Jay Jaffee

Eric E. Erickson

The steep downward angle in this picture of a little girl reinforces her diminutive stature and, by concentrating on her face, calls attention to her slightly bemused expression.

Robert Frereck/Woodfin Camp

The surging perspective in this picture of California redwoods, achieved by pointing a wide-angle lens almost straight up, powerfully describes their grandeur. The way the trees seem to disappear into the clouds also suggests their Olympian dimensions.

Strengthen by framing and cropping

To draw the viewer's attention to the main subject, photographers sometimes rely on a simple compositional device known as framing. Positioned around the subject, trees, a window, or even a rocky crevice can create a visual frame of sorts within the picture's physical frame. Framing is not only a highly effective means of directing the eye; it also serves to obscure unattractive foregrounds or other distracting details. At the same time, a framing device can create a sense of depth in a photograph and identify its setting.

Cropping an image in the darkroom (see page 280) is a more direct way to focus attention on the primary subject and to eliminate extraneous detail. But because the higher degree of enlargement often required can compromise the technical quality of your print, you should make an effort to compose your image as you would like it to appear.

The dramatic framing effect of a rock crevice makes this landscape stark and dramatic. It also directs our attention to the unexpected lone tree protruding triumphantly from the inhospitable clifftop.

Martin L. Taylor

Nathan Benn/Woodfin Camp

The grand natural arch formed by the stately trees sets off the façade of the mansion and evokes an antebellum feeling.

Charles Derek Paget-Clarke

Two pictures of the same subject illustrate the dramatic effect that framing and cropping techniques can have on the way an image is seen. Because it shows more of the exterior of the building, the photograph at left seems to be about nothing more than an elderly man sunning himself by a window. But because the image at right is more tightly cropped, we are invited inside, and our attention is directed to the man's expression. In this way we become more personally involved with the photograph.

Study the language of light

Light is the photographer's medium, just as oils are the medium of the painter. An artist must learn the properties of paint to bring ideas to life on canvas. Similarly, a photographer must understand the characteristics of light in order to create an effective photograph. Light creates the hues we see in a color photograph and the tones of a black-and-white one. Even the most subtle variations in the quantity, quality, color, and direction of light can greatly affect the emphasis and mood of a picture.

As you'll see, the most available source of light—the sun—affords countless opportunities to the alert photographer. The character of sunlight changes dramatically with the seasons, but even in the course of a day its quality can range from soft, misty luminescence to blinding midday brilliance to the oblique rosy rays of sunset. And at dusk, sunlight bounced off an evening sky creates a color scheme in which pastel shades have a stunning vibrancy.

But other light sources, from ordinary incandescent and fluorescent lights to the intense mercury vapor lamps of sports arenas or the neon signs that color city streets, can produce intriguing results.

By understanding light, you will be able to take advantage of its enormously varied forms and utilize the many technical options available for controlling it as described in Part II. Often this may simply be a matter of waiting for favorable conditions and making the proper exposure; other times it will involve creative or corrective filtration or the use of supplementary light sources; and sometimes even thoughtful composition will help you control its tonal play. As you perfect your technique, you will apply each of these and more.

The image at right of a stream cascading down a rocky palisade is as much about light as it is about rocks and water. The mist from the agitated water diffracts "white" sunlight into the full spectrum of its component colors—in other words, it makes a rainbow.

Timothy Eagan/Woodfin Camp

In this vividly impressionistic study of a nighttime street scene, red neon light is smeared across the wet pavement in painterly swatches. The photographer's use of a fairly long exposure to blur movement and soften edges, thus minimizing detail, gives the colors independence from content.

Gary Whelpley

Sense the mood of colors

Whether warm or cool, bright or subdued, riotous or somber, color often establishes the mood of a photograph. Although we frequently take color for granted—as a feature over which we have no control—it is possible to manipulate it by judicious choices of subject, considered composition, technical controls such as filtration, and most important, careful thought about lighting possibilities.

What we perceive to be the color of an object is a function of how it reflects and absorbs light. But light itself varies in color composition, depending on its source, and can have a pronounced effect on a subject's color. You may have noticed, for example, that a face seen in the harsh glare of fluorescent lighting looks pale, yet seems more ruddy or even-toned by daylight or under an incandescent bulb. And, of course, different atmospheric conditions change the color of daylight itself, and thus of things illuminated by it.

When we look at an object in different kinds of light, our brain automatically makes the necessary adjustments. If we know a building is white by day, we tend to see it as white even when it is rose-tinged at sundown or faintly blue in the failing light of dusk. Only by training our eyes to see such differences, as the camera does, can we compensate for them, or use them to produce a certain image or mood.

Good color photographs are rarely accidental. With careful technique, you can bring some colors to the fore and subdue or neutralize others. While there are no absolute rules regarding the use of color, generally, the photographs that please us most are those in which one color or a group of closely related hues predominates. This may take the form of a bright, primary-colored object against more neutral shades or softer hues that permeate the entire scene, like the blues in the moonlit scene at right.

Above, a gradient of cool blues is interrupted only by the luminescent moon and the fisherman's tiny presence.

The sky and water merge here, accentuating the serene emptiness of the scene.

In each of these exceptional outdoor scenes, photographer George Silk uses one prevailing color to create a mood. At left, a flock of geese is silhouetted against a blood-red dawn sky which merges so seamlessly with the ocean that waves could pass for clouds.

. . . the beauty of black and white

In a black-and-white photograph, light is recorded as a range of tones rather than colors. Although black-and white film is more sensitive to some colors than others, in general, the more light an object reflects, the lighter its tone will be in the final print. Tonalities in a black-and-white image must do double duty, suggesting both the substance and form of objects (a task largely carried out by hue in a color image) and the direction and character of light itself.

Any two-dimensional representation of reality such as a print is necessarily an interpretation, but because black-and-white photography can reduce a subject to pure tonal intensities, it has exceptional interpretive possibilities. This is both its strength and, if not properly addressed by the photographer, its weakness. A red sign, for example, may stand out brightly against a grey clapboard wall, but in a black-and-white photograph its tone may be almost the same. However, black-and-white technique —from exposure in the camera to manipulation in printing—allows the photographer to alter the normal tonal relationships of a subject to give more or less emphasis to its specific parts. And frequently, qualities that do not depend on color can be better portrayed in black-and-white: highlights and shadows, strong shapes, textures, and patterns. This ability to reduce the world to such basic elements is what has traditionally given black-and-white photography its reputation for powerful realism. Furthermore, because our understanding of perspective in a flat image is usually based on tonal gradations and linear cues, a black-and-white photograph often has more three-dimensionality than a color image.

A black-and-white image can also have a flat, strikingly graphic quality that color is rarely capable of, however. Many great photographers have exploited this characteristic, using it to abstract their subjects in new and interesting ways.

A good photographer, ironically, needs to cultivate two contradictory skills: patience and spontaneity. The great photographer Ansel Adams possessed both. Frequently he was willing to wait, even for days, until all the elements in a scene were just right. But here he had neither the time nor the luxury for deliberate planning or calculation. Instead, relying on his superb photographic instincts, he reacted quickly to capture the last vestiges of a setting sun, glimmering off the gravestones of a tiny New Mexican town. He also understood the importance of composition, as shown in the way the massive expanse of black sky creates a powerful sense of space and isolation.

. . . the intensity of tonal values

Russell Hart

In this image, the photographer has isolated the elegant shape of a boat's sunlit hull by filtering the sky to make it black. The slightly off-center composition and the tilt of the boat's prow save the picture from being too severe.

Although a color image may be soft or harsh in its range of brightnesses, you can't change the essential character of its values. A black-and-white image, on the other hand, can be made to have either a long scale of grey tones or an abrupt, limited range of dark and light values. To some extent, each subject and the negative it produces will determine which treatment is most appropriate, but there is still tremendous interpretive latitude in black-and-white technique.

For instance, one photographer may print a negative with a contrasty range of tones, opting for a strong, graphic effect, while another will print the same negative with a much fuller spectrum of greys. Or one may choose to make the tone of the sky darker than the other would. Individual taste will have a noticeable effect on the final print.

In assessing the light in your black-and-white subject, try to envision how the tones it produces will be rendered in a finished print. This ability to previsualize is particularly important in black-and-white photography. Both photographs shown here, for example, depend for their success on strong contrast between light and dark areas. But the image at right uses it to create an active, intensely busy effect, while the image above relies on broad areas of black, white, and deep grey to achieve its dramatic spareness.

The staccato play of brilliant light and deep shadow in the photograph at right has an almost noisy quality, and as such is a perfect visual metaphor for the auditory experience of being underneath an elevated train as it rumbles and screeches by.

Investigate the direction of light

The direction of light can have a profound effect on a subject's appearance. Principally, a subject can be front-, back-, or sidelighted, but the variations within and between these categories are limitless.

Frontlighting, in which the sun is behind you when you take a picture, provides the most even kind of direct illumination. Because it creates few shadows on the surface of your subject, though, an image produced by frontlighting tends to lack a sense of volume and depth. Hazy sunlight may soften this effect, but ordinarily it is useful only when you want to emphasize broad, flat shapes.

The illusion of three-dimensionality is more convincingly achieved when the subject is lighted primarily from one side. Indeed, for most photographs, whether portraits or landscapes, sidelighting is the most effective kind of illumination. Sidelighting renders surfaces in a more sculptural way than frontlighting, revealing both contours and texture. And at more extreme angles, it even can exaggerate texture and form.

Illumination from behind a subject, or backlighting, is tricky to use, but its effect is often dramatic. If the light is strong, the silhouette it produces can be a powerful simplifying device, as in the photograph of a man and his boat at upper right. If it is weak, or at more of an angle to the subject, its effect may be rimlighting, which highlights the edges of a shape. Rimlighting works best when balanced by reflected light filling in its shadowed front, as in Ernst Haas's fountain scene at far right.

Lighting from above, most commonly seen at midday when the sun is directly overhead, creates shadows that are generally unflattering to human subjects. This is true of most landscapes too, but the toplit scene on page 57 proves the exception.

Sébastien Marmounier

Backlighting simplifies this Venetian scene by silhouetting the man and his boat. Hazy illumination from a high sun softens the distant land mass, giving the foreground shapes importance. It also lends a sparkling texture to an otherwise flat water surface.

Martin L. Taylor

In this photograph of an industrious little girl, strong sidelight and a dark and out-of-focus background immediately draw our attention to her face. The character of the light adds visual drama to an otherwise commonplace scene.

In the photograph at right of a woman and children at a fountain, master photographer Ernst Haas has come in close to capture their gleeful, spontaneous expressions. The low sun behind the subjects causes rim lighting, which highlights the texture of their hair and adds sparkle to the photograph.

Ernst Haas

. . . soft and reflected

Barbara McCluskey

The pleasantly engaging expression of this woman feeding pigeons would have been consumed by shadows on a sunny day. In the softer light of an overcast sky, however, detail is preserved. Depending on the film you use, diffused light may require longer exposure times than bright, directional light (see page 90), and in this case, its effects proved interesting, blurring the birds' wings to give the image an animation that it would not have otherwise had.

In this portrait of a father and his sons on an outing, the gentle light of a shady setting is in keeping with the familial harmony we sense. And on a more practical level, the light has spared the subjects the need to squint, thus preserving a directness in their faces crucial to the success of the photograph.

John Ficara/Woodfin Camp

Frank D. Bruce

Some directional light mixed with a more prevalent diffused light can provide an effective visual accent in certain subjects. The cool, subtle sidelighting on the face of this wide-eyed youngster combines with soft, warm ambient light to play up the rounded form of his face.

Light has character as well as direction, and in exploring it you must develop an eye for both. The photographs here show that light needn't be direct to provide a sense of substance. In fact, soft, diffused light—whether from an overcast sky, a window, or a shaded setting—may actually accentuate the solidity of forms. And contrary to what many people think, it often increases the intensity of colors, revealing their nuances more effectively than direct light.

Because it diminishes contrast, indirect light is especially flattering to human subjects. By eliminating harsh shadows on people's faces and preventing the need to squint, it softens facial features. And in all kinds of subjects, diffuse light can prevent the loss of detail that sometimes occurs with harsh, direct light.

But either kind of light has its usefulness, and it would be inaccurate to suggest that you will have to choose between one or the other. There are countless combinations of the two, and each will affect the mood and atmosphere of a scene in a unique way. You can observe this by studying a familiar scene over the course of a day, from the mellow light of dawn to the cool blue of twilight. And, as we will see on the following pages, the seasons of the year lend specific characteristics of lighting, altering both mood and atmosphere.

. . . day and night

Martin L. Taylor

Because of its warm hues produced by atmospheric diffusion, sunset has always been a favorite time for photographers. In shooting all but the most spectacular sunsets, however, you should include other elements to give the image structure and depth. In this picture, silhouetted trees fragment the sky's rich color, making it even more tantalizing.

Martin L. Taylor

In this dreamlike image of dawn on a river, soft light, mist, and the river's glassy surface combine to obliterate the distinction between sky and water. The photographer has reinforced this ambiguity by showing us more of the river than the sky, so that we see the reflections of clouds beyond the top of the frame. The light of dawn offers many such impressionistic possibilities.

Derek Doeffinger

The ultramarine half-light of this bleak winter landscape helps unify its isolated components—stop sign, tree, and moon. Although the apparent lack of color in such nocturnal settings may dissuade you from using color film, in fact they can often yield a stunning monochrome effect.

. . . spring and fall

Hans Wolf/The Image Bank

The palette of spring is cool and green, punctuated by the intense hues of flowering plants. Here, the broad light of a cloudless spring day has turned grass and sky into flat bands of color, divided by the bright wedge of a mustard field, accented by a fruit tree in full bloom.

Autumn light is well suited to the brilliant amber shades of changing foliage. As days shorten and the sun sits lower in the southern sky, it lends an enveloping warmth, and the defining slant of its rays gives the landscape a sparkling clarity. In photographs of foliage such as this, it is often the contrast between turned leaves and the deep green of pines that dazzles the eye.

Shinzo Maeda/The Image Bank

. . . winter and summer

Don Cornelius

Winter light, in most parts of the world, is as stark and severe as the season's effects on nature. Its low sun renders the landscape in high relief, giving textures an extraordinary presence. Snow enhances its brilliant contrast, yet adds detail to its long shadows by reflecting open skylight, as in the picture at left of a ptarmigan. Even in the leaden light of overcast sky, snow simplifies and adds contrast to a scene.

The intensity of summer light can either flatten or add volume to an object, depending on its direction. But in the broad light of noon, colors can lose their brilliance, so you may prefer to shoot during the cooler morning hours or the lingering evening twilight when the light is more angular. A shady setting is another solution. Yet the sun's parching toplight is effective in the photograph at right, giving a contour to the landscape and providing a striking blue background for the browns and beiges of the rock and sand, and enhancing a feeling of intense dry heat.

Peter Gales

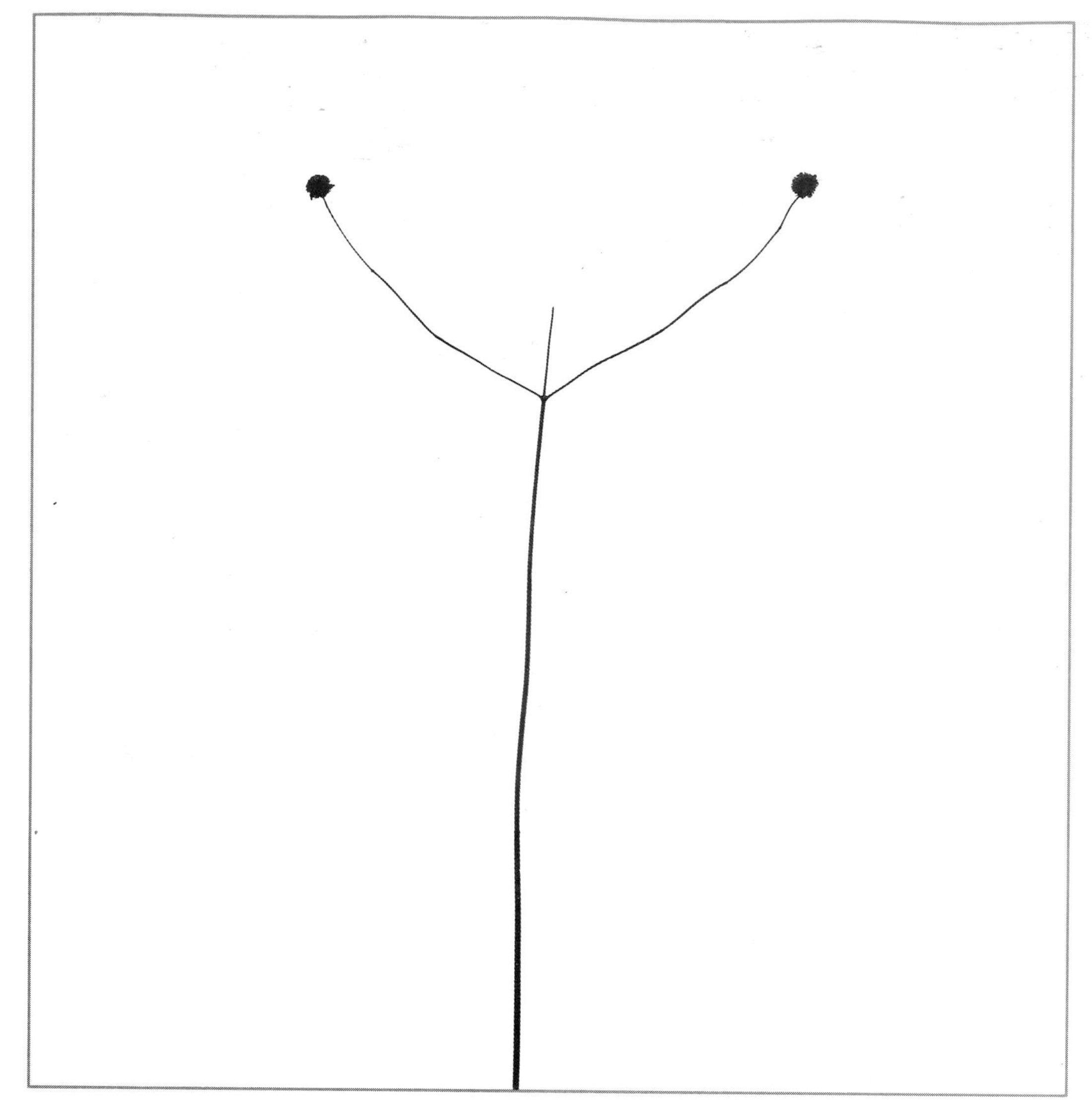

Detroit, 1941

The Personal Style of . . . Harry Callahan

Harry Callahan's modesty belies his stature as one of the greatest living photographers. For over forty-five years, he has photographed his world with a patience and devotion that has often been called religious. His work reflects a strong sense of direction and purpose. "Photography gave me something to believe in . . . I feel that by snapping the shutter I'm making a decision," he says.

Callahan's beginnings in photography were as unassuming as his manner. Bored by an unfulfilling job, he joined a Detroit camera club in 1940. "It was a hobby deal for me. I was really very ignorant in terms of the medium," he recalls. Nevertheless, the club was an important creative catalyst. Callahan can trace his decision to devote his life to photography to a single week in 1941, after a visit to the club by Ansel Adams. "It just opened up a whole world to me. It was then that I saw what a print could be. [Adams's] prints were small then, and they were each beautifully printed—sort of precious, a fact which hit me just right."

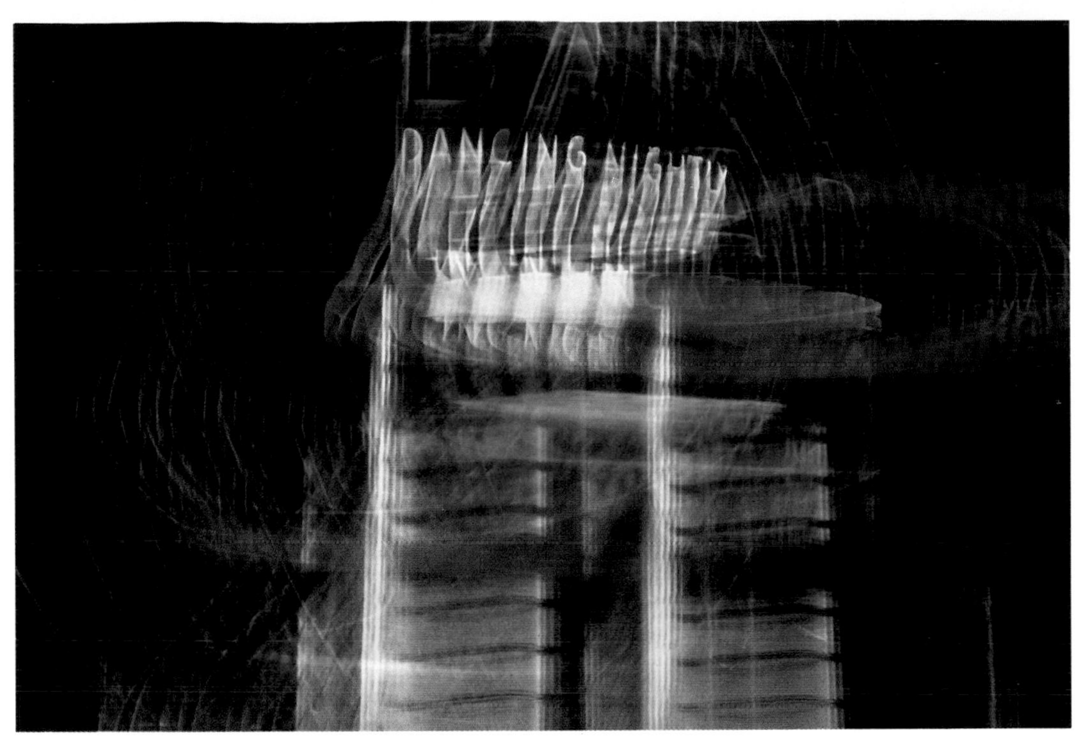

Detroit, 1948

Eleanor, ca. 1947

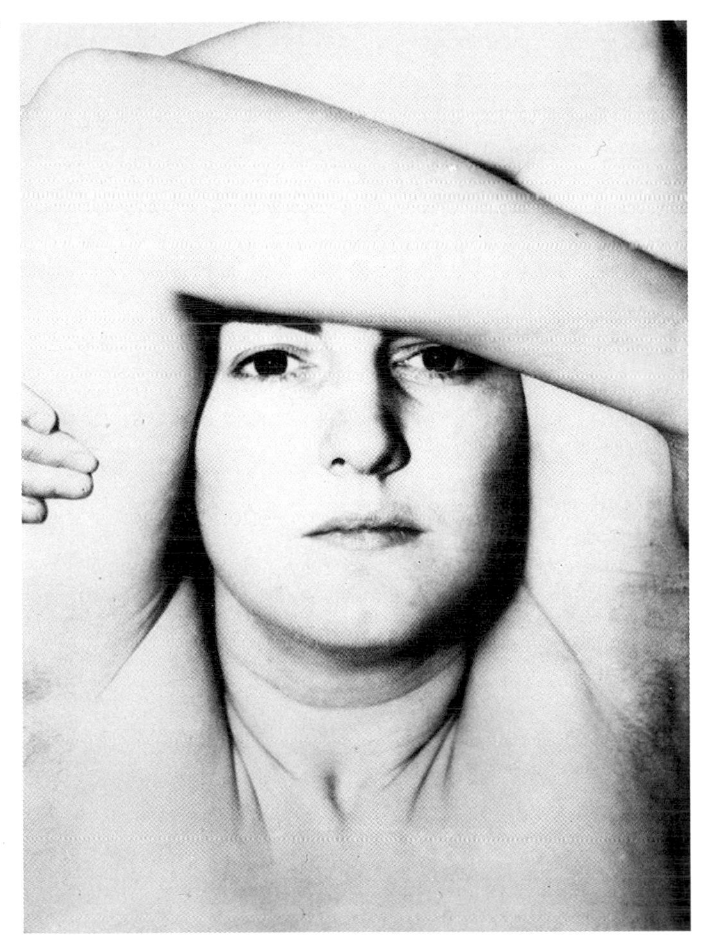

Callahan was less moved by the expansive landscapes that have since established Adams's fame than he was by his photographs of leaves, ferns, and natural details. Inspired, Callahan went on to photograph the close-ups of weeds in water and snow or against the sky for which he is so well-known. He went on to take Adams's approach a step further, abandoning its rich detail and subtle tonalities for a more linear, high-contrast effect. "When I made those pictures of weeds in the snow, it just seemed like a sin to leave out the texture in the snow . . . it was a really big step for me. But it's exciting when you see you can break the rules."

The exceptional variety of Callahan's work is testimony to the number of times he's broken the rules. His willingness to experiment, and to fail in the process, is a rare thing in an art world that often confuses sameness with artistic vision. "If you keep up with the same sort of thing, it's a dead end," says Callahan. "I've always felt the need to move on, even though it's hard to give up something you're good at."

Callahan started taking color photographs decades before it was fashionable in art photography circles. And although he has photographed his wife, Eleanor, constantly over the years, he has used an impressive range of formats and styles to capture the same subject matter. Callahan's work reflects his assessment that artistic vision is an organic, evolutionary process, rarely—if ever—repeated. In the early 1950s, he did a series of pictures of people on the street in Chicago, using a long lens set at its closest focusing distance and filling the viewfinder with their faces. "They were all lost in thought," he says. "I've gone back to that a little bit, but it never seems to work." Callahan's street photographs of ten years later have a very different feeling. Photographed from a low point of view with a wide-angle lens, the figures take on an imposing, almost ominous quality.

Callahan subscribes to the belief that inspiration has a life of its own, and that the element of surprise is part of what sustains a creative artist. "Sometimes you work at something, and work at it, and you think you know what you're doing, and it comes out in a different way . . . and it's probably the real thing coming out."

In 1941, for example, after hearing Ansel Adams talk about photographer Alfred Stieglitz "as if he was a god," Callahan undertook a pilgrimage to New York City to meet him and see his work. He was particularly impressed with the photographs of cloud formations that Stieglitz called "Equivalents." Callahan remembers, with typical self-effacement, "I thought I'd make water my thing, like Stieglitz made sky, and I photographed water for a couple of years. Most of it was with a view camera, and the only things that held up were where I left the camera open and the water moved and the highlights wrote on the film . . and I wasn't even looking for that."

Chicago, 1950

Eleanor

Callahan's working method is a seemingly improbable combination of intuition and hard work. He has had no formal training in photography and is interested in technique only as a means to achieve a certain kind of image. Any analytic approach to the medium, he claims, "goes right over my head. As a photographer, I'm sort of like a naive artist." The technique of multiple exposure, which Callahan has experimented with throughout his artistic life, is a case in point. His multiple exposures are not meticulously previsualized. "I just keep shooting and putting things together, and finally it works . . . if I'm really wrapped up in it, I don't quit until it does work. And when it works, I don't know what makes it work, it just works."

Chicago, 1951

Portugal, 1982

Part of Callahan's strength as a photographer is that he can be his own critic. "I'm not the kind of photographer who sets up the camera and snaps the shutter and says 'I got it.' On a good day, I shoot maybe three rolls. I might have one good picture on a roll if I'm lucky. I've just got piles of pictures that I don't consider good." His careful selection of images also helps to further define the shape and character of his work. "When I get down to serious editing," he comments, "I find I've got even more junk."

Callahan was a teacher for thirty years, first at Chicago's Institute of Design, then at the Rhode Island School of Design. He is considered by many to be the single most influential teacher of his generation, having fostered an exceptional number of successful younger photographers. Yet he is as modest about his achievement as a teacher as he is about his photographic genius. He feels that he has taught as much by his own example as by conventional pedagogy, and his Socratic methods are consistent with his approach to the medium. "I got wonderful results from the students, even though I didn't say much. To try to explain things was just as weird as trying to explain my photography, and I understand that what I am is some kind of mystic . . . to myself and to other people."

Perhaps Harry Callahan is such a good teacher because he believes that photography—like any means of creative expression—is a way to learn about yourself and your place in the world. "It can happen in anything that allows you to think and to put things in some kind of form. When you first go out, you don't know much, but if you're lucky you can make something that means something to you. If you get a few of these, and they keep piling up . . . you broaden yourself and you grow, and you have something that gives you real satisfaction."

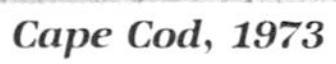

Cape Cod, 1973

Meryl Streep, 1981

The Personal Style of . . . Annie Leibovitz

Annie Leibovitz's portraits of famous people —rock stars, actors, athletes, writers—have been featured in magazines all over the world, displaying her trademark blend of color, originality, and intimacy. Her pictures express warmth, humor, and sensuality to a degree that is all the more remarkable, given that her state-of-the-art technique means working with a complex camera, tripod, lights, props, and an assistant or two.

Although she works in the journalistic tradition—unlike many portrait photographers of her generation, who come from a background in fashion photography —a Leibovitz portrait is rarely predictable or merely descriptive. "It's not real life . . . it's taken from real life and it's more like theatre," she says. "It's someone coming to terms with how they're going to present themselves."

Timothy Hutton, 1981

Paloma Picasso, 1982

Annie Leibovitz's images linger in the mind. Striking and forceful with a distinct flair for the outrageous, they present us with new insights into an already well-known face or figure. Whether the setting or mood is deliberately stylized or spontaneous, each picture makes an unmistakably personal statement—not only about the individual behind the celebrity, but about those unique qualities that have made him or her famous. "I don't try to over-intellectualize my concepts of people," she says. "I normally start with an idea and then hope. I go into [a session] with some sort of structure and some sort of discipline, but if something else happens, well, then that's exciting, too. You have to be ready for that." The photograph of Paloma Picasso, taken in her Paris apartment, was visualized long before it was taken, inspired by André Kertesz's famous image, "Satiric Dancer." Yet many of Leibovitz's photographs have a distinctively collaborative air. When Steve Martin, who had just purchased a Franz Kline painting, told Leibovitz, "I see myself in that picture," she featured it prominently in the portrait. The result is a wonderful blend of solemn humor that also typifies Martin's special comedic gifts.

Leibovitz prefers to approach a portrait assignment by getting as close to the subject as she can, for as long as she can (even up to a number of days, if possible), to observe and develop ideas. Nevertheless, due to the exigencies of deadlines, Leibovitz has been known to get the picture in as little as twenty minutes. Meryl Streep, for instance, came into the studio complaining that everyone was trying to turn her into the next glamorous star. She was nobody, she insisted; all she was was an actress. Leibovitz had just been looking at a book of drawings of clowns and suggested the traditional white face makeup of the mime. After shooting a couple of rolls in less that ten minutes, the resulting picture became one of her most famous. (On the other hand, what is probably Annie Leibovitz's most well-known image, of John Lennon and Yoko Ono lying together, came about at the end of a session that had taken several days and was, says Leibovitz, a picture that had really taken ten years—the time she had known and worked with Lennon—to make.)

Yoko Ono and Sean Ono Lennon, 1981

Carl Lewis, 1983

Although she originally wanted to be a painter, Annie Leibovitz was still in college when she decided to become a photographer. Inspired by the work of Jacques-Henri Lartrigue and the style of photography then being practiced at the San Francisco Art Insititute (work strongly influenced by Henri Cartier-Bresson and Robert Frank), she began to carry her camera with her wherever she went, recording the sights and scenes of San Francisco in the 1960s. She describes her own early style as "more like sophisticated street photography. I had a facility to put something in a frame and make something of it." She put her pictures in a portfolio and took them to *Rolling Stone* magazine. The editor, Jann Wenner, liked her photographs, commissioned her to take a portrait of John Lennon for an interview she was doing, and within a month her work was on the cover of the magazine.

What is surprising in the case of Annie Leibovitz is how much of her technique is self-taught. For although her use of color and lighting is extremely sophisticated, her choice of equipment and format developed in many ways as a response to the requirements of her job as chief photographer for *Rolling Stone*. She began to use color when the magazine decided to have color covers and changed from the 35 mm format to the 2¼-inch format as the reproduction and paper qualities of the magazine improved.

Although many of her photographs can be viewed as highly original set pieces, Leibovitz says that the direction she is likely

Steve Martin, 1981

to take in the future lies with the subjects themselves. "In the beginning my portraits were often to do with wanting a lot of information, more information than you normally got. Now I'm more interested in the photograph not competing with the person, just letting the person come forward."

Annie Leibovitz's portraits have conveyed the essence of famous personalities for more than a decade. They've shaped our perceptions and echoed our fascination with the power and excitement of fame itself. Wherever the future takes her, her bold and innovative style will no doubt continue to command attention and admiration.

Dunhuang, 1980

The Personal Style of . . . Eliot Porter

"Every photograph that is made, whether by one who considers himself a professional, or by the tourist who points his snapshot camera and pushes a button, is a response to the exterior world, to something perceived outside himself by the person who operates the camera."

So speaks Eliot Porter, whose personal response to the external world has led to a career as one of this century's foremost color photographers. Looking at the saturation of his well-known landscapes, as well as the exquisite detail of his close-ups, one can see why it has been said of Porter that he has

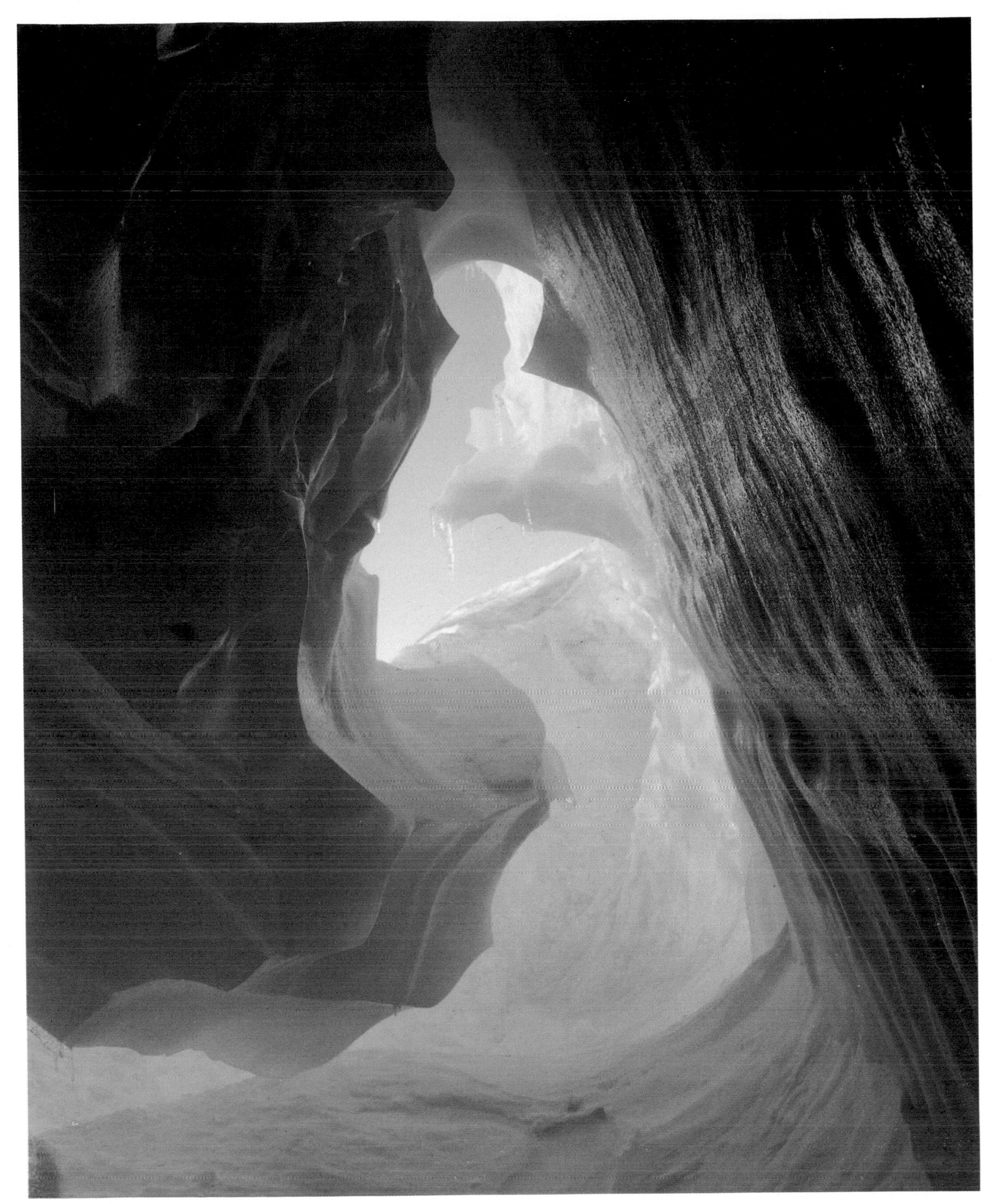

Ross Island, 1975

Holl's Creek, Glen Canyon, 1962

"absolute color pitch," the ability to find that point at which color and light meet in perfect harmony to record nature's greatest beauty. Indeed, since childhood, Porter's perceptions of beauty have been intimately associated with nature, and his work is a translation of his love for that subtle beauty into images.

Perhaps the greatest influence on Porter's career as photographer and conservationist were the summers he spent as a boy on Great Spruce Head, the family island off the coast of Maine. "It matters not what theme, what emotional commitments, or even what financial considerations motivate the photographer," Porter says. "He responds to the same kind of stimulus—to what he sees." It was on Great Spruce Head Island where Porter as a youth first saw and photographed the birds, plants, and forests that would remain his favorite subjects throughout his career.

During Porter's undergraduate years at Harvard University where he earned a degree in chemical engineering in 1924 and an M.D. in 1929, photography was relegated to a minor interest. His first serious black-and-white photographs were taken about ten years later while teaching at Harvard. Porter used an Ernst Leitz Leica camera and continued to focus on natural subjects and, in particular, birds. His first exhibit included 37 of his black-and-white photographs at Delphic Studios in New York in 1936.

Porter's career took a dramatic turn when his brother Fairfield Porter—a well known painter—introduced him to Alfred Steiglitz. Soon after, Steiglitz arranged to exhibit Porter's photographs at his gallery, An American Place, providing the young artist his official entrée into New York photography circles. In 1939, Porter quit his teaching position and devoted his attentions

Glen Canyon, 1961

almost exclusively to photography, with particular emphasis on color photography of birds and details of nature. During the 1940s and 1950s he continued to use black-and-white for landscape and architectural photography in the southwest where he had established his residence in Santa Fe.

Gradually, the switch from black-and-white photography to color seemed to tap in Porter an entirely new source of inspiration. A practical matter at first (Porter's photos of birds were turned down by publishers who needed color for identification purposes), he became increasingly fascinated by the complexity of the natural world, which he felt could be captured only through color. He also became a staunch defender of color photography as an art form, not a popular notion during the forties and fifties, when the most respected photographers, including Steiglitz, Steichen, and Ansel Adams, worked primarily in black-and-white. "To say that because a photograph is in color it is less creative than one in black and white," Porter has claimed, "is to manifest a poverty of perception no less egregious than to condemn photography as a whole because it is the product of an optical instrument."

Great Smoky Mountain National Park, 1968

Balanced Rock Canyon, Glen Canyon, 1962

Pavilion at Pure Sound Temple, Sichuan, 1981

Throughout the fifties and sixties, as Porter became more and more attuned to the living things he photographed, he also became more indignant over man's utter ignorance of the ecosystem of which he is a small part. In no uncertain terms, Porter spoke out against the abuses of technological developers. "It has been established beyond doubt," he once said, "that the highly exploitive practices of strip mining, clear-cut lumbering, overgrazing, stream pollution, and predator extermination all cause disbalances which result ultimately in the destruction of the soil, which carries away with it the plant and animal life dependent on it in a downward spiral toward desolation." Almost as if to remind us of what we risked losing if we continued these practices, Porter took some of his most vivid and breathtaking photographs on wilderness expeditions in Glen Canyon, the Galapagos Islands, and Antarctica.

It was during the early fifties, too, that Porter began rereading the works of Henry David Thoreau, whom he had first discovered as a young boy on Great Spruce Head. Thoreau's works, and expecially his vehement defense of and love for things of the earth, seemed more and more to be in harmony with what Porter was attempting to express through his color photographs. At his wife's suggestion, Porter began taking photographs for a book to illustrate and complement selected passages from Thoreau's writings. After being turned down by a score of trade publishers, *In Wildness Is the Preservation of the World* was finally published in 1962 by the Sierra Club, which would publish several more of his books throughout the sixties.

But Porter's career did not end with his becoming simply a "conservationist" photographer. Today, he continues to travel, to photograph, to challenge our notions of space and scale and color. Whether we are looking at a close-up of rose petals on a beach or a dramatic view into the depths of a canyon, Porter's images reflect a philosophy born of observation and experience.

Great Spruce Head Island, Maine, 1971

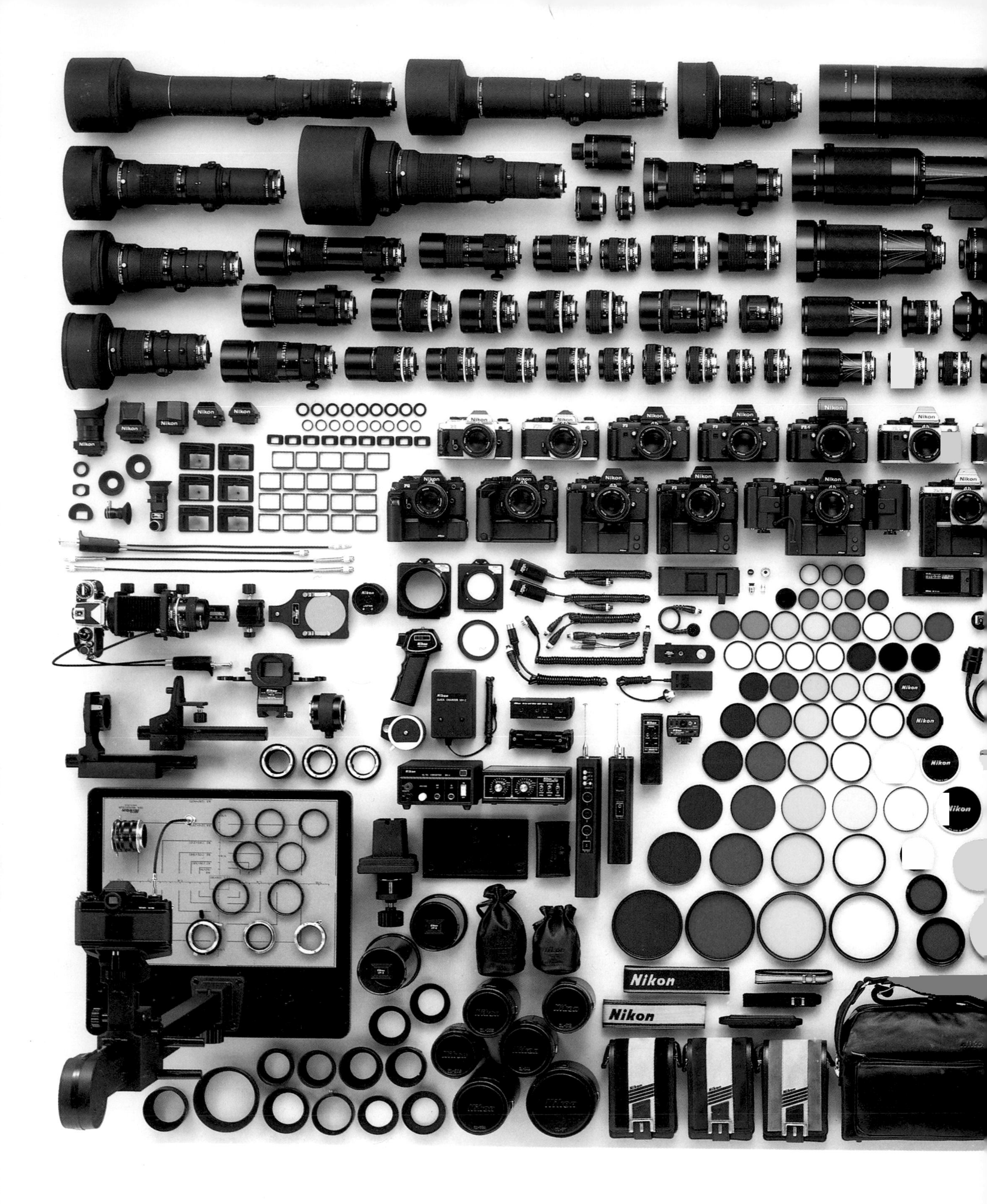
Nikon
Nikon

Courtesy Nikon Inc.

Part II

The Tools

Cameras
Film
Lenses
Filters
Flash
Accessories
The Photographer's Most Common Problems

The family of 35 mm camera equipment is large. Cameras come in a variety of models, and most manufacturers also offer a wide array of accessory equipment—lenses, filters, cases, flash attachments, and other devices. In some instances, equipment from one manufacturer's line can be used with cameras from another maker, although you may need to invest in adapters. Before you buy a camera or other photographic equipment from any manufacturer, read the tips on buying a camera on page 79.

Cameras

Types of Cameras

The extraordinary popularity of the 35-mm camera is a fairly recent phenomenon. Although it was once the choice of amateurs alone, technical improvements in optics, camera design, and film have brought many professionals into its camp. Developed in the 1920s by the E. Leitz Optical Company of Germany, and originally designed to accept existing movie film, the 35-mm camera's combination of versatility, convenience, and high image quality is unrivaled. Although there are countless varieties of 35-mm cameras, from simple vest-pocket models to sophisticated systems, there are only two basic types: the rangefinder, or non-SLR camera, and the single-lens reflex, or SLR.

Although the original Leitz camera was a rangefinder model, most current rangefinders are quite different. The feature that distinguishes either from the SLR is that the viewfinder optics, used for framing and focusing, are separate from the lens. But unlike earlier models, today's non-SLRs are largely automatic: most have fully automatic exposure and built-in flash, and many offer automatic focus and film advance as well. The permanently mounted lens usually has a relatively wide field of view, which makes it useful for general picture-taking purposes, but it can be a limitation in many specific applications. And although the scene you see through the viewfinder is more or less the image that the lens will record on your film, when you move very close to a subject there is a discrepancy between the two. Models capable of such close-up work usually have compensating marks to guide you in this situation, but even so, you must be careful to avoid inadvertently cropping any part of your subject.

The single-lens-reflex camera solves these problems, however, with a built-in mirror and prism that allow you to view a subject through the same lens that takes the picture. Although this addition makes the camera heavier and more complex, as well as more expensive, it dramatically increases the camera's potential. In a close-up, for example, you'll be able to see exactly what you are shooting, and even in general photography the SLR gives you a more precise viewfinder image. Furthermore, the viewfinder shows the effect of the many interchangeable lenses available for SLRs, from wide-angles that encompass large scenes to telephoto lenses that bring distant objects near. And most SLRs accept a multitude of accessories, such as those shown in the system on the preceding pages, for all kinds of specialized applications.

Although some mechanical models are still available, most current rangefinder and SLR cameras are electronic, depending on power from a battery to run their various mechanisms. In either kind, though, a battery powers a built-in light meter that measures the intensity of light in a scene. Some cameras require you to set both the shutter speed and aperture manually in accordance with this reading, which is usually indicated by a needle or diode that responds as you change one or the other setting. Other models give you this option but also offer automatic exposure modes in which miniaturized circuitry controls the shutter speed, the aperture, or both. In some cases, you set the shutter speed and the camera sets the aperture; modes or models that work this way are described as shutter-priority. Other cameras offer aperture-priority exposure, in which you adjust the aperture, and the meter dictates to the camera which shutter speed to set for proper exposure. A programmed automatic camera sets both the shutter speed and aperture for you. Some models give you a choice of automatic exposure modes in addition to a manual mode, although these tend to be the more expensive ones.

Tom Beelmann

The camera that started the 35-mm boom—the Leica, introduced in 1924—is shown in the foreground above. Behind it is a recent automatic single-lens-reflex camera.

Many newer SLRs also have an exposure compensation control that gives you the freedom to deviate from the camera's meter reading, a particularly useful device in a camera without a manual mode. Other models have a feature that locks in an exposure, allowing you to take a reading off the most important part of your subject, then to step back to include a broader scene that might otherwise give an incorrect meter reading. Either of these features is helpful in compensating for unusual lighting situations.

Jerry Antos

At left are two current 35-mm cameras. In the foreground is a rangefinder model, in which all camera functions are automatic. Behind it is an electronic single-lens-reflex camera with automatic exposure control.

Buying a Camera

When you buy a camera, here are some things to ask yourself:

▶ Do you want the compactness and convenience of a rangefinder model or the more extensive flexibility of a single-lens-reflex? They use the same films and can give virtually identical results in normal situations. If you are primarily interested in everyday situations—friends, vacations, family gatherings—an inexpensive non-SLR may suit your needs. If you want a broader range of creative options, including interchangeable lenses, you should have an SLR.

▶ Do you want a camera with automatic or manual exposure control? Automatic cameras may save you some technical decisions and camera operations that might otherwise cause you to miss a shot, but manual cameras or cameras with a manual option give you more control. You should also ask yourself what other automatic functions, if any, you want.

▶ Research what models are available. Talk to other photographers, read photo magazines, and send for manufacturers' test reports and brochures. Additional features usually cost more. Decide whether you need a top shutter speed of 1/1000 second instead of 1/500, or a maximum aperture of f/1.4 instead of f/2 (see pages 80 and 81).

▶ If you are getting an SLR, you'll probably want to add lenses and other equipment eventually. Be sure that the model you're buying will be compatible with the kinds of accessories you will want.

▶ When you've narrowed the field to a few models, take ample time to check out the cameras themselves. Are the controls easy for you to operate? Is the viewfinder sufficiently bright for easy focusing in dim light? Is the light meter display clearly discernible?

Cameras

A Camera's Lens

Without a lens, a camera would be nothing more than a glorified box. The lens collects light from the subject and produces a sharp, correctly colored (on colored film) image for the film to record.

You've probably noticed that objects viewed through an ordinary magnifying glass have a rainbow-colored fringe. This is because the component colors of white light are actually focused on slightly different planes. The high-quality, complex lens in a camera literally bends these divergent light rays back into place, through an intricate arrangement of glass elements of varying shapes. Distortions in the shape of a subject that occur with simple lenses are also corrected in this way. A refinement of recent years is the application of microscopically thin optical plastics to the front of the lens to control flare, a loss of contrast that occurs when light strikes the lens directly. In addition, the barrel, or housing, of the lens is a sophisticated piece of engineering, designed not only to reposition the glass elements internally when focused, but also to regulate the amount of light passing through the lens.

The mechanism on the outside of the lens that allows you to adjust the amount of light reaching the film is called the ***aperture ring.*** It is usually right next to the camera body, although on some models it may be the most distant ring. The aperture ring controls an adjustable diaphragm—a series of overlapping metal blades that operate together much like the iris of the eye. The size of the opening created as the blades open and close determines the amount of light admitted. The diaphragm can be opened to let in all the light the lens collects, or it can be closed down to let only a tiny shaft of light through. And, of course, it can be adjusted for any amount of light in between.

The size of this opening, or aperture, is indicated by its *f*-number, which is inscribed on the aperture ring. The sequence of *f*-numbers is typically 1.4, 2, 2.8, 4, 5.6, 8, 11, 16 and sometimes 22. You simply align the *f*-number of the aperture you want with a fixed mark on the lens barrel. For reasons explained below, the larger the *f*-number, the smaller the opening. On most lenses for 35 mm cameras the smallest aperture is *f*/16 or *f*/22, although many telephoto and special purpose lenses offer *f*/32. The largest aperture varies, but on many compact rangefinders it is *f*/2.8, and on the normal lens supplied with current SLRs it is at least *f*/2. Lenses with a wider maximum aperture such as *f*/1.4 (often called "faster" lenses because they admit more light than lenses of smaller maximum aperture) may be substituted at substantial extra cost. There are times when this extra speed can mean the difference between a possible picture and an impossible one—for example, when shooting in dim light or when you need a very high shutter speed to freeze action (see page 182). But you have to weigh this advantage and the likelihood of encountering such situations against the price difference.

The relationship between apertures, called *f*-stops (and denoted by *f*- numbers), is simpler than their numbers might suggest. At any setting, the next largest aperture (smaller number) doubles the amount of light entering the camera; the next smallest aperture (larger number) halves it. For example, if you adjust the aperture from *f*/8 to *f*/5.6, you double the light entering the camera; if you adjust it from *f*/8 to *f*/11, you halve it. This is true for all but a few odd maximum apertures, such as *f*/1.7 and *f*/3.5, which are half-stops.

Norman Kerr

The 35 mm camera above was sliced in half to expose the intricate workings of the lens and camera body. Notice the seven glass elements and the aperture diaphragm in between them. The geared plates in the lens barrel are for focusing the lens.

Norman Kerr

An overhead view of a normal lens on a 35 mm camera shows, from top to bottom, the focusing ring (with distances indicated in both feet and metres), the depth-of-field scale, and the aperture ring. This lens is focused on infinity, with the aperture set at f/4.

F-numbers are based on the ratio between the diameter of the aperture opening and the focal length of the lens. Focal length is an optical measurement that determines the degree of magnification and the field of view, but in simple terms, it is the distance between the lens and the film when the lens is focused on infinity. Thus, the diameter of the aperture of *f*/4 is one fourth the length of the lens. The lens on most compact rangefinders has a focal length between 35 and 45 mm, whereas a standard lens for an SLR has a focal length between 50 and 55 mm, usually described as a "normal" lens.

Both the focal length and the maximum aperture of a lens are engraved on the ring around the front of the lens. The lens in the picture at right, for example, has a focal length of 50 mm and a maximum aperture of f/1.4. Note that the aperture is usually written as a ratio, in this case 1:1.4. The serial number is also often inscribed on the front of the lens, as in the camera at left.

Donald Buck

Lenses for 35 mm cameras with a focal length longer than 55 mm are telephoto lenses. A photograph taken with a telephoto lens makes the subject appear to be closer than it actually was. As a result, less of the total scene is recorded than would be captured with a normal lens from the same point. Lenses with a focal length shorter than 45 mm are wide-angle lenses. They encompass more of a scene than a normal lens would. For this reason, objects appear to be farther from the camera than they actually are. (See pages 104 to 107 for more information on telephoto and wide-angle lenses.)

The other control on the lens is the ***focusing ring,*** which repositions the glass elements in the lens to produce a sharp image of your subject. Usually it is the ring closest to the front of the lens. The numbers inscribed on the focusing ring indicate camera-to-subject distance in both feet and metres. Most normal lenses can focus from as close as two or three feet to as far away as the eye can see, which is usually called infinity and marked ∞ on the distance scale. When you rotate the focusing ring until your subject is sharp in the viewfinder, the number at the top center of the lens, opposite a stationary slash or dot, is the distance between camera and subject.

Surrounding the top center mark on most SLR lenses is a series of lines with numbers (or colors) corresponding to the *f*-stops. This is the depth of field scale, which indicates the amount of picture area in focus at a particular *f*-stop and camera-to-subject distance. In general, when you focus on a subject using a small aperture, such as *f*/11 or *f*/16, much of the area in front and in back of the subject will also be sharp; with a large aperture, on the other hand, such as *f*/2.8 or *f*/2, very little more than what you focused on may be sharp. How to read this very useful scale is explained in detail on page 92.

Inside a Camera

When you look in the ***viewfinder*** of a single-lens reflex camera, you are actually seeing through the lens. The cutaway section at right shows how an image is transported through the lens to both your eye and the film. If you follow the red and white lines, you will see that as the light rays collected by the lens enter the camera body, they are reflected upward by an angled mirror into a prism housing on top of the camera. The image coming through the lens, however, is reversed, with the white line on top and the red on the bottom. It is also backwards, with the right and left sides of the image reversed in a similar manner. The mirror turns the image right side up, and the prism turns it around and reflects it into the eyepiece. By the time it reaches your eye, the scene looks like the one that you see without the camera which will then appear in the finished photo.

When you press the shutter button to take a picture, the angled mirror flips upward to permit light to pass to the back of the camera, where the film is. Simultaneously, the ***shutter,*** a pair of curtains just in front of the film, opens to let the light hit the film. The shutter remains open for a precise amount of time, which is determined when you set the shutter speed. At 1/250 second, for example, exposure time will be far shorter than if the shutter speed is set at 1/8 second. As soon as the shutter closes, the mirror drops back into its normal viewing position. Because the mirror rises to allow the image to pass through to the shutter and then to the film, the viewfinder goes black momentarily when you take a shot.

Most modern SLRs have a built-in ***exposure meter.*** One or more photocells located in the light path measure the intensity of the light reflected by the subject and admitted by the camera. On an automatic camera, the shutter speed or lens aperture, or both, are set automatically, according to this measurement. On a manual camera, or an automatic camera in the manual mode, you set the shutter and the aperture by hand to achieve a proper exposure. Correct combinations of the two are indicated in the viewfinder by a match-needle, light-emitting diode (LED) or liquid crystal display (LCD). On an automatic camera, the aperture or shutter speed or a combination of the two chosen by the camera will usually be displayed in the viewfinder. Refer to your instruction manual for an explanation of your camera's viewfinder display.

A rangefinder camera works quite differently from an SLR. Its viewfinder window is optically separate from the lens —usually just above it. With current compact autofocus rangefinders, this window is used simply for composing the picture. In non-autofocus (or system) rangefinder cameras, it is also used for focusing, supplemented by another, smaller window that provides the binocular effect to determine distance and sharp focus. When you look through the viewfinder, you see a bright image of your subject with a second, fainter image superimposed on it. You focus by turning the focusing ring until the two images coincide. The viewfinder in a rangefinder camera doesn't have the characteristics of a complex lens, so everything looks sharp through it. The lens and its variable aperture, on the other hand, allow you to increase or decrease the area of sharpness. (These effects are observable in the viewfinder of an SLR because you are seeing through the lens. Certain SLRs will

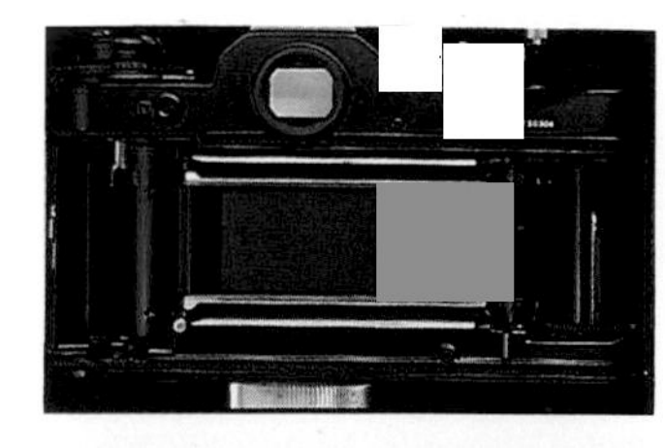

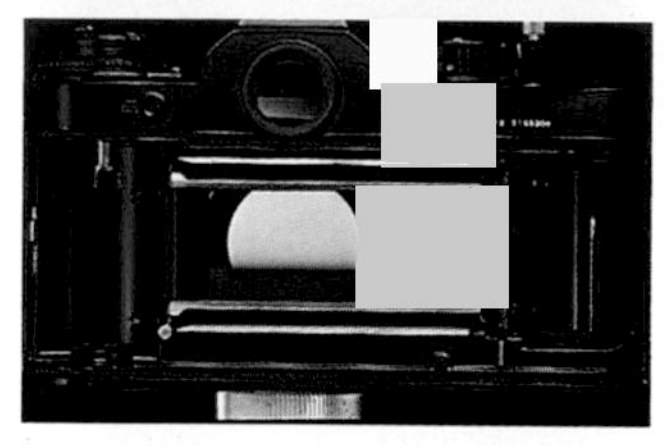

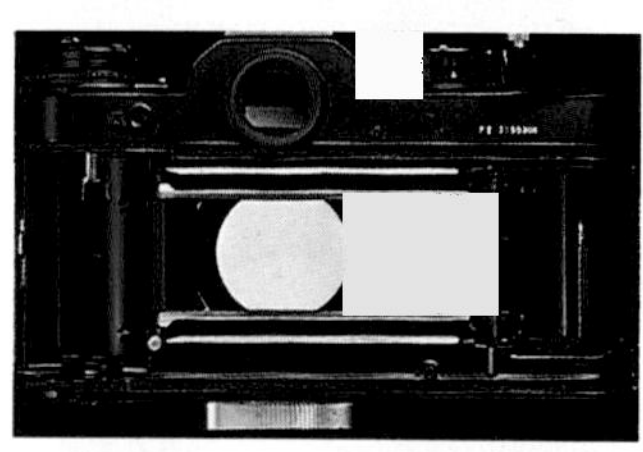

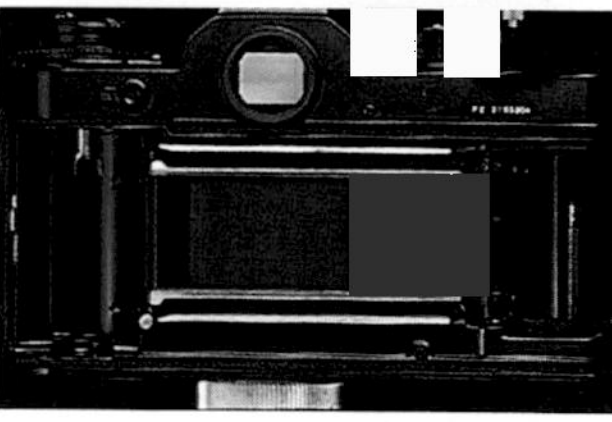

Norman Kerr

The SLR's focal plane shutter is composed of two curtains. One curtain (top) covers the film opening before exposure. When the shutter is released, it is rapidly pulled downward (second and third pictures) to uncover the film (fourth picture). A second curtain (bottom picture) follows the first from the top to complete the exposure, thus insuring that all parts of the film receive light for the same amount of time. At higher shutter speeds, the second curtain begins to move across the film before the first has completed its transit, and the two curtains often form a small slit that crosses the film surface to make the exposure.

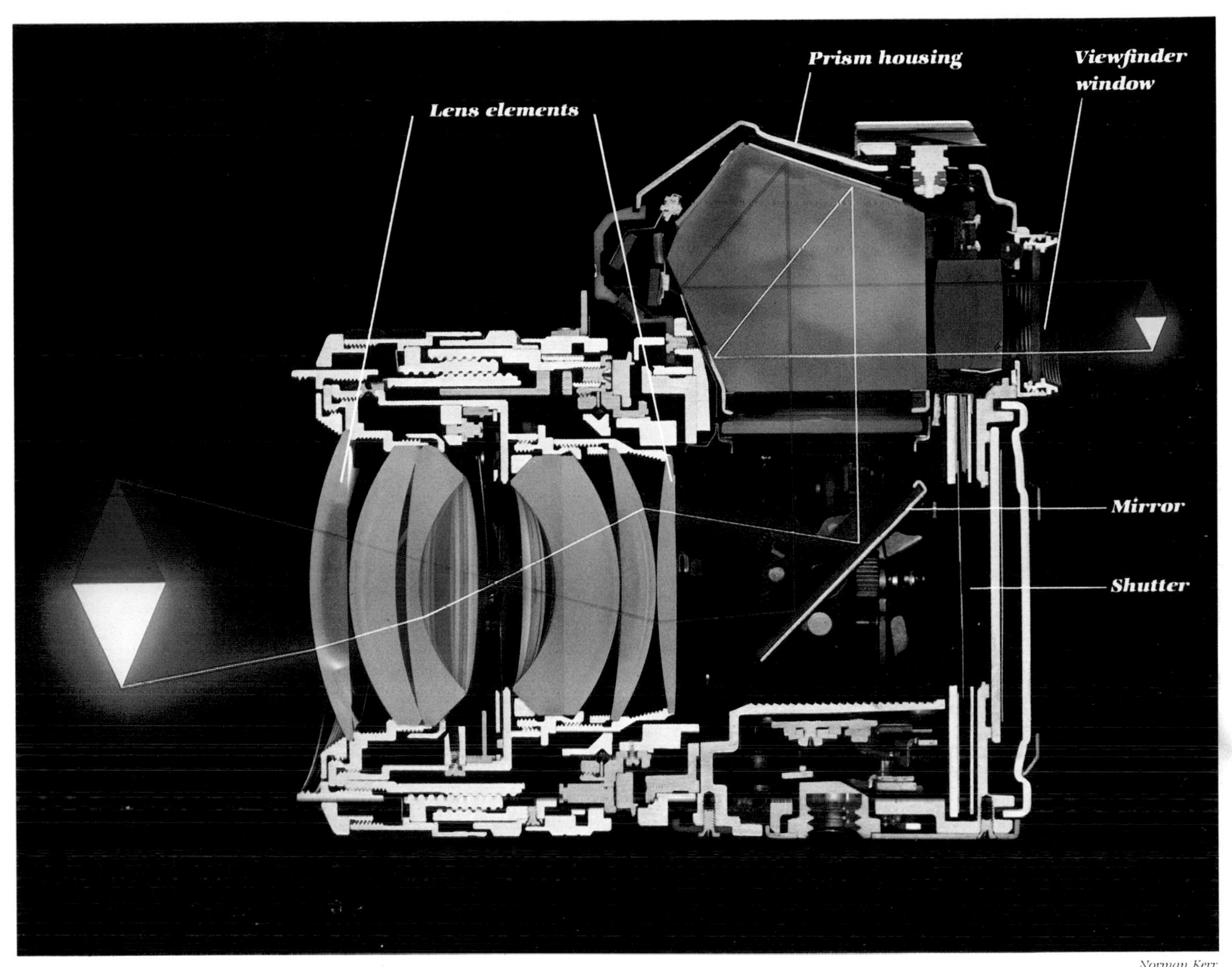

Norman Kerr

The combination of an angled mirror in the camera body and a prism housing on top of the camera allows you to see through the lens of a single-lens reflex camera. The red and white lines in the cutaway view indicate the path of light from the lens to the window of the viewfinder. During exposure, however, the mirror flips up, permitting light to pass directly through the shutter and onto the film.

allow you to see this zone of sharpness precisely with a depth-of-field previewer. See page 85 and pages 92–93).

The rangefinder also differs from the SLR in its shutter. Instead of a curtain-type shutter right in front of your film, as in the SLR, rangefinders have metal blades that are located inside the lens and look somewhat like the aperture diaphragm. This is an advantage in a camera you can control manually because it allows you to use flash with a greater number of shutter speeds (see page 136). Also, most compact automatic rangefinders do not display any exposure information in the viewfinder, and the photocells for their metering systems are usually located on the outside of the camera, near the lens or viewfinder.

To move the film out of the magazine, across the picture area, and onto the take-up spool, both types of cameras have similar ***film transport mechanisms,*** as we will see in the section on loading the camera (see page 87).

Outside a Camera

The exteriors of most 35 mm cameras have an almost bewildering array of dials, levers, rings, and other controls. But they are all easy to use once you understand their functions. Two basic controls, the focusing and aperture rings, are on the lens; their functions were described on pages 80 and 81. The other basic control, for shutter speed, allows you to choose the amount of time that the shutter will remain open. On an SLR, the ***shutter-speed dial*** is usually a small cylindrical control on top of the camera, to the side of the prism. (Some newer models have buttons that change an LCD display; on certain older models, a ring on the lens barrel itself may control shutter speeds.) Shutter speeds are usually marked or displayed as 1000, 500, 250, 125, 60, 30, 15, 8, 4, 2, 1, and B. Most represent fractions of a second—1000 stands for 1/1000 second, 500 for 1/500 second, and so on down to 2 for ½ second. The number 1 represents a full second. Some newer models offer both faster and slower shutter speeds. If you set the control on B, the shutter stays open as long as you hold down the shutter release button, useful when making long time exposures (see pages 244 and 245). One shutter speed that is usually distinguished from the others is the flash synchronization—the fastest shutter speed recommended for taking pictures with electronic flash. Speeds of 1/30, 1/60, 1/125, and 1/250 second are typical (see page 136).

You activate the shutter by pressing the familiar ***shutter release button.*** It is located on top of the camera, where you can press it easily with your right index finger. Most shutter release buttons are threaded to accept cable releases, an accessory that enables you to trigger the shutter without touching and jiggling the camera, often at a distance (see page 146). Many cameras also have a ***self-timer*** lever, which delays the exposure for eight to ten seconds for you to include yourself in the photograph.

Most SLRs have a device called the ***film-advance lever,*** located on the right side of the top of the camera. When you move the lever, an unexposed frame of film moves forward out of the cartridge, into position for the next picture. Many compact rangefinders advance the film automatically after each exposure with a small built-in motor. In either case, advancing the film changes the ***film-frame counter,*** which is adjacent to the lever or the shutter button and indicates how many pictures have been exposed on the roll. On the left side of the camera top is the ***rewind knob,*** used for winding the film back into its cartridge. (Some compact rangefinders also rewind the film automatically at the end of the roll.) Before this knob will work, you must disengage the film advance mechanism, in most cases with a small ***rewind release*** button on the bottom of the camera. When you've rewound the film, the same knob is usually pulled up to open the back of the camera so that you can remove the film.

Most modern cameras also have several controls for their built-in exposure meters. One is simply a switch for turning the meter (and the camera itself) on and off and is usually on the top of the camera. Another lets you adjust the meter for the sensitivity, or speed, of your film. On most SLRs this ***film-speed dial*** is located around the rewind knob, and on rangefinders usually near the front of the lens. You should set this dial according to the ISO number of the film you use (film speed is explained on page 98). On many cameras the dial also has an exposure compensation feature built into it (marked 0, +1, -1, etc.), often engaged with a small release button that allows you to override the automatic exposure system or bracket your exposures. Finally, the meter of an automatic camera may be affected by an ***exposure mode selector switch,*** which allows you to choose between automatic and manual

The two cameras shown here, an SLR (top) and a compact automatic rangefinder (bottom), represent the extremes of complexity and simplicity available in the 35 mm format. The SLR's many controls give you a wide range of creative options and let you adjust the degree of automation to suit specific shooting situations. The rangefinder, on the other hand, frees you from the need for any technical decisions, but is a less versatile instrument. Some camera controls, such as the film advance lever and the rewind knob, are the same on most cameras, but the location of others varies from model to model. The best guide to a particular camera is the instruction book that comes with it. If you purchase a used camera, or if you have lost the manual, you can write to the manufacturer for another copy.

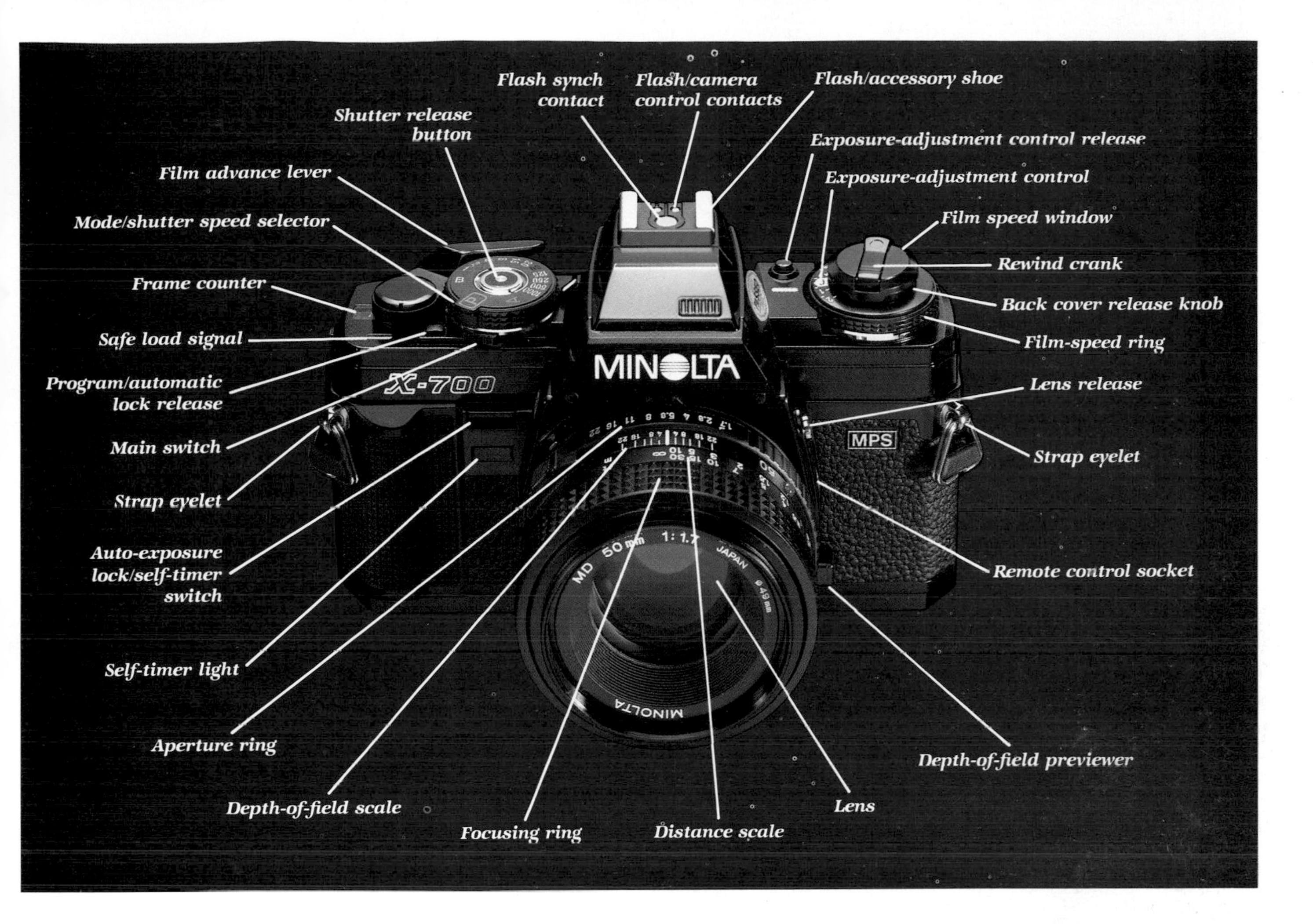

exposure modes and is frequently integrated into the shutter speed dial (see pages 88-89).

There are two ways to connect an electronic flash unit to a camera, both of which establish electrical contact, synchronizing the flash with the shutter. One is the ***hot shoe*** outlet, almost always located on top of the prism. On most SLRs you can also plug a cord from the flash unit into an outlet on the front of the camera. Many SLRs have a ***depth of field preview button*** or lever that lets you view the scene through the aperture you've selected to examine the zone of sharpness it will provide in the scene, and a ***lens release*** button that permits you to unlock and remove the camera's lens. The back and bottom of a camera are described on the next page.

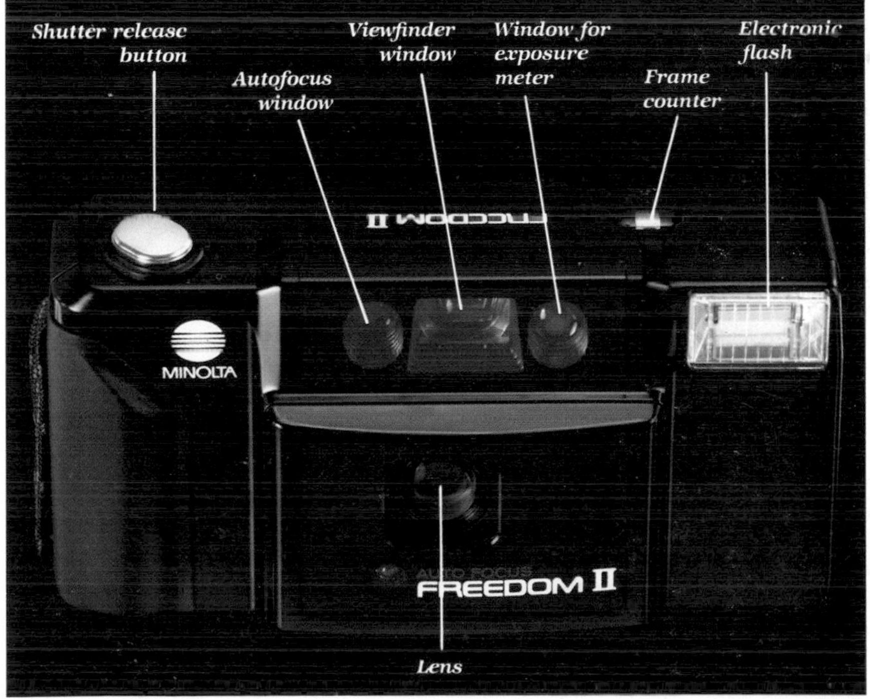

Donald Buck

Cameras

Outside a Camera

Although there are far fewer elements on the back and bottom of a 35 mm camera than on the front and top, it is just as important to understand their functions. The most significant feature on the back is the ***viewfinder eyepiece,*** through which you compose and focus a picture. On a single-lens-reflex camera such as the one shown here, the viewfinder eyepiece is located behind the prism in the center. On most rangefinders, the prism and viewing windows are found more toward the left, although on some, like the one above,they are centered. If you wear glasses and have trouble seeing through the viewfinder with them on, you may wish to investigate the possibility of getting a corrective lens for your camera's eyepiece. Rubber eyecups are also available to prevent the camera from scratching your glasses.

Beside the viewfinder of the rangefinder shown here is the ***flash-wait*** (or ***flash-ready***) ***light,*** which indicates whether or not the camera's built-in flash is adequately charged. The window below and to the right of the viewfinder shows the type of film you are using. On the SLR, insert the end of the film box in the ***film tab holder,*** a metal frame in the center of the back, for a handy way of remembering the kind of film you have in the camera. To disengage the take-up spool so that the film may be rewound, most SLR's have a small button on the bottom, but the rangefinder shown here has a switch which also activates its automatic rewind function. Film speed is set with a control right beside it. On this model, the camera back is opened with a switch to its left, and a built-in protective cover for the lens is opened or closed with a sliding control on the bottom of the lens mount. This switch also turns the camera on and off.

On the bottom of nearly all modern 35 mm cameras is a ***battery compartment*** that houses the battery used to power the exposure meter or the camera itself. On an

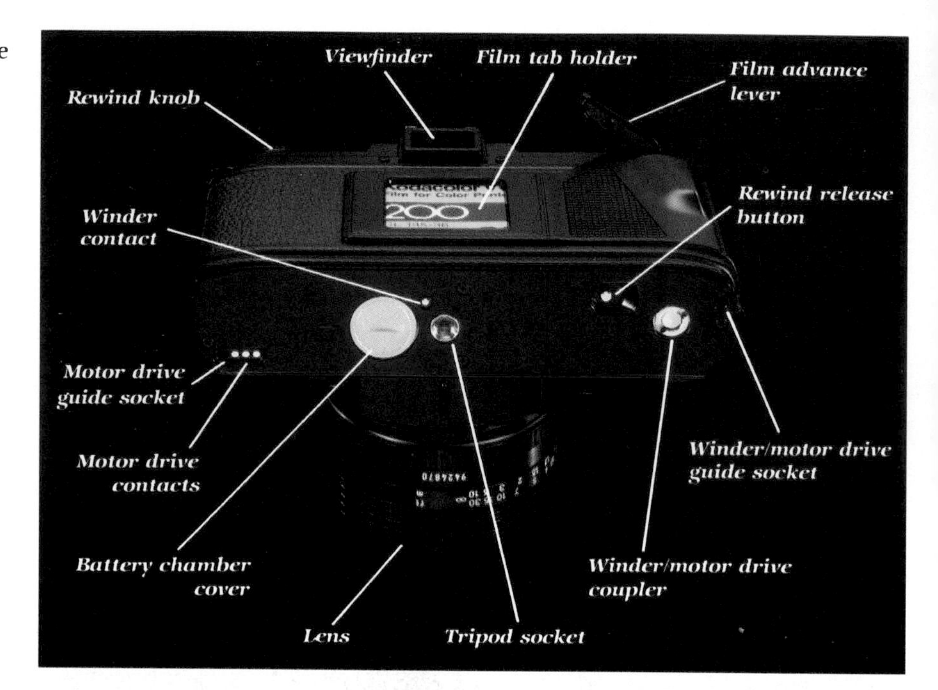

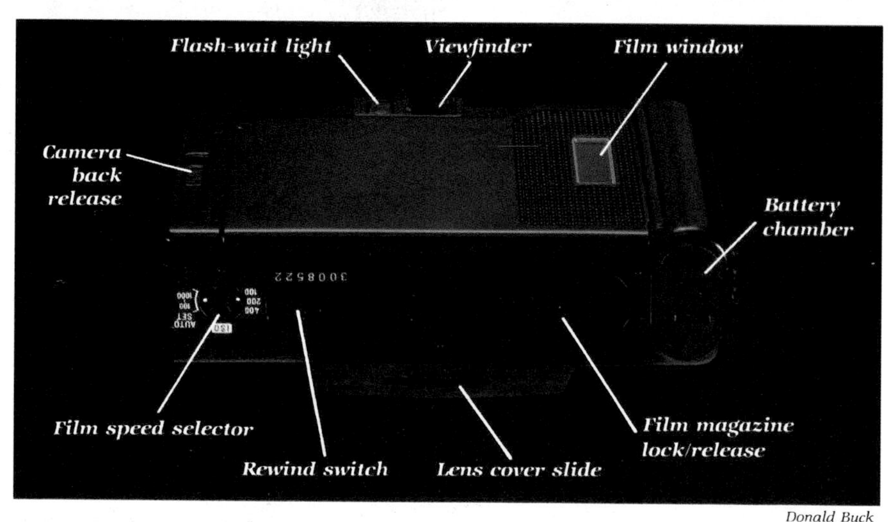

Donald Buck

These views show the back and bottom of a typical SLR (above) and rangefinder. This rangefinder has more of its relatively few controls on these surfaces than an SLR does.

SLR, the lid covering it can usually be unscrewed with a coin. You should replace the battery at least once a year; leaving it in any longer may cause corrosion. Rangefinder cameras with built-in electronic flash typically feature a different type of door that covers one or two AA batteries that power the exposure meter, camera, flash, and automatic film advance, if available. If you use the flash frequently, you will have to replace the batteries more often. Most cameras also have a ***tripod socket,*** which is used not only for mounting the camera on a tripod but also (on an SLR) for attaching a motor drive or an automatic winder, devices described on page 146. The bottom of an SLR may also have electrical contacts for attaching either of these units and another screw-out lid covering the opening where they connect with the camera's film drive.

Unless you are using a camera with automatic film engagement, be sure that the film leader is secure in the take-up spool and that the film's top and bottom perforations are engaged by the sprockets.

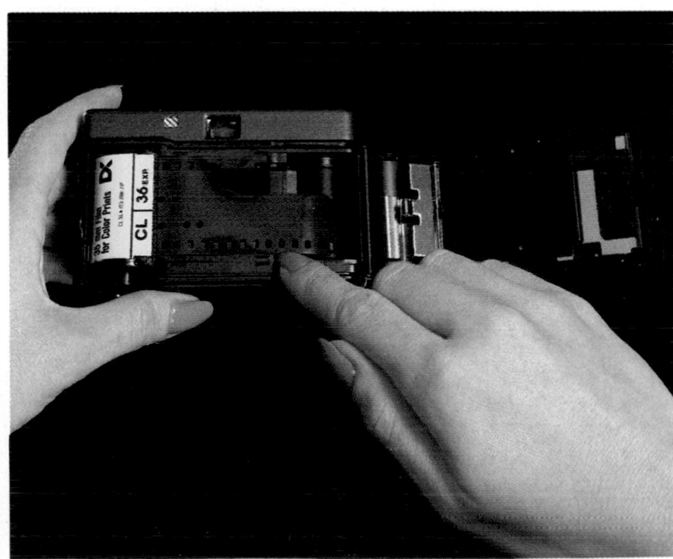

Donald Buck

Loading a Camera

Many of the newer compact automatic rangefinders and some SLRs engage the film leader from a 35 mm magazine automatically when you place the film across the sprocketed spool and close the back. The motorized film advance then advances it to your first exposure. But even loading a camera by hand becomes almost automatic after you do it a few times. Although the specific design of the take-up mechanism may vary from camera to camera, the procedure here applies to most.

▶ ***Set the camera's film-speed dial to the ISO number indicated on the film instructions, packaging, or magazine. (A few cameras will be programmed automatically for film speed by the DX encoding on the side of the magazine.)***

▶ ***Take the film magazine out of its packaging and open the back of the camera.***

▶ ***Pull up the rewind knob and insert the magazine in the left side of the camera. Make sure that the spool end coming out of the magazine is pointed downward and that the leader strip—the narrow strip of film sticking out of the magazine—is pointed toward the take-up spool on the right.***

▶ ***Secure the magazine in place by pushing down on the rewind knob. Turn the knob slightly until you feel it drop into place.***

▶ ***Pull a small amount of film out of the magazine and thread the leader strip over the sprockets onto the take-up spool. These spools engage the film in different ways, so follow your camera's instructions.***

▶ ***Using the film-advance lever, move the film forward one frame, as shown above, to make sure the take-up spool has a good grip on the film. It's a good idea to advance the film one or two more frames until both sets of perforations are engaged by the sprockets next to the take-up spool.***

▶ ***Close the back of the camera. Then, to take up any slack in the film, gently turn the rewind knob clockwise until you feel a slight tension. Advance the film and press the shutter release two or three times until the number 1 appears in the film-frame counter on top of the camera. To make sure that the film is moving smoothly through the camera, check the rewind knob as you advance it. It should be turning in a counterclockwise direction.***

▶ ***To remove the film after you finish the roll, activate the rewind release, which is usually a button on the bottom of the camera. Fold out the crank on the rewind knob, and turn it slowly clockwise to reel the film back into the magazine. When you feel the tension on the film as it pulls off the take-up spool, turn the rewind knob several more times to retract the leader. Open the back and remove the magazine. Particularly when using faster films (ISO 400–1000 and faster), load and unload film in dim light; outdoors shield the film from the sun.***

The effect of one-stop changes in aperture setting is clearly illustrated at right. At the same shutter speed, the aperture settings range from f/1.4 (top left) to f/16 (lower right). The camera's meter indicated a proper exposure of f/5.6. The setting on the camera is shown beneath each shot. One-stop changes in shutter speed would have resulted in similar changes in exposure.

Setting the Exposure

Films differ greatly in their sensitivity to light. Some require a lot of light to record an acceptable image, while others need much less, as we will learn in the section on film (see pages 94 to 101). If your film receives the proper amount of light, the final image will reproduce your subject in its proper tones and colors. But as this series of pictures shows, if the film gets too much light (overexposure), the image will be pale and lacking in detail; if it gets too little light (underexposure), the image will be dark and muddy. To avoid overexposure or underexposure, it is important to understand how to use the two controls that adjust the amount of light reaching the film—the shutter speed and the aperture.

Exposing film to light has been compared to filling a bucket with water from a faucet. You can open the tap wide and fill the bucket quickly, or open it only a little and let the water trickle slowly. The two variables are how much you open the faucet and how long you leave it on. The two exposure controls on the camera work in much the same way. Like the valve in the faucet, the aperture controls the size of the opening in the lens that admits light. The shutter speed determines the length of time that the shutter will stay open to let light pass through.

The exposure meter in your camera reads the total quantity of light reflected from the subject and tells you—or the camera—which combinations of shutter speed and aperture will produce a proper exposure on the particular film you are using. In a well-lighted scene, this may be a combination of a large aperture and fast shutter speed, such as *f*/2.8 and 1/1000 second, or a small aperture and slow shutter speed, such as *f*/22 and 1/15 second. Both combinations will admit the same amount of light. A wide aperture, however, such as *f*/2.8 severely limits the zone of sharpness in a picture (see pages 92 and 93) and a slow shutter speed such as 1/15 second may make it virtually impossible to keep the camera steady in your hands. You will usually want a combination of a relatively small aperture and a moderately fast shutter speed. A setting of *f*/8 and 1/125, for example, would minimize the chance of blurring the image by misfocusing or shaking the camera. You won't always be able to use such a combination, however, even in a well-lighted scene. And although there is some flexibility with either variable, you must make thoughtful decisions about which combinations are best suited to your subject. The effects of different apertures and shutter speeds are explained on the following pages.

The mechanics of setting an exposure vary according to the camera. On manually operated cameras, or on an automatic camera in the manual mode, you must set both the aperture and the shutter speed until the light meter indicator in the viewfinder shows proper exposure (see pictures at right). Which you set first depends on the nature of your subject and the effect you want to achieve with it. With a fairly stationary subject of normal size in good light, using a lens of average focal length and low-speed film, the *f*/8 and 1/125 second setting mentioned above would make a good starting point. Avoid shutter speeds below 1/30 second when holding the camera by hand. For most films, the exposure table in the instructions that accompany the film is a good guide for initial settings.

Some automatic exposure systems require you to set only one variable. On shutter-priority automatics (or in a shutter-priority exposure mode), you set the shutter speed and the camera automatically adjusts the aperture. On an aperture-priority automatic (or in an aperture-priority mode) just the opposite is true—you set the aperture. With programmed automatics (or in the program mode), the camera sets both controls within a safe range for normal pictures.

Below, the viewfinder of a programmed-automatic exposure camera shows operating mode (program, aperture-priority automatic, or manual), shutter speed, and aperture. Middle, similar information is given by this aperture-priority automatic camera—mode (automatic or manual), shutter speed, and aperture. Bottom, for a manual camera, the bracketed centering needle indicates correct exposure settings. Shutter speed is shown at the bottom.

Neil Montanus

Norman Kerr

Neil Montanus

Neil Montanus

Donald Buck

Neil Montanus

Donald Buck

Setting the Exposure

The different light levels of the many things you will want to photograph call for changes in exposure settings. A park scene on an overcast day, for example, requires a wider aperture or a slower shutter speed or both than does the same park on a sunny day. This is because film of a specific sensitivity to light (or speed) needs more or less the same amount of light in each case to produce a well-exposed image. If the illumination is even and not too dim and the subject reflects an average amount of light, your camera's meter is fairly reliable in selecting the proper setting. Keep in mind, though, that a light meter is only a mechanical device designed to take a general reading of the light in a scene. In some situations, this reading will not produce the results you want.

Your meter may be particularly prone to error in measuring strongly lighted scenes with bright highlights and deep shadows. In such cases, it may be best to take local readings from both dark and light areas, then choose an exposure midway between. The meter assumes that the tones in anything you show it will average to a medium grey and recommends an exposure that will make a subject conform to this average. But in a subject such as a beach scene, where most tones are light, this will result in underexposure—the meter will try to make the white beach grey. If you have manual exposure control, you can take a reading off a photographic grey card, which is what the meter is calibrated for, to avoid this error. Caucasian skin is about twice as bright as this card; if you take your meter reading off it, and open the lens or increase your shutter speed one stop, you will arrive at approximately the same exposure. With slide film, sometimes a meter reading off a grey card will produce a light result, so you may want to decrease the indicated exposure by one-half stop. With any film, to be on the safe side in tricky lighting situations, you should *bracket*—that is, take extra pictures that give you one-half or one stop more and less exposure than indicated.

A sidelighted human subject, or one against a bright background such as the sky or a sunlit wall, may require one extra stop of exposure over what the meter recommends for flesh tones to look normal. A backlighted subject is likely to require two more, and a subject against a dark background may need one less. The best practice is to move close to take a reading of the light on the most important part of your subject. Then, set your camera for that reading and resume your original picturetaking position. The same approach may be necessary when the lighting is uneven or when the element you wish to emphasize is small. If manual control isn't possible, some automatic cameras have a button or lever that allows you to lock in this reading and that also permits convenient bracketing. Otherwise, an automatic camera (or a camera in an automatic mode) will continue to compensate both for changes in the scene presented to it and your changes in aperture or shutter speed. You can also use the exposure compensation device, adjusting the exposure for your overall scene until the settings in the viewfinder correspond to those of your close-up reading.

If your automatic camera doesn't have these provisions for overriding the meter, you can get the equivalent of a one-stop increase in exposure by turning the ISO film-speed dial to the setting closest to one-half the film's normal ISO rating. (Reduce exposure with similar increases in ISO.) With a manual camera, remember that a one-stop change in shutter speed is the equivalent of one *f*-stop change in aperture. If you want to increase the exposure of a scene by one stop, you can open the aperture one *f*-stop—say, from *f*/16 to *f*/11—or switch to a slower shutter speed—from 1/250 to 1/125 second, for example. In either case you are doubling the amount of light reaching the film.

1

2

3

4

Neil Montanus

The camera's meter is usually fairly reliable in the exposure it recommends for direct frontal light (1) or the light of open shade (2). But you may have to override the meter's reading in other kinds of light, increasing it by one stop for sidelighting (3) and by two stops for backlighting (4).

Emiel Blaakman

Derek Doeffinger

Extreme situations call for extreme exposure combinations. The dimly lighted interior above, for example, required both a wide aperture and a slow shutter speed. Photographing the motorcyclist at left, on the other hand, called for a fast shutter speed to freeze his movement, which has also isolated the spray of snow from his tire. Strong backlighting made a high shutter speed possible without requiring a very wide aperture to compensate.

Focusing

Proper focusing is as important as setting the correct exposure in getting a technically good picture. Recognizing this, many current compact rangefinder cameras have an automatic focusing capability—particularly useful when you want to catch a fast-moving subject and manual focusing might slow you down. A very narrow beam of infrared light, indicated by a spot in the center of your viewfinder, is emitted to determine the distance to the subject. This spot must be aimed at your subject to obtain correct focus. When you want your subject out of the center of the picture, you may still be able to get sharp focus by using the focus lock, if your camera is so equipped. Many autofocus cameras have this feature, which lets you prefocus by placing the viewfinder spot on your primary subject, activating the focus lock, then reframing the image.

Most SLR lenses have to be focused manually with a ring on the lens barrel. You focus a non-autofocus rangefinder by turning the ring to align two viewfinder images, one bright and one faint. The subject seen in the viewfinder of an SLR becomes sharp or fuzzy as you turn the focusing ring. The image you see is actually reflected to your eye from a special glass screen above the mirror. The screen breaks up the light in ways that allow you to focus more carefully. A common feature is a circular center area called a microprism, which shows very slight differences between sharp and less sharp images. On some viewfinders this microprism may be supplemented or replaced by a central split-image finder, such as the one shown at right.

Understanding Depth of Field

In focusing a camera, it is important to know that the depth of field—the zone in acceptably sharp focus in front and in back of the main subject—varies enormously depending on the size of the aperture, the subject's distance from the camera, and the focal length of the lens. The decisions you make about depth of field will have a dramatic effect on the appearance of the scene you are photographing. In simple terms, a shallow depth of field results in a blurry background or foreground, whereas a greater depth of field results in overall sharpness. The series of pictures at far right illustrates this.

Aperture is critical for depth of field. The smaller the aperture, the greater the depth of field. At *f*/16, for example, most normal (50 mm) lenses focused on a subject twelve feet away will make everything sharp from five and a half feet in front of the camera to infinity. At *f*/2, only the subject will be sharp; both the foreground and the background will be blurred. Midway between, at *f*/5.6, sharpness will extend from about three and a half feet in front of the subject to eight feet beyond it.

Subject distance also affects depth of field. In general, the closer your subject, the shallower the depth of field. Even at *f*/16, if you focus on a subject three feet away with most normal lenses, the depth of field will be less than a foot. And at *f*/2, your subject's eyes may be in focus while the nose and ears are blurred. As you back away from a subject, the depth of field increases rapidly. With *f*/16 at six feet, the zone of sharpness will extend from a foot in front of the subject to about three feet behind. And as mentioned, at about twelve feet at *f*/16, the depth of field extends to infinity. This is the maximum range of sharpness for most normal lenses. Focusing any farther away only reduces foreground sharpness. Although this point of diminishing return varies with different focal length lenses (at

Peter Culross

In the out-of-focus and in-focus examples of an SLR viewfinder above, the center circle is a split-image finder, while the ring surrounding it is a microprism. The entire surface of the viewing screen also serves as a focusing aid.

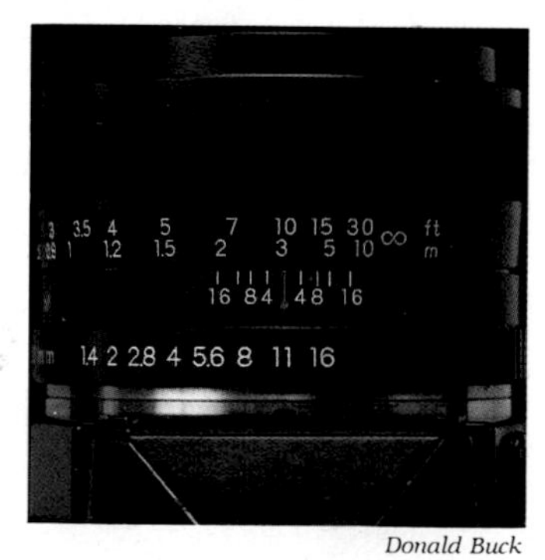

Donald Buck

The aperture ring on the lens above shows it is set on f/11, and the focusing ring indicates that the subject is ten feet away. The color-coded pair of lines for that aperture on the depth of field scale (the middle ring) shows that everything from about seven feet to twenty feet away will be sharp.

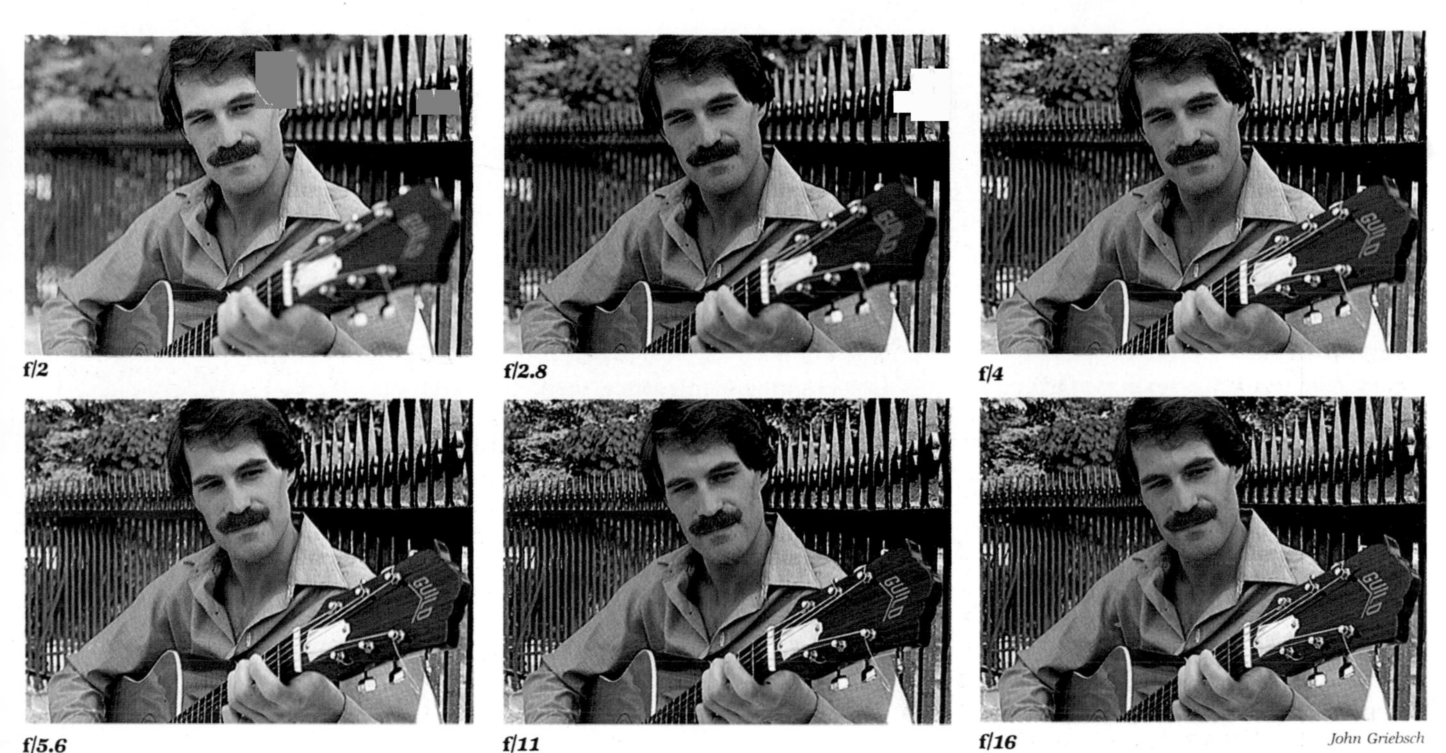

f/2 **f/2.8** **f/4**

f/5.6 **f/11** **f/16**

John Griebsch

The pictures above show the effect on depth of field of changes in aperture. In each, the lens was focused on the face of the guitar player. (The shutter speed was changed with each change in aperture to keep the exposures consistent.) Notice how smaller apertures improve the sharpness of both the distant fence and the head of the guitar, encouraging us to look at them more closely. Changes in depth of field are often an effective way to manipulate the viewer's eye.

the same camera-to-subject distance), it is important to be aware of it—especially when you want to get the greatest possible range of sharpness in both foreground and background, as in a landscape.

The focal length of the lens plays a role in depth of field too. The shorter the focal length, the more depth of field you'll get at a given aperture at the same subject distance. Thus, a wide-angle lens gives more depth of field at *f*/11, say, than a normal lens, and a normal lens gives more depth of field than a telephoto lens. Likewise, to get the same depth of field with a 100 mm lens that you are getting at *f*/5.6 on a normal lens, you would have to stop down to a much smaller aperture.

Many lenses have a simple depth of field scale inscribed next to the focusing ring. The scale on the normal lens in the picture at left, for example, has two lines representing each aperture between *f*/4 and *f*/16. (Most manufacturers inscribe the actual *f*-numbers under the lines; some color-code the lines to match the color of the *f*-numbers on the aperture ring.) As you turn the focusing ring, the distances falling between these lines are in acceptable focus. You may have noticed that when you change the aperture ring on your camera, neither the brightness nor the depth of field of the viewfinder image changes. This is because an SLR keeps the lens open to its maximum aperture until you click the shutter, so that you have the brightest possible viewfinder image. Thus, the depth of field visible in your viewfinder is that of the lens at *f*/2, or whatever its maximum aperture is, not the smaller aperture that you may be planning to use. To compensate for this, many SLRs provide a depth of field preview button. When you press it, the aperture closes down to the *f*-stop you have set. Although the viewfinder will become noticeably darker unless you are shooting with the lens wide open, you can see the actual zone of sharpness at your selected aperture. Use this feature carefully, though, because objects that appear sharp when you preview depth of field may not end up sharp in the enlarged print or projected slide.

At times you will have to compromise on depth of field. If you are trying to freeze the motion of a racing cyclist on an overcast day, for example, you can't expect great depth of field—the fast shutter speed required to stop action calls for a large aperture, with its minimal depth of field. In a case such as this, film speed also becomes a factor in depth of field. A more light-sensitive, high-speed film will also permit you to use the smaller apertures that give a deeper zone of sharpness.

Film

A hundred years ago, most photographs were made individually on large, cumbersome glass plates. The photographer planning to take twenty or thirty pictures had to lug about a considerable burden. In addition, each plate had to be carefully coated with a light-sensitive liquid emulsion just before exposure and developed immediately afterward. By comparison, today's 35 mm film is truly amazing—a long, flexible strip of lightweight film only 1-3/8 inches (35 mm) wide, able to capture up to thirty-six images on a single roll, and packaged in a compact, light tight metal spool known as a magazine, cassette, or cartridge.

Although far more convenient, 35 mm film works on the same principle as a glass plate negative. Its flexible plastic base is coated with a light-sensitive emulsion consisting of fine particles of silver halide and other compounds. When light strikes the film, it causes a change in the chemical structure of the particles, creating an invisible record—or latent image—of the subject matter that is later made visible by chemical action during processing. Black-and-white film has only one layer in its emulsion; all light reaching it, whatever its color, is reproduced as black, white, or shades of grey. Color film has additional layers that respond to the three primary colors in the light spectrum—blue, green, and red.

After processing, the image recorded on black-and-white film is a negative, which then must be printed onto light-sensitive paper to produce the positive image that we call a photograph or print. Depending on the type, color film will produce either negative images, for making prints, or positive transparent images—slides—which can be projected onto a screen or looked at in a hand viewer. You can make prints from slides in a color darkroom (see page 269), as can a photofinisher, who can also produce slides from negative film.

Each of these three general categories—black-and-white negative, color negative, and color slide—includes several different types of film. On the pages that follow, we discuss their characteristics and their suitability for various conditions and picture-taking situations. It's wise to experiment with several different films. Once you have found a particular film you like, however, the best way to become really familiar with its characteristics is to use it almost exclusively for a long time. You will soon acquire an eye for its potential in different situations, and that familiarity will give you the confidence for creative approaches.

Whatever type of film you use, certain precautions should always be observed. First, expose and process film before the expiration date printed on the box. After that, its color and speed may be unpredictable. Store film in a cool, dry place. Keep it away from direct sunlight, heaters, or radiators and out of automobile glove compartments. In damp climates, put your film in a sealed plastic bag along with moisture-absorbing silica gel crystals. Although refrigeration is recommended for some professional films, most others are intended to keep well in normal room temperatures. When advancing and rewinding film, use smooth, steady movements. In extremely dry atmospheres, rapid movement can create static electricity, which may produce streaks on your

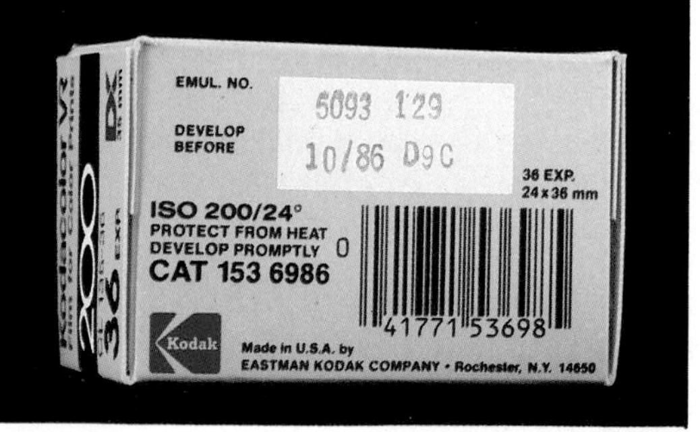

Jerry Antos

There are three kinds of 35 mm film from which to choose. The positive strip in the center here is color slide film. To the right of it are color negative film and a contact print made from it. To the left are black-and-white negative film and a black-and-white contact print made from it. Below is the bottom panel of a box of film, which indicates the type of film, its ISO speed, the number of exposures, and the date by which you should process it.

Jerry Antos

pictures; in frigid weather, film can become brittle and break. Airport security x-ray baggage scanners can also damage unprocessed film, particularly the newer very high-speed negative films. The effects of x-rays are cumulative; avoid repeated exposures at different stopovers. (Outside the United States, avoid x-ray inspection if possible.) Lead bags for film that block x-rays are available, but the attendants may ask to inspect them when they can't see into them. The best solution is to pack your film in a clear plastic bag, arrive early, and ask for a hand inspection. You can also mail your exposed film home or to a laboratory in prepaid envelopes. If you develop your film yourself (see Part IV, The Process), always handle it in complete darkness once you've removed it from its light tight cartridge.

Film

Types of Film

Different light sources emit different colors of light. But our eyes adjust quickly to the difference between the yellowish hues of incandescent light bulbs indoors and the more bluish color of sunlight outdoors. Film is not as adaptable. Even with black-and-white film, artificial and natural light render colors with different intensity. But because black-and-white film records all colors as tones of grey, the differences are acceptable to our eyes.

With color film, however, even subtle gradations of color must be reproduced accurately if the image is to look correct to the eye. To achieve this, color film is adjusted, or "balanced," for a particular light source. Because the color can be altered somewhat in the printing process, color negative film is usually balanced for only one source—daylight. This includes direct and reflected sunlight, as well as the light provided by electronic flash and blue flashbulbs. But color slide film, which becomes the final image when processed, cannot be corrected after the fact. Thus, while some slide films are balanced for daylight, others are balanced for one of two different kinds of artificial light source.

For photographic purposes, the color of light is described by its "temperature" on the Kelvin thermometric scale, and thus noted by a "K." Some special color slide films, called type A, are designed to be used with photolamps with a color temperature of

When daylight film is used in the outdoor light for which it is designed, the result (far left) seems correct to our eye. But when tungsten film is used outdoors (below), the image has a strong blue cast, giving skin an unattractive pallor. Indoors under incandescent light, tungsten film provides the color balance that we expect (below right). When daylight film is used instead (far right), the picture looks too amber in tone, although this is less detrimental to skin tones than some other colors. To avoid using film improperly, read the instructions that accompany every roll. The instructions shown at right are printed inside the film box.

Daylight film outdoors

Tungsten film outdoors

Michele Hallen Infantino

3400 K. But color slide film balanced for tungsten light of 3200 K color temperature, known as type B, is more commonly used. Although 3200 K tungsten light is slightly brighter in intensity and cooler in hue than normal room lighting, you can use type B film with excellent results in a scene that is illuminated by ordinary household incandescent bulbs.

To compensate for the shortage of blue hues in yellow-red incandescent light, tungsten film is especially sensitive to the blue end of the spectrum. As a result, if you use tungsten film outdoors in the more even mix of colors provided by sunlight, your slides will have a pronounced bluish cast. Conversely, if you shoot daylight-balanced film indoors under household incandescent bulbs, it will record the scene as more golden in hue than you perceive it. The four shots of the man below show the effects of using tungsten and daylight film in both types of light. As a rule, you should match your film to the prevalent light source in any scene you are photographing. However, the high speed of many recent color films invites their use in low-level artificial light, even though they are balanced for daylight. In particular, slide film should be corrected for this discrepancy with filters (see pages 118 to 121), although color negative film will also benefit by filtration in artificial light. You can also use filters to adjust the color of any light when you have the wrong kind of film in the camera.

KODAK EKTACHROME 400 Film (Daylight)

Load and unload your camera in subdued light.

EXISTING-LIGHT EXPOSURE: Cameras with automatic exposure controls—Set film speed at ISO (ASA) 400. **Cameras with manual adjustments**—Determine exposure setting with exposure meter set for ISO (ASA) 400 or use table below.

Interiors with Bright Fluorescent Light*	1/60 f/4
Ice Shows, Circuses—spotlighted acts (carbon-arc)	1/250 f/2.8

*May require corrective camera filters for optimum results.

Home Interiors at Night—Areas with Bright Light Areas with Average Light	1/30 f/2.8 1/30 f/2
Brightly Lighted Downtown Street Scenes at Night	1/60 f/2.8
Neon and Other Lighted Signs at Night	1/125 f/4
Floodlighted Buildings, Fountains, Monuments	1/15† f/2
Night Football, Baseball, Racetracks	1/125 f/2.8
Basketball, Hockey, Bowling	1/125 f/2
Stage Shows—Average Light (Bright—2 stops less)	1/60 f/2.8
Circuses—Floodlighted Acts	1/60 f/2.8
Ice Shows—Floodlighted Acts	1/125 f/2.8
Church, School—Stage and Auditorium	1/30 f/2

†Use a camera support.

☐ Tungsten light renders yellow-red cast.

Light	Film Speed	Filter
DAYLIGHT	**ISO (ASA) 400**	**None**
3400 K photolamps	ISO (ASA) 125‡	No. 80B
3200 K tungsten	ISO (ASA) 100‡	No. 80A

‡For through-the-lens exposure meters, see camera manual.

PROCESSING: Have this film processed by Kodak or other laboratory. Or process it yourself with KODAK EKTACHROME Film Processing Kit, Process E-6. You can increase speed to ISO (ASA) 800 with KODAK Special Processing Envelope, ESP-1. See your dealer.

If you have questions about this film: In the United States, write to Eastman Kodak Company, Dept. 841C, Rochester, N.Y. 14650. Outside the U.S., write Kodak in your country. See *KODAK Films* (AF-1) book at dealer.

Tungsten film indoors

Daylight film indoors

Michele Hallen Infantino

Film

Film Speed

In addition to color balance, film has other characteristics that can affect your pictures. Most notably, all film has a specific sensitivity to light. This sensitivity, or speed, is denoted by an ISO number. ISO is an abbreviation for the International Standards Organization. (In this country, for years the speed index was noted by ASA numbers, and in parts of Europe you will still find a DIN number used for a different speed index.) The ISO speed is clearly indicated on the film box and instructions, as well as on the film magazine itself. Some film magazines have a patterned code printed on them that programs the ISO number into the camera automatically.

ISO numbers range from 25 to 1000 and higher for the most commonly used films. The higher the number, the more sensitive the film is to light. For convenience, the ISO numbers are usually classified into the following categories: low speed (ISO 10 and below to 50), medium speed (ISO 64 to 200), high speed (ISO 250 to 640) and very high speed (ISO 800 to 1600). A doubling of the number indicates a doubling of the sensitivity of the film. Thus, a film with an ISO 400 rating needs only half as much light for proper exposure as a film rated ISO 200. Conversely, an ISO 100 film is half as fast, or sensitive, as an ISO 200 film, and it requires twice as much light for proper exposure. Not all film is rated in uniformly doubling multiples, but any such doubling or halving of ISO numbers is the equivalent of a one-stop change in either aperture or shutter speed on your camera, since these controls also work by doubling or halving the light. For example, if an ISO 200 film needed an exposure of 1/125 second at *f*/5.6, an ISO 400 film could be exposed at 1/125 second at *f*/8, or 1/250 second at *f*/5.6.

Since high-speed film requires less light for proper exposure than slower film, it allows you to take pictures in low light both outdoors and indoors, pictures that might otherwise be impossible. In particular, it may allow you to hand hold your camera in light levels that would otherwise require shutter speeds too slow for hand holding. Furthermore, because less light is needed, you can use smaller apertures and faster shutter speeds, which give you the benefit of greater depth of field or good action-stopping ability.

Medium-speed film (ISO 64 to 200) is intended for general picture-taking. In reasonable light, it allows flexibility in choice of aperture and shutter speed combinations, while yielding a sharp, fine-grain image with smooth tonality. It can be enlarged to a high degree without sacrificing these qualities, and its additional sensitivity often outweighs the slightly finer grain of low-speed films as an advantage.

The exceptional sharpness, fine grain, and rich tonal scale of low-speed film (ISO 10 and below to 50) make it an excellent choice for portraits, landscapes, still lifes, or any shot in which you want to show fine detail or textural nuances. Its relatively low sensitivity to light, however, requires that you use it in bright conditions or mount your camera on a tripod so that slower shutter speeds are possible.

In extreme conditions—very dim light, for example, or a combination of low light and a moving subject—certain black-and-white and color transparency films can be "pushed" for extra speed, either commercially or at home. (See the film's processing instructions or ask your photo dealer for information.) When you are shooting a roll that will be push-processed, you should set a higher ISO number on your camera. If you plan to increase the sensitivity of ISO 160 film by one stop, set 320 on the ISO dial. If you plan to push-process ISO 400 film one stop, set 800 on the dial; for one and a half stops, set 1250; and for two stops, 1600.

When you push film, extra development makes up to some extent for the reduced exposure you give the film, but at some cost to the image. Because highlights and lighter values are most affected by this technique, shadow detail may be poor. The image also tends to be grainier, more contrasty, and with slide film, slightly warmer in color than a normally processed image. KODAK EKTACHROME P800/1600 Professional Film (Daylight) is especially designed for push-processing, so that these sacrifices are minimized. Color negative film can't be pushed with much effect, and the new very high-speed films (ISO 1000) have reduced the need. With black-and-white film, special compensating developers (see page 274) can be used to minimize the loss of shadow detail. Remember that when you push film, the whole roll is pushed; any frames that received exposure at the film's normal ISO will be overdeveloped.

Finally, if your pictures consistently look washed out and overexposed or dark and underexposed, run a meter test. Bracket a normal exposure two full *f*-stops more and less than your meter recommends, using half-stop increments. If your results indicate that you need more exposure than you are getting with the meter set at the film's normal ISO number, compensate by setting a lower ISO speed; for less exposure, set a higher ISO speed. For each full stop of exposure you need, double or halve the ISO speed accordingly.

William M. Johannes

High-speed black-and-white film's sensitivity to light makes it useful for shooting in low light or freezing action with high shutter speeds, such as in this picture. It also permits using smaller apertures for better depth of field. If the negative from such a film is processed carefully, an 8 × 10 enlargement will not be objectionably more grainy than one from a lower-speed film.

Film

Film Characteristics

A film's definition, or ability to render a sharp, clear image, also varies with the chemical composition and thickness of the emulsion and the film's plastic base and backing. All of these affect the tendency of light to scatter in the emulsion. When light scatters, the boundaries between light and dark detail blur. As a general rule, this blur is least likely to occur with low-speed film.

Thus, when you require the utmost definition in a picture, a fine-grain, low-speed film is highly recommended. More often, however, you will probably opt for the convenience of medium- and high-speed films. Given modern advances in film technology, today's high-speed films provide very satisfactory results.

Norman Kerr

Norman Kerr

Color negative films are available in a range of speeds from ISO 100 to 1000, and just as with black-and-white film, graininess and sharpness are a function of film speed. ISO 100 film (above left) is a good choice for subjects that are rich in detail, but usually must be used in relatively bright light or with flash; ISO 400 color negative film (above right) is useful for more active subject matter; and ISO 1000 film (at right) is especially suited to subjects in dim light, particularly if you must hand hold the camera. In an 8 × 10 enlargement made from a negative of this very high-speed film, graininess will be quite pronounced.

Donald Maggio

Thomas Dell

Bob Clemens

Low- and medium-speed black-and-white films, ISO 25 to 125, are a better choice than high-speed film if you want to show fine detail and render textures precisely. Medium-speed film's moderate sensitivity to light makes it somewhat more versatile than low-speed film, while still yielding smooth tonalities and fine grain, such as in this lake scene (upper left). Low-speed film may require the use of a tripod, even in reasonable light. The watch detail above is from a small section of a negative made on Kodak Technical Pan Film 2415, ISO 25, enlarged 15 ×. This film affords the ultimate in fine grain and sharpness.

When you set the exposure on your camera, keep in mind that black-and-white and color negative films have a fairly wide exposure latitude. Slight underexposure or overexposure can be corrected in printing, although the results will never be as good as from a properly exposed negative. Generally, these films are more tolerant of overexposure than underexposure, even by a stop or two, although they will still show a loss of sharpness, increase in graininess, and distortion of contrast. The exposure for color slide film is far more crucial. As the series of pictures on page 89 shows, a one-stop change can make a noticeable difference. Because of this, you should bracket important color slide shots in uncertain lighting conditions by shooting at one-half and a full stop both over and under the recommended exposure. When in doubt, slight underexposure is best with slide film.

All film is designed to be exposed within a range of shutter speeds. These "reciprocity characteristics" vary from film to film and are often indicated in the information provided with the film. If not, the manufacturer will provide them on request. But in general, if low light or other factors require that you use an exposure of a second or more, you exceed the film's acceptable range, and its sensitivity decreases. With black-and-white film, you can compensate by increasing aperture size or using an even longer exposure. With color film, however, there may also be a shift in color when you stray outside the film's limits. Tungsten films are usually designed for the longer exposures artificial light requires and tend to shift less than daylight films with long exposures. Although slide films can be filtered on the camera to correct for such shifts if you test for them in advance, and color negative films can be corrected in printing, sometimes uncorrectable "color crossovers" occur. Thus, it's best to avoid extremely long exposures, except for special effects.

The progressive loss of sharpness as you move from low- to high-speed films can be explained in terms of the silver and dye particles in the film's emulsion. The faster a film is, the larger these particles must be. In higher-speed films, the particles tend to form irregularly distributed clumps that give the photo a sand-like or granular appearance. This quality, known as graininess, is most pronounced in extreme enlargements.

Neil Montanus

Color slide films, as explained on pages 96 and 97, are designed for different kinds of light. Daylight-balanced slide films, such as the ISO 64 film shown here, come in a greater range of film speeds than tungsten-balanced slide films.

Lenses

One of the great advantages of single-lens-reflex cameras is their ability to accept a diverse range of lenses. This gives the photographer an important creative control, because as we will see on the following pages, the lens has a powerful effect on the way the subject is presented. Lenses are described primarily by their focal length. Simply put, focal length is the distance between the lens and film when the lens is focused on infinity. In today's sophisticated compound lenses, though, it may not be the actual distance because they have been designed for compactness and to accommodate the presence of the SLR mirror. Focal length is measured in millimetres, and the standard (or "normal") lens on most SLRs is 50 mm. This lens is supplied with the camera because it represents the elements of a scene in the same size relationships that appear to the unaided eye and gives a reasonably broad angle of view. (The fixed 35 or 40 mm lenses provided on most rangefinders are probably closer in their wider angle of view to our own eyes. But the 50 mm lens's natural perspective may make it somewhat more versatile.)

To understand how focal length affects the angle of view of a lens, imagine a small hole in a solid wooden fence. Your eye is the film and the hole is the camera's lens. The closer your eye gets to the hole, the more you see on the other side. Sophisticated optics notwithstanding, the principle is the same for a lens: The closer it can get to the film, the wider its angle of view will be, and the more it will be able to fit on the film.

Lenses with a narrower angle of view than a 50 mm lens are called telephoto lenses. They have longer focal lengths and bring distant subjects closer. Wide-angle lenses have shorter focal lengths than 50 mm and encompass more of a scene from the same point. Zoom lenses provide a continuous range of focal lengths between their specified maximum and minimum limits, and other specialized lenses are designed for taking close-ups and for correcting perspective distortions.

Learn to use the lens that your camera is equipped with and fully explore its potential before you purchase accessory lenses. When you are ready for an additional lens, keep in mind that lens quality varies and that there is no reason to pay for more lens than you need. For example, if you will be shooting in bright daylight only, it doesn't make sense to pay a premium for an extra stop of maximum aperture. Also be aware that lens mounts differ. You can get adapters, but any time you buy a lens not designed for your camera's mount, test it to see if it connects properly to the camera and meter. Finally, lenses are delicate instruments that must be handled with great care. Keep your front lens cap on when not shooting, and use a UV or skylight filter (see page 116) to protect the lens when you are shooting. Keep front and back lens caps on all detached lenses. When you change lenses, do it in the shade and carefully read your camera's instruction booklet as to the proper method. Be sure, too, to keep your lenses dust- and fingerprint-free.

These beach-going photographers are using some of the longest telephoto lenses available to the single-lens-reflex user, but Ernst Haas chose a more versatile medium telephoto lens to take this shot.

Ernst Haas

Telephoto Lenses

Telephoto lenses, which have a focal length longer than that of a normal lens, enlarge a subject in the same way that a telescope does. As the focal length increases the degree of magnification increases, and a number of other interesting things happen that affect your image. The lens's angle of view becomes narrower, for example, and, provided that the camera-to-subject distance remains constant, the depth of field becomes shallower. There is also a change in perspective. These effects can be useful, depending on the kind of image you desire. The narrow angle of view enables you to isolate a detail or eliminate a cluttered foreground. Although it makes more careful focusing necessary, the shallow depth of field is great for blurring distracting foregrounds and backgrounds. And the perspective change can make distant elements in a landscape appear closer together or let you get a tight close-up of a face without distortion.

By far the most useful of the long lenses is a medium telephoto—any lens with a focal length between 75 and 135 mm for a 35 mm camera. Many have fairly large maximum apertures, such as *f*/2 or *f*/2.8. Because they minimize facial distortion and allow a comfortable distance between photographer and subject while still providing a full-frame image, medium telephotos are ideally suited to portraits. In addition, they are needed in many situations in which you have to keep a moderate distance away from your subject—when you are taking a candid street shot, for example, or photographing architectural details.

Strong telephoto lenses—those with focal lengths of 180 mm or longer—have much more specialized uses. Most notably, they are used by sports and wildlife photographers. Both these types of photography rely on the powerful magnification of a strong telephoto, even though these lenses are practical only in

Neil Montanus

Norman Kerr

50 mm normal lens

Neil Montanus

Donald Buck

100 mm medium telephoto lens

Taken from the same vantage point, these photographs compare the effects of a normal 50 mm lens (upper left) with a moderate 100 mm telephoto lens (lower left), a stronger 200 mm telephoto (upper right), a powerful 400 mm lens (middle right), and a 500 mm mirror telephoto lens (lower right). Since the focal length of each lens was twice the previous one, with the exception of the 500 mm lens, the magnification of the subject doubles with each image. Also note the decreasing depth of field with the longer lenses, especially apparent in the trees on the other side of the lake.

200 mm telephoto lens

Norman Kerr

Neil Montanus

400 mm telephoto lens

Norman Kerr

Neil Montanus

500 mm mirror telephoto lens

Donald Buck

Neil Montanus

brightly lighted situations. They usually have a relatively small maximum aperture, often *f*/4 or smaller, and since they accentuate the effect of camera movement, a fast shutter speed is necessary. This means that these lenses, for which depth of field is already limited by focal length, are often used near their maximum aperture, so that careful focusing becomes even more important. Increased magnification also increases the possibility of blurring from camera movement. To avoid this, the rule of thumb is to use a shutter speed at least as fast as the reciprocal of the lens's focal length. For a 200 mm lens, for example, this would be 1/250 second. With slower speeds use a tripod, monopod, or brace to steady the camera. Often, however, the active subjects typically photographed with these lenses require higher shutter speeds anyway.

Telephotos of 500 mm or longer are bulky, heavy, and awkward to use and nearly always require a tripod. (Many such lenses have tripod sockets in the middle of the lens for extra stability.) The mirror telephoto lens greatly reduces these problems. Following a principle used in the design of observatory telescopes, this lens has two curved mirrors that bounce the light rays back and forth—in effect "folding" them to pack a longer focal length into a shorter lens barrel. Although the lens is larger in diameter than a regular long lens, it is far more compact and lightweight. The price of this convenience, however, is an unchangeable aperture, usually around *f*/8 for a 500 mm lens. Further, with this lens there is a tendency for bright, out-of-focus points of light to become doughnut-shaped rings in the final image.

To obtain greater magnification with most lenses, you can also use tele-extenders—relatively inexpensive tube-like attachments that fit between the lens and the camera either to double or triple the focal length of the lens. Tele-extenders reduce the effective aperture of the lens and usually cannot match the sharpness achieved with a real telephoto, but they may be useful in certain situations.

Lenses

Wide-Angle Lenses

When you want to encompass more of a scene than would be possible with your normal lens, you should use a wide-angle lens. With its shorter focal length and broader angle of view, the wide-angle lens achieves an effect opposite that of a telephoto. Instead of enlarging and isolating a part of a scene, the wide-angle lens reduces its apparent size and takes in more of its surroundings from the same vantage point. This characteristic can be very useful when you are physically unable to get further away from your subject to include more of it, or when getting further back would mean including a visual obstruction or other unwanted element. A wide-angle lens also has much better depth of field at a given aperture with camera-to-subject distance constant than does a longer focal length lens, making it a good choice for a scene in which you want a deep zone of sharpness.

Like telephoto lenses, wide-angle lenses alter the perspective of a scene, but in a different way: Elements appear to be more distant from one another than your eyes perceive them to be. This change in perspective can cause distortion if your subject is too close to the lens or at an angle to it. An object or person may appear longer, taller, or wider than in reality, and this attenuation of space may cause protruding elements, such as a person's nose, to loom. (For this reason, be especially careful when using a wide-angle to take close-ups of people.) Parallel vertical lines, in particular, will converge (toward the top of the image) if the lens is pointed up, diverge if it is pointed down. These effects are controllable; keeping the camera level, for example, will keep vertical lines parallel. But sometimes the distorting effects of a wide-angle lens can be interesting and dramatic, if used thoughtfully.

Neil Montanus

A moderate wide-angle lens, one with a focal length of 28 or 35 mm, is the most useful. These lenses generally have a fairly large maximum aperture, *f*/2 or *f*/2.8, making them especially helpful when shooting indoors in limited space and low light. Extremely wide-angle lenses, 16 to 24 mm, can be very effective in creating an expansive space or for deliberate distortion of shapes. Ultra-wide-angle lenses, known as fisheyes, take in 180 degrees or more, far beyond what the unaided eye can see, but their shorter focal lengths will produce only a circular image. If you are considering purchasing a fisheye lens, you will have to weigh the limited usefulness of its spectacular distortion against the high price its outsized optics command.

Donald Buck

35 mm wide-angle lens

Neil Montanus

Donald Buck

20 mm wide-angle lens

Lonald Buck

8 mm fisheye lens

The scene shown on the preceding page—taken from the same vantage point—is used to illustrate the effects of a 35 mm moderate wide-angle lens (at left), a 20 mm extremely wide-angle lens (upper right), and an 8 mm fisheye lens (right), which takes in a hemispheric 180 degrees. In lenses of focal length shorter than 28 or 24 mm, depth of field is virtually limitless.

Neil Montanus

Lenses

Zoom Lenses

Rather than being limited to just one focal length, a zoom lens has movable optical elements that make possible a whole range of focal lengths. The control used to adjust the focal length of the lens varies. On some lenses, it is a separate ring that you turn to enlarge or reduce the image of your subject. In more recent zooms, it is incorporated into the focusing ring, and you slide the ring up and down the length of the lens barrel to change focal lengths. One of the advantages of these "one-touch" zooms is that you can focus once, then slide the ring without turning it, and the lens will remain focused on the subject throughout the changes in focal length. Both styles of lens have their advantages.

Zoom lenses are available in a variety of focal-length ranges. The telephoto range offers focal lengths from 70 or 80 mm to 200 or more, although some makers now offer lenses in the 150 mm up to 600 mm range. Another group ranges around the normal 50 mm focal length, many having moderately wide-angle to medium-telephoto capabilities, such as 28 or 35 mm to 80 mm and beyond. Some wide-angle zooms range as short as 24 mm, although their upper end is more limited.

Early zoom lenses were awkward to operate and often were not very efficient in sharpness or contrast. Today, however, zooms are both easy to use and often of superb optical quality, and they are tremendously practical. By adjusting the focal length and image size, you can make a subject fill the frame without changing your position or lens, an advantage with an active subject that moves closer to and farther from the lens, as in a sporting event. You should be wary, though, of relying on this feature too heavily because there are times when a simple change in magnification won't bring about the desired perspective rendition that a change in position might. On the other hand, a zoom lens can take the place of two, three, or more separate lenses, the combined cost of which makes its higher individual price seem quite reasonable. Most current zooms have built-in close-up capability, which makes them even more versatile and useful.

Neil Montanus

The unusual effect in the picture above was achieved by "racking" the zoom lens—that is, changing its focal length—during a relatively long exposure.

The adage that you get what you pay for is particularly true of zooms; you may find inexpensive zoom lenses are not as satisfactory as more costly ones. But even high-quality zooms have certain drawbacks. They are bulkier than conventional lenses of comparable outside focal length, and have a smaller maximum aperture, usually *f*/3.5 or less. This may limit their use to fairly well-lighted scenes, particularly at the higher shutter speeds required by longer focal-length settings. Thus, if you usually shoot outdoors—or indoors with a flash—a zoom lens makes good sense, but if you take a lot of pictures in low existing light, your best bet would be to stick to single-focal-length lenses.

28 mm setting — *Neil Montanus*

Donald Buck

28 to 85 mm zoom lens

80 mm setting — *Neil Montanus*

Wide-angle zoom lenses, which can range in focal length from 21 mm through 35 mm and on up to 50 mm, are one of the most recent major advances in optics. For most photographers, however, the handiest zoom lens ranges on either side of the normal 50 mm lens, covering focal lengths between 28 mm and 100 mm (above). A zoom lens that runs between 80 and 200 mm (right) is especially useful for sports, nature, and candid photography.

200 mm setting — *Neil Montanus*

Norman Kerr

80 to 200 mm zoom lens

Special-Purpose Lenses

Nearly all photographers have had occasion to lament the limitations of their standard lenses. Two situations in particular are frustrating: when you want to move in for a tight close-up and you find that your lens won't focus that close; and when you take a picture of a building and discover that its sides converge so much toward the top that it looks more like a pyramid than a rectangular structure. The special lenses designed to handle these problems will be more expensive than a standard lens, but if you frequently encounter situations where these lenses are needed, they may well be worth the investment.

The problem of sloping building sides, known as keystoning, occurs when you must tilt the camera upward to take a picture of a tall building. This distortion is most apparent with wide-angle lenses—which are frequently used to photograph architecture—because of the way they exaggerate perspective. The ***perspective-control lens*** (PC) is a special wide-angle lens with a front that can be shifted up or down or side to side, in its rotating mount, so that you can encompass the top of the building while keeping the camera level for minimal distortion.

When photographing high buildings, even if you shift the PC lens's front all the way up, you still may not be able to include the very top, and you may have to tilt the camera in addition to shifting the lens. Even so, the convergence of the sides won't be as severe as if you had been using a standard lens. Many photographers feel that a little convergence is natural-looking. The top of a fully-perspective-controlled building can sometimes look oddly stretched out because of the extreme angle at which the image of that portion of the building has struck the film. The PC lens can be used to correct distortion occurring in other directions too.

A 28 mm wide-angle lens is useful in architectural photography, but it often causes parallel lines to converge unnaturally. This is particularly apparent in vertical subjects when you point the camera up. By using a 28 mm perspective-control lens and shifting its front up instead, the photographer has eliminated distortion in this courtyard wall of Boston's Gardner Museum.

Russell Hart

Donald Buck

28 mm perspective control lens

The convergence to the side of the top and bottom of a facade that must be photographed at an angle because of an obstructing tree, for example, can be partially or fully corrected by shifting the lens sideways.

There are two main limitations to the PC lens: It doesn't connect to the camera's built-in meter, and because it must be stopped down manually before shooting, causing the viewfinder to become dim, you may need to use a tripod with it. (A tripod will also allow you freedom to adjust camera position and lens correction accurately and maintain both while you take the picture.)

The lens that lets you focus closely on a small subject, such as the flowers shown here, is usually known as a ***macro lens.*** Strictly speaking, this lens should be called a close-focusing lens, since the term *macro* implies making an image life-size or larger on film. When used by themselves at their closest focusing distance, these lenses can produce a film image that is about half the size of the subject. For most close-up subjects—flowers, insects, coins, stamps, or documents—this range is more than adequate. With the addition of extension tubes or bellows between the camera and the lens, the range of the macro lens can be extended even further to reproduce subjects at two, three, or more times larger than life.

Most macro lenses are of normal focal length, although longer lenses in the 100 to 200 mm range are also available. (Many zoom lenses have a macro function, making close-up work over a wide range of focal lengths possible.) Most also focus to infinity, making them useful in general photography as well. In close-up work, you must be particularly careful in focusing because depth of field is very shallow (see page 194). Because these lenses focus on a flat plane rather than the curved surface (formed by all points that are the same distance from the lens) that regular lenses focus on, you should keep the important parts of your subject in a plane parallel to the film itself. And, if your subject has much depth at all—like a flower or an insect, for example—you must decide which part of it you want to be in focus. Such selective focusing isn't necessarily undesirable, since a soft blurring of the foreground or background can make the central aspect of a subject stand out and appear three-dimensional.

The macro lens allows you to focus very closely on a small subject and get a near life-size image without distortion. The first picture at left was taken with a 50 mm lens at its closest focusing distance; the second, below, only inches from the flowers using a macro lens.

Neil Montanus

Donald Buck

55 mm macro lens

For the photographer who only occasionally takes close-ups, there are alternatives to the macro lens. Extension tubes and bellows can be used with your regular lenses for very close focusing (see page 196). Another, less effective, method is the filter-like, close-up attachment that screws onto the front of your regular lenses.

Filters

If you've ever looked at a professional's photographs and wondered why they looked so much more realistic, intriguing, or dramatic than your own, the answer may well be filters. As the sampling here shows, a wide array of these simple attachments is available, and each can make a unique contribution to your pictures.

#0

#1A

#29

#11

#50

#80A

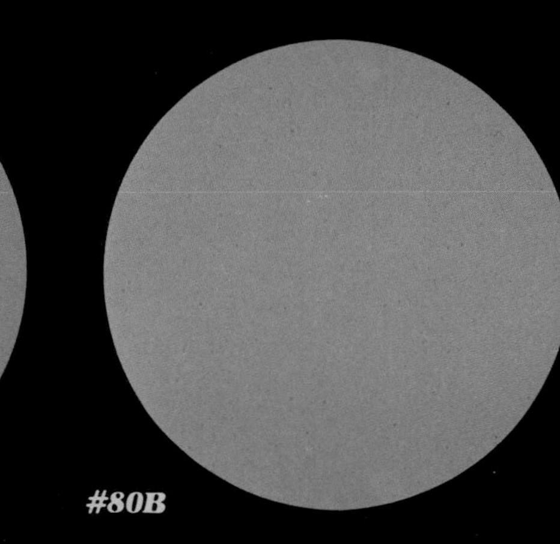

#80B

#82A

#25

#58

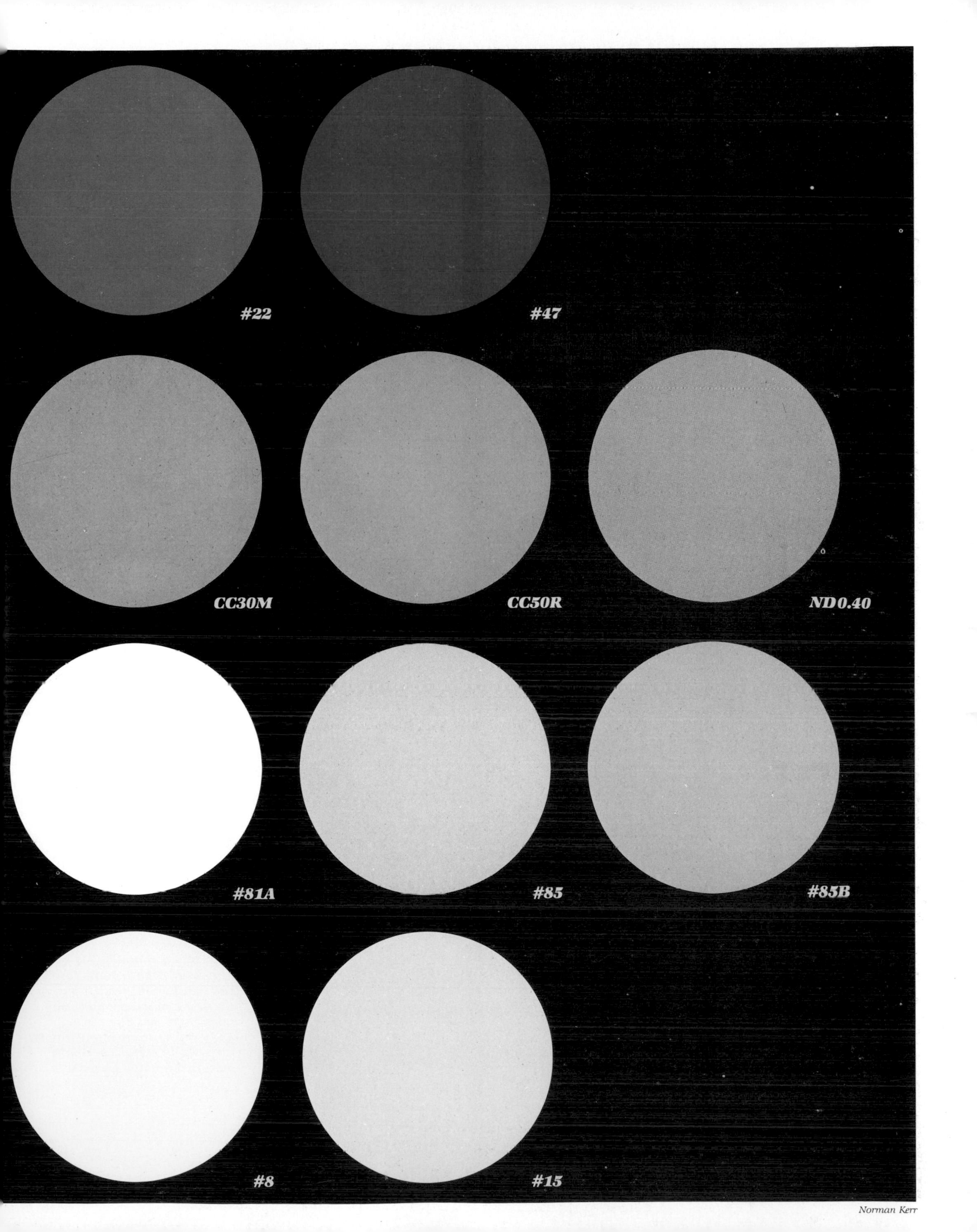

Norman Kerr

Filters

How Filters Work

Because film cannot adjust for the different colors of light the way the human eye can, filters are often essential in making the hues and tones of a photographic image correspond to those we see with our eyes. A color filter permits light of its own color to pass through it and, to varying degrees, absorbs or blocks the light of other colors. The extent to which this occurs depends on the intensity of the filter color as well as its position in the spectrum. In general, closely related hues are permitted to pass through, while complementary colors are stopped. Thus, a yellow filter absorbs blue but lets most orange pass through. Only the light that gets through, of course, is recorded on film.

Nearly all filters, because they reduce the light entering the camera, require the use of a larger aperture or a slower shutter speed to ensure that the film receives just as much exposure as it would have received without a filter on the camera. The change, although now frequently given in *f*-stops, is traditionally specified as a filter factor—a number that indicates by how much you must increase your exposure. Filter factors for some common filters are given in the table on page 122. A filter factor of 2, for example, tells you that you must double your exposure—the equivalent of a one-stop change. A factor of 4 indicates that the exposure must be increased four times—the same as a two-stop increase. These factors are useful in situations in which a through-the-lens exposure meter might not provide a reliable reading with a filter on the lens. For example, if you are using a red filter to darken a blue sky (see "Filters for Black-and-White Film," page 122), and your subject includes a lot of green foliage, the filter will block so much light from the scene that the meter might recommend overexposure to compensate. On the other hand, a through-the-lens reading taken with a yellow filter (or any other filter of relatively pale color) on the lens is usually fairly reliable. If in doubt take a meter reading before attaching the filter and adjust it with the filter factor. Compare the adjusted reading to a reading taken with the filter on the lens. Although it is inconvenient to constantly attach and reattach a filter you are using regularly, be aware of situations in which readings may be thrown off by the filter's presence. Bracket your exposures if there isn't time to double-check your reading.

The size of a common glass disk screw-in filter is usually expressed as a number representing its diameter in millimetres. When you purchase a filter, be sure it is the same size as the diameter—not the focal length—of your lens. You can purchase adapters that allow you to attach larger filters to smaller-diameter lenses, to save yourself the cost of several sets of filters. However, manufacturers are making an effort to standardize their most commonly used lenses so that you have to purchase only one set of filters. This is only practical, though, with focal lengths ranging from about 20 mm to 100 mm and this usually doesn't include bulkier zooms. Gelatin filters, which are less expensive but also more delicate than glass filters, will attach to most lenses with a special holder. As discussed in the following pages, some filters come only in gelatin form.

Norman Kerr

You can buy glass-mounted filters that screw directly into lenses (top). Different lenses, however, may require different-size filters. Rather than buy a complete set of filters for each lens you own, you can buy all your filters in the same diameter and use adapter rings, like the one shown at bottom. Many filters are sold in series especially designed for this purpose.

Norman Kerr

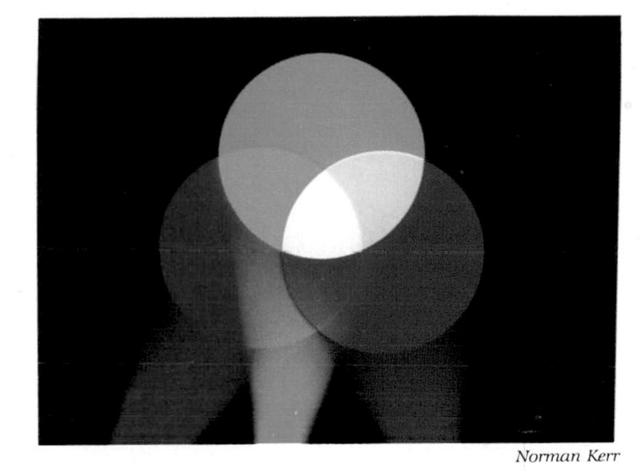

Norman Kerr

As the picture above shows, the primary colors that constitute white light are red, green, and blue. What happens when filters of the complementaries that block them—magenta, yellow, and cyan—are overlapped can be seen at left. Note that when all three overlap at center, the result is no light transmission—or what we call the color black.

Filters

UV, Skylight, and Polarizing Filters

UV and Skylight Filters: The two most commonly used basic filters are the colorless ultraviolet (UV) or haze filter and the faintly pinkish skylight filter. Because their effect on a color or black-and-white image is extremely subtle, and they require no exposure change, many photographers simply leave one of them on the camera at all times to protect the lens's vulnerable front element from airborne matter and scratches. If scratched, a filter is far less expensive to replace than the lens, and it is more resistant to repeated cleanings.

The UV filter absorbs ultraviolet radiation—wavelengths shorter than the blue-violet end of the visible spectrum. Although we can't see UV light, film records it along with visible light, often as an unexpected haze (bluish in a color shot) in the background of a distant scene. The UV filter blocks out this ultraviolet radiation, making the scene recorded on film look more like what we see. It will not eliminate visible haze, as often believed. The skylight filter is similar in its effects to the UV filter, but its slight tint can also reduce the bluish cast of light in open shade and on overcast days, which is exaggerated by certain films.

Polarizing Filter: Like the UV and skylight filters, the polarizing filter can be used with either black-and-white or color film. But it has a greater variety of uses, and its effects are much more dramatic.

Some light reflected from nonmetallic surfaces is polarized—that is, it vibrates in only one plane. The polarizing filter is a grid of microscopic crystals. It rotates in its mount, and as you turn it, the grid prevents light not traveling parallel to it from entering the lens. Thus, the polarizing filter allows you to monitor and select the amount of non-parallel reflected light recorded on film.

Neil Montanus

By eliminating reflections, either diffuse or direct (as in this picture), the polarizing filter can increase the intensity of colors dramatically.

If you've admired the almost unnaturally rich colors of photographs in travel magazines, it's a good bet they were achieved by the use of a polarizing filter. This is because the filter increases the color "saturation" of many surfaces, ranging from foliage to skin, by eliminating reflections that lighten their tone. Likewise, the polarizer is the only way to deepen a blue sky in a color photograph, but it will accomplish this just as effectively in a black-and-white photo. It does so by blocking the polarized light reflected by tiny airborne particles of dust and water vapor. For the same reason it's a more effective way to penetrate haze than the UV filter, for color or for black-and-white.

But the polarizing filter is perhaps most effective in dealing with highly reflective

To use a polarizing filter effectively, keep in mind the following points:

- ***For maximum effect, the handle or mark on the polarizing filter's rotating ring should point toward the main light source or toward the source of the reflection.***

- ***With a single-lens reflex, you can monitor the effect of a polarizing filter through the viewfinder as you turn the filter and as you change camera angle. With a rangefinder, on the other hand, you must hold the filter to your eye, turn it until you get the effect you want, and then mount it on the camera with the handle or mark pointing in the same direction.***

- ***Reflections from metallic surfaces cannot be eliminated with a polarizing filter. This includes mirrors, which have a metal-leaf backing. However, if the metal is painted, such as on a car, the polarizer will work.***

Neil Montanus

A polarizing filter is the only way to darken a blue sky in a color photograph. You can vary the degree of darkening by rotating the filter in its mount, the effect of which will be visible in the viewfinder if you are using an SLR. Here, the darker sky in the picture taken with the polarizing filter accentuates the shapes of the boat hulls, and makes their whiteness seem brighter. The filter has a similar effect on clouds.

surfaces like water or glass, such as in the pictures shown here. At the correct camera angle, with the filter properly set, you can eliminate or tone down reflections that would otherwise prevent you from seeing through those surfaces. The filter can suddenly reveal a log on the bottom of the lake, or a mannequin in the store window. Nevertheless, the polarizing filter should be used with discretion. Reflections provide a great deal of information about the physical world, and without them surfaces might appear dull or even ambiguous. They can also be used as an interesting pictorial device. Thus, in some instances, it's better to filter out reflections partially, toning them down rather than eliminating them. Don't forget that reflections can be an interesting pictorial device too.

Surprisingly, the degree of polarization has no effect on exposure. In fact, a through-the-lens meter is often fooled by a polarizing filter in a less-than-full effectiveness setting. The standard procedure is to meter the scene without the polarizing filter and then increase exposure by one and one third stops. (The polarizing filter always has a factor of 2.5 no matter what extent the polarization [degree of rotation].)

Neil Montanus

Although the polarizing filter has an extraordinary ability to reveal, sometimes it's best not to use it at all. In these pictures of a submerged alligator, not only is the reflection necessary in defining the water's surface, but the disembodied protrusion of the alligator's head is a more familiar image than the whole animal, and more evocative of its deadly stealth.

Filters

Color Correcting Filters

Ideally, the color film you use in a given situation should be balanced for the type of illumination available. But color film can also be used successfully with other light sources if you filter it to adjust for the color of the light. The cost, as with most filters, will be an increase in the exposure required. This correction is crucial with slide film, since it is processed directly into a final image after shooting. In most cases, the images from color negative film can be partially corrected during printing.

The color correction filters specifically designed for adjusting the color temperature of light are the yellow- and blue-tinted filters known as color conversion filters. There are about eighteen color conversion filters in the series 80 (darker blue) and 85 (darker yellowish orange) for major adjustments, and in the series 81 (paler yellow) for more minor changes. The most commonly used of these are the No. 85B and No. 80A.

These two filters are designed for the color-balance discrepancy situations you are most likely to encounter, as illustrated in the picture sequences at right. The first is outdoors on a sunny day with a half-exposed roll of tungsten-balanced film in your camera. Since tungsten film produces a bluish image if used in daylight, the filter that corrects for this—No. 85B—is yellowish-orange in color. It filters out the excess blues and heightens yellow-red hues. The same filter should be used when shooting tungsten film with an electronic flash, since the flash simulates daylight.

The second situation is just the reverse—indoors in incandescent light with daylight-balanced film. Uncorrected, pictures taken on daylight film in these conditions will appear unaturally golden. The solution is a blue-colored filter, No. 80A, which absorbs some of the overly abundant yellows and reds and enhances the scarce blues. Although this filter requires a two-stop increase in exposure, an ISO 1000 film will still have an effective speed of ISO 250 if you use it. But if you know you will be shooting a roll of film half indoors and half outdoors, your best bet is to select a high-speed tungsten film (push processed ISO 320), which you can use unfiltered indoors where the light is dimmer. In brighter sunlight, the two-thirds of a stop exposure increase required by the No. 85B filter shouldn't give you any trouble.

If you do much work with photolamps, there are four filters you might want to consider. With a blue No. 80B filter, you can use daylight-balanced film under photolamps, while a yellowish orange No. 85 will allow you to use photolamp-balanced film outdoors. This adjustment is very similar to the adjustment required for tungsten- and daylight-balanced film and light sources shown at right, since there is a relatively small difference between tungsten illumination rated at 3200 K and photolamp light rated at 3400 K. There are, however, filters that adjust even for this slight difference. A faint yellow No. 81A filter corrects photolamp light for tungsten film, and a pale blue No. 82A adjusts tungsten light for photolamp film. Exposure increases for these filters are given on page 120.

If you think that the effect of any of these filters is too yellow or too blue, use the next lightest filter. Although some of the other color conversion filters are rarely needed, each has its purpose. If you shoot indoors under normal room lighting with tungsten film and find that the results are too amber, then try a pale blue No. 82B or 82C filter. Similarly, if you feel that your photos shot on cloudy, rainy, or hazy days are too cool in color—even with a skylight filter—experiment with a light yellow No. 81 or 81A filter. In both cases, the adjustment is likely to result in a final image that corresponds more closely to the way your eye perceives the scene.

When daylight film is shot outdoors on a sunny day, the result (top) looks much the way we see it. With tungsten-balanced film (middle), however, there is a pronounced bluish cast. When a No. 85B yellow-orange filter is used with the tungsten film (bottom), the color balance is almost the same as with daylight film. The filter required a two-thirds-stop increase in exposure.

Using tungsten-balanced film with incandescent light indoors (top) gives a natural-looking image. When daylight-balanced film is used instead (middle), the result is too amber in tone. But with a blue No. 80A filter (bottom), a picture taken on daylight film is virtually indistinguishable from the image on tungsten film. The correction, however, required a large exposure increase—two stops.

Daylight film outdoors

Tungsten film indoors

Tungsten film outdoors

Daylight film indoors

John Griebsch

Tungsten film outdoors—filtered

John Griebsch

Daylight film indoors—filtered

Filters

Color Correcting Filters

The table at top right will help you determine the appropriate filters and exposure changes for different film and light-source combinations. It is particularly useful if your camera has an external photocell because it tells you by how much you should lower the ISO setting on the camera to adjust for the light the filter blocks. Although the through-the-lens meter in an SLR will give reasonably accurate readings through many filters, as mentioned, the stronger filters may throw it off. In such cases, a safer bet is to set the lower ISO for the filter shown in the table and adjust your camera before putting on the filter and shooting. Alternatively, you can first meter the scene without a filter at the film's normal ISO. Then, when you put on the filter, increase the indicated exposure by the *f*-stop change shown here.

For the other most common type of illumination, fluorescent lighting, color conversion filters are helpful. Fluorescent tubes are too deficient in red to fit into the spectrum of colors for which film is balanced, and a strong addition of red and yellow is needed to make the image appear natural in tone. The most widely used kind of fluorescent light, cool white, can usually be corrected with two commonly available screw-in filters—FLD (fluorescent daylight) for daylight film and FLT or FLB (fluorescent tungsten) for tungsten film. Both filters require a one-stop increase in exposure. For other types of fluorescents you can use color compensating (CC) filters, most of which are available only in gelatin form. These filters are made in graduated densities for the three primary colors—red, blue, and green—and for the three complementary colors, cyan, yellow, and magenta. Some suggested combinations of these filters for different kinds of fluorescent light are shown in the lower table at right.

Michæle Hallen Infantino

These three pictures were taken in the same cool white fluorescent light but with two different types of film. Tungsten-balanced film (top) gives the greatest distortion—a pronounced greenish cast. Daylight-balanced film (middle) provides much better results, although the image is still off color. The most natural looking shot (bottom) was taken with color correction filters and daylight film.

If you plan to take pictures in a specific situation, such as for a party or a ceremony with unusual or mixed lighting, you can shoot a test roll with a preliminary correction based on the recommendations in these tables, then assess the result on the color-corrected lightbox often found at most custom photo labs. If the film has a noticeable color cast to it, place CC filters of that color's complement and of progressively higher densities over the slide until the cast is eliminated. Then when you do your final shooting, add to your first filter pack the filter (or filters) that does this most effectively. (You can and may need to use light-balancing as well as color compensating filters. If your slides seem too yellow-brown, for example, a color conversion filter of the light blue 82 series might be appropriate.)

In using color compensating filters, keep in mind that each primary color blocks the other two primaries—a red filter, for example, blocks blue and green. Each of the complementary colors blocks one of the primaries: A cyan filter blocks red, a magenta filter blocks green, and a yellow filter blocks blue. The extent to which they block the colors depends on their density, which is indicated by their number. Thus, a CC30M (magenta) filter blocks 30 percent of the green in the scene. This filter might be useful if you are shooting through a green-tinted, plate glass window. A CC30R, which blocks 30 percent of the blues and greens, may be helpful in underwater photography.

Conversion Filters and Exposure Changes for Color Films

Film color balance	*Film speed*	*Daylight speed or f-stop change 5500 K*	*Photolamp speed or f-stop change 3400 K*	*Tungsten speed or f-stop change 3200 K*
	Filter type ▶	*No filter*	*No. 80B*	*No. 80A*
Daylight film	25	25	8 or + 1⅔ stops	6 or + 2 stops
	64	64	20 or + 1⅔ stops	16 or + 2 stops
	100	100	32 or + 1⅔ stops	25 or + 2 stops
	200	200	64 or + 1⅔ stops	50 or + 2 stops
	400	400	125 or + 1⅔ stops	100 or + 2 stops
Tungsten film	*Filter type* ▶	*No. 85B*	*No. 81A*	*No filter*
	160	100 or + ⅔ stop	125 or + ⅓ stop	160
Film for photolamps	*Filter type* ▶	*No. 85*	*No filter*	*No. 82A*
	40	25 or + ⅔ stop	40	32 or + ⅓ stop

Filters and Exposure Change for Fluorescent Light

Fluorescent lamp	*Daylight film* KODACOLOR VR 1000*, VR 400*, VR 200, VR 100 EKTACHROME 200 and 100 KODACHROME 25	*Daylight film* EKTACHROME P800/1600 *(Professional)* EKTACHROME 400 KODACHROME 64	*Tungsten film* EKTACHROME 160
Daylight	40M + 40Y + 1 stop	50M + 50Y + 1⅓ stops	No. 85B + 40M + 30Y + 1⅔ stops
White	20C + 30M + 1 stop	40M + ⅔ stop	60M + 50Y + 1⅔ stops
Warm white	40C + 40M + 1⅓ stops	20C + 40M + 1 stop	50M + 40Y + 1 stop
Warm white deluxe	60C + 30M + 2 stops	60C + 30M + 2 stops	10M + 10Y + ⅔ stop
Cool white	30M + ⅔ stop	40M + 10Y + 1 stop	60R + 1⅓ stops
Cool white deluxe	20C + 10M + ⅔ stop	20C + 10M + ⅔ stop	20M + 40Y + ⅔ stop
Unknown fluorescent †	10C + 20M + ⅔ stop	30M + ⅔ stop	50M + 50Y + 1⅓ stops

**For critical use.*
†These filters are for emergency use only, when it's not possible to determine the type of fluorescent lamp in use. Color rendition in pictures taken with these filters will be less than optimum.

Filters

Filters for Black-and-White Film

Because black-and-white film records colors as shades of grey, an enormous variety of color filters can be used to change the appearance of a black-and-white print, either subtly or dramatically. Nearly all widely used black-and-white films are panchromatic—that is, they will record all the colors in the visible spectrum. But they do not reproduce each of these colors with the same relative brightness we perceive them to have. In particular, black-and-white films are less sensitive to yellow and more sensitive to blue than is the human eye. They are also fairly sensitive to ultraviolet radiation, which we can't see. The most noticeable result of this disparity is that a blue sky appears much lighter in tone in a black-and-white print than we actually see it. Sometimes it ends up so light that any tonal separation between clouds and sky is lost, or the difference is less dramatic than it originally appeared. By using a light yellow No. 8 filter, which blocks a certain amount of blue light, this relationship can be restored, and the sky given a more natural-looking tone. A No. 15 deep yellow filter will make the sky reproduce somewhat darker than it appears, and No. 21 orange and No. 25 red filters will yield progressively deeper skies with more dramatic clouds. Always be aware, though, that these filters will also lighten colors similar to their own and thus minimize other tonal separations.

Filter Factors for General Picturetaking with Black-and-White Films

		Daylight		Tungsten light	
Filter number	Color of filter	Filter factor	Open the lens by (f-stops)	Filter factor	Open the lens by (f-stops)
3	Light yellow	1.5	$\frac{2}{3}$		
4	Yellow	1.5	$\frac{2}{3}$	1.5	$\frac{2}{3}$
6	Light yellow	1.5	$\frac{2}{3}$	1.5	$\frac{2}{3}$
8	Yellow	2	1	1.5	$\frac{2}{3}$
9	Deep yellow	2	1	1.5	$\frac{2}{3}$
11	Yellowish green	4	2	4	2
12	Deep yellow	2	1	1.5	$\frac{2}{3}$
13	Dark yellowish green	5	$2\frac{1}{3}$	4	2
15	Deep yellow	2.5	$1\frac{1}{3}$	1.5	$\frac{2}{3}$
23A	Light red	6	$2\frac{2}{3}$	3	$1\frac{2}{3}$
25	Red	8	3	5	$2\frac{1}{3}$
29	Deep red	16	4	8	3
47	Blue	6	$2\frac{2}{3}$	12	$3\frac{2}{3}$
47B	Deep blue	8	3	16	4
50	Deep blue	20	$4\frac{1}{3}$	40	$5\frac{1}{3}$
58	Green	6	$2\frac{2}{3}$	6	$2\frac{2}{3}$
61	Deep green	12	$3\frac{2}{3}$	12	$3\frac{2}{3}$
Polarizing screen—grey		2.5	$1\frac{1}{3}$	2.5	$1\frac{1}{3}$

Because the filters described above work by blocking blue light, the density of the sky in the negative is reduced. This area of reduced density lets through more light when the print is made, resulting in a darker value. Conversely, objects of color similar to the filter's produce relatively greater densities on the negative, making them lighter in tone in the black-and-white print. This effect can be used in a similar fashion to heighten the contrast between elements in a scene. It is useful when two elements of equal brightness but different color might be recorded as almost identical

These pictures show the effects of different filters for black-and-white on a blue sky. Although the picture at left, taken without a filter, shows tone in the sky, quite often a pale blue sky will reproduce as a blank white in a print. A yellow filter can restore tone to it or darken its tone to match that of the scene, as it has in the second picture below. For a deep sky with dramatic clouds, use a red filter, as in the picture on the right.

Neil Montanus

Neil Montanus

When photographed in black and white, red flowers appear the same shade of grey as their green stems. With a No. 25 red filter, the flower petals become lighter, but the stems seem unnaturally dark. A No. 58 green filter, on the other hand, lightens the stems by increasing their exposure on the negative and darkens the flowers by blocking the red light they reflect. Because in a black-and-white print tonal separations must represent color differences as well as differences in brightness, this added contrast seems natural.

greys. Unfiltered, red flowers will tend to merge with their green leaves, but with a red filter, they will appear light against dark foliage. If a green filter is used, the flowers will appear dark against light foliage. In addition to lightening foliage, a No. 58 green filter will darken a blue sky about as much as a yellow filter, making it a good alternative for outdoor work.

Keep in mind that filters can affect overall image contrast as well as specific tonal relationships; stronger filters such as orange and red will increase it considerably. Even a yellow filter increases contrast slightly. Also, some manufacturers of glass filters have their own designations for filters. Check with your photo dealer to find out how they correspond to the table at right.

Filter Recommendations for Black-and-White Films in Daylight

Subject	*Effect desired*	*Suggested filter*
Blue sky	Natural	No. 8 yellow
	Darkened	No. 15 deep yellow
	Spectacular	No. 25 red
	Almost black	No. 29 deep red
	Night effect	No. 25 red, plus polarizing screen
Marine scenes when sky is blue	Natural	No. 8 yellow
	Water dark	No. 15 deep yellow
Sunsets	Natural	None or No. 8 yellow
	Increased brilliance	No. 15 deep yellow or No. 25 red
Distant landscapes	Addition of haze for atmospheric effects	No. 47 blue
	Very slight addition of haze	None
	Natural	No. 8 yellow
	Haze reduction	No. 15 deep yellow
	Greater haze reduction	No. 25 red or No. 29 deep red
Nearby foliage	Natural	No. 8 yellow or No. 11 yellowish green
	Light	No. 58 green
Outdoor portraits against sky	Natural	No. 11 yellowish green No. 8 yellow or polarizing screen
Flowers—blossoms and foliage	Natural	No. 8 yellow or No. 11 yellowish green
Red, "bronze," orange, and similar colors	Lighter to show detail	No. 25 red
Dark blue, purple, and similar colors	Lighter to show detail	None or No. 47 blue
Foliage plants	Lighter to show detail	No. 58 green
Architectural stone, wood, fabrics, sand, snow, etc., when sunlit and under blue sky	Natural	No. 8 yellow
	Enhanced texture rendering	No. 15 deep yellow or No. 25 red

Color Filters for Special Effects

The pictures at the far left and second from right were taken without a color filter. On the other shots, the filters used were, from left to right: orange, deep red, and dark blue.

Peter Gales

Peter Gales

The same filters that can bring a sense of realism to black-and-white photographs can be used in excitingly interpretive ways with color film. Even the denser color compensating filters, ordinarily used to make the color scheme more natural-looking, can create a vividly impressionistic palette. The effect of such a strong overall hue on a scene is shown in the seascapes above, which range from a burning red that suits a setting sun to an icy blue that hints at frigid waters. You can vary the intensity of the effect by using paler or stronger filters; use colors and intensities that are appropriate to the subject. A desert setting, for example, is more suited to a warm color, a snow scene to a cool one. For such special effects, it is wise to use slide film because a well-meaning processing lab may struggle to print your negative with natural tones. If you want a print, the lab can make it directly from the attached slide.

Filters

Split-Field Filters

There is no need to limit yourself to just one hue when you're using color filters for special effects. Split-field filters, which divide the filter surface into two or more different colors, can help you add interest to many scenes. There are three basic types of split-field filters, all of which are available commercially. You can also make your own, however, by cutting up filter gelatins and either using them in a filter holder or taping them over a colorless UV filter, as shown in the picture below.

On the first type of split-field filter, which is used mostly to emphasize the sky, only half of the filter is tinted. The second type of split-field filter is half one color and half another, to create an effect such as the one in the picture of the sphinx at right. On the third type, there is a clear circle in the center of a tinted filter to produce a color vignetting effect.

With all of these filters, the line between the different colored areas will be much softer and less distinct if you use a wide aperture and a long lens. Commercial dual-color filters are usually designed so that both halves require the same exposure increase, and if you make your own, you should try to do the same. Exposure with split-field filters is still largely experimental, however. If your camera has a meter that measures light passing through the filter, you can use it as a starting point, but it's still a good idea to bracket by several stops.

Split-field filter

Norman Kerr

Paul Kuzniar

This scene of a sphinx and a pyramid, shown at top as it would normally appear, was dramatically transformed with the use of an amber-purple split-field filter. In making a dual-color filter, be careful to butt the edges evenly.

Gary Whelpley

By rotating a two-color polarizing filter, you can change the overall tint of a scene from deep red to deep blue, with interesting color combinations in between.

Color Polarizing Filters

Color polarizing filters are another device that allows you to change the overall hue of a scene. With the single-color type, for example, you can gradually change the color of a scene from light pink to deep scarlet. With a two-color polarizer, such as a red-blue one, you can color a scene with a tint that goes from deep red to light red through magenta, and then on to light blue and dark blue.

Norman Kerr

Color polarizing filter

Filters

Neutral Density Filters

Neutral density (ND) filters are greyish filters that reduce the amount of light entering the lens. Since they do not change the hues or relative intensities of the colors in a scene, they can be used with any black-and-white or color film without altering the appearance of the subject. They are invaluable in situations that require you to reduce exposure. If you go on vacation and want to be be able to photograph in varied conditions on the same roll of film, for example, you can put high-speed film in your camera and use it without filters for most lighting. When you want to shoot a very bright scene—a sunny beach, say—using an ND filter on the camera will reduce the light entering the lens to a level that will produce an acceptable exposure on high-speed film. For that matter, you may wish to use the graininess of high-speed films for deliberate artistic effect; an ND filter will let you do so even in bright conditions.

William Hill

By cutting down the light reaching the film, a neutral density filter allows you to use slower shutter speeds in bright light without overexposing the final image.

Neutral density filters will also let you combine a greater range of exposure variables for achieving certain special effects. If you want to use a large aperture, such as *f*/2, for shallow depth of field to blur out a background but find that you don't have a shutter speed that's fast enough, an ND filter will enable you to blur it out. And as the picture above demonstrates, neutral density filters can be used to prevent overexposure of the film with a slow shutter speed or long exposure, if the smallest aperture on your lens isn't small enough to compensate for the length of the exposure. As the chart at right shows, ND filters are graded by their density, and the gradations translate into *f*-stop reductions. Using an ND 0.10 filter, for example, means you should increase your exposure setting by one-third stop. The three handiest gradations of filters are 0.30, 0.60, and 0.90, as they represent full *f*-stops—1, 2, and 3, respectively. To increase the effect of neutral density filters, add two or three together. You can also use a polarizing filter as the equivalent of an ND 0.40 filter.

Neutral Density Filters

Density	Number of f-stops to increase exposure
0.10	$\frac{1}{3}$
0.20	$\frac{2}{3}$
0.30	1
0.40	$1\frac{1}{3}$
0.50	$1\frac{2}{3}$
0.60	2
0.70	$2\frac{1}{3}$
0.80	$2\frac{2}{3}$
0.90	3
1.00	$3\frac{1}{3}$

Norman Kerr

Neutral density filter

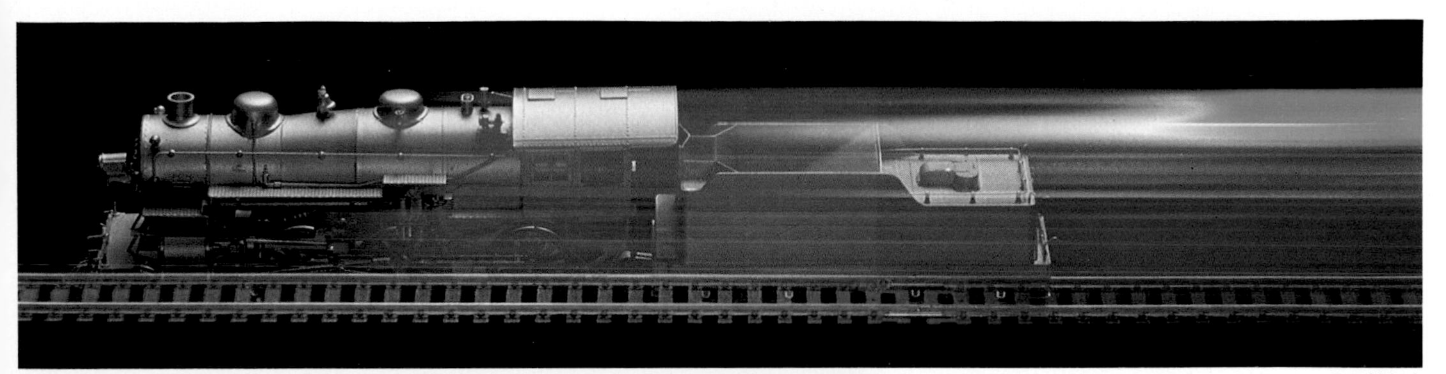

Donald Buck

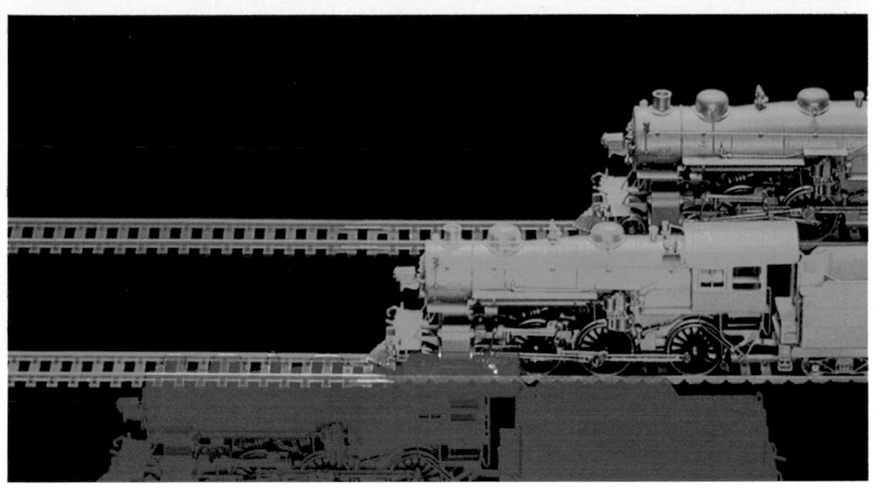

Donald Buck

Two views of a model train illustrate the effects of recording multiple exposures with three different color filters (left) and of using a Harris shutter (top).

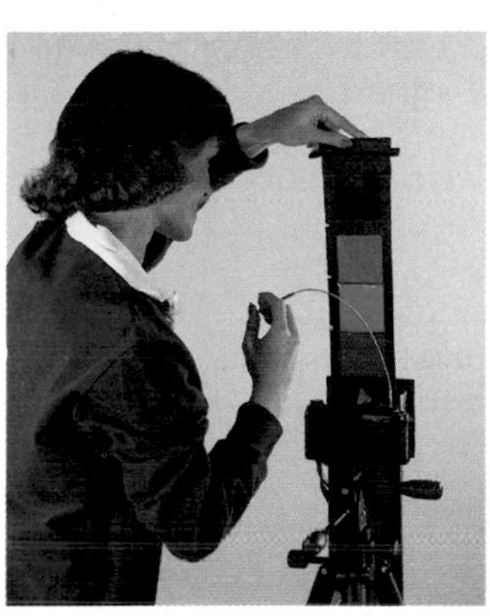

Donald Buck

Harris shutter

The Harris Shutter

You can get striking images with multiple exposures when you take each exposure through a different color filter, and this is easy to do with the basic techniques and exposure times for multiple exposures explained on page 242. Move the camera slightly for each new exposure so that the colors overlap, as in the picture immediately above. To get the right amount of light on the film, decrease exposure by one stop for each exposure. If a scene calls for a setting of 1/250 second at *f*/8, a double exposure through filters would require 1/250 at *f*/11 for each of the two exposures.

Although you can use any combination of filters, you will get the most interesting results when you use red, green, and blue filters—the primary colors that constitute white light. When you shoot a scene such as a landscape through No. 25 deep red, No. 61 deep green, and No. 38A blue filters, most of the scene will look normal, because the original color has been restored by the primary combination. Anything in the scene that is moving, however, will be recorded with rainbowlike colors.

Putting on and taking off three filters can be cumbersome, so to get the same effect with much less bother, you can use a simple device known as the Harris shutter. The Harris shutter, pictured at right, is three gelatin filters taped side by side, with pieces of black cardboard attached at both ends. The entire filter strip fits in a frame on the front of the lens. When you take a picture using the Harris shutter, set the camera on B for time exposure and start with one of the pieces of black cardboard over the lens to block light. While the shutter is open, let the Harris strip drop until the cardboard piece at the other end covers the lens. The Harris shutter allows you to make multicolored time exposures of moving subjects, as the picture of the toy train at top shows. Your exposure time will depend on how fast you let the strip fall. It's wise to bracket your exposure and to use color negative film, which can be corrected to a certain degree in printing if you've made an exposure error.

Filters

Lens Attachments for Special Effects

There are a great many other filters and filterlike attachments that can be used to produce striking results on film. Perhaps the best known of these are diffusion filters, which produce an overall misty, soft-focus effect, and vignetting filters, which produce a similar effect around the edge of the picture but leave the center sharp. You can obtain a similar type of diffusion by stretching a piece of nylon hose over the lens (pictured below) or by smearing a thin coat of petroleum jelly on a colorless UV filter. The effects vary quite a bit, so it is best to experiment. A wide aperture and backlighting enhance diffusion.

Two other common lens attachments shown here work by bending or breaking up light rays. The starburst filter is a screen that causes bright pinpoint lights or reflections to look as if they are emitting long, pointed rays. A diffraction grating attachment breaks a light source into a prismatic rainbow of hues in a pattern across the picture. If your camera's meter reads light passing through the filter, you don't need to make any exposure adjustments for these attachments.

Stephen Kelly

Norman Kerr

Starburst filter

Starburst, or cross-screen, filters (above) contain a fine metal mesh that turns points of light into four-pointed stars —or eight pointed ones if two filters are placed at an angle to one another.

Norman Kerr

Whether you stretch a piece of nylon hose over the lens (above) or smear petroleum jelly on a colorless filter, homemade diffusers and vignetting filters are fine for the photographer who only occasionally takes a soft-focus picture.

John Murphy

Norman Kerr

Diffraction grating lens

A diffraction grating lens (above) has thousands of tiny ridges in its surface that act as prisms, breaking strong light into bands of spectral colors.

Gary Whelpley

Most diffusion filters such as the one at right have a fine pebbly surface that causes the light to reflect slightly and spread, creating a soft-focus effect, as in the picture above.

Norman Kerr

Diffusion filter

Derek Doeffinger

The filmy aura surrounding the vase and flowers at left was cast by a soft-focus lens, a simple lens (often with interchangeable apertures) that creates a romantic effect similar to that of a diffusion filter.

Lens Attachments for Special Effects

Another popular group of screw-on filterlike attachments features multiple-image lenses. They have prismlike surfaces that cause images to repeat in parallel, concentric, radial, and other patterns. They require no exposure adjustments and usually work best with subjects isolated against a simple background.

Repeating lens

Norman Kerr

A parallel, repeating multiple-image lens, such as the one above, was used to produce the picture of the skier below. The lens can also be turned to make images that repeat vertically or diagonally.

Multiple-image lens

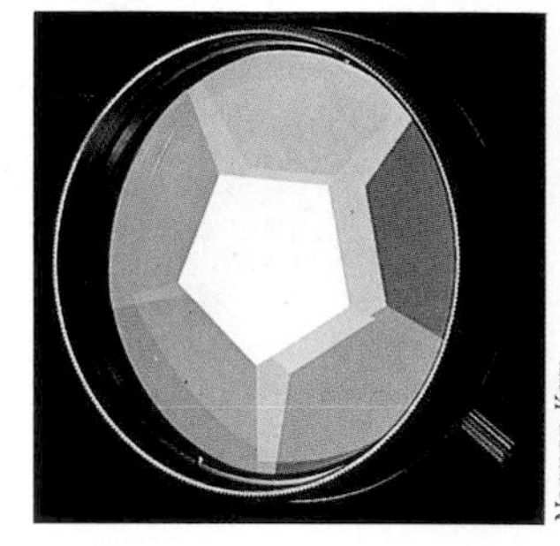

Norman Kerr

Multiple-image lenses such as this one produce one main image surrounded by slightly fainter repetitions. In the picture at right, the effect was enhanced by using multicolor filters at the same time.

Norman Kerr

G. Whelte

Accessories

Flash

For most of us, snapshots have been the traditional province of flash photography because flash overcomes many of the limitations of shooting in the relatively low-level existing light found at home. Although fast films and lenses now make it possible to take pictures in very dim light, flash still offers many technical and creative advantages. Because it provides so much more light, you can use fine-grain, low-speed films and auxiliary lenses with smaller maximum apertures. The smaller shooting apertures it allows also give you greater depth of field. And because the duration of a flash burst is so short, it's extremely effective in stopping action. Although flash bulbs are still practical for some photographs, they have been almost completely eclipsed by automatic electronic flash units, which are more convenient to use and cost less per flash.

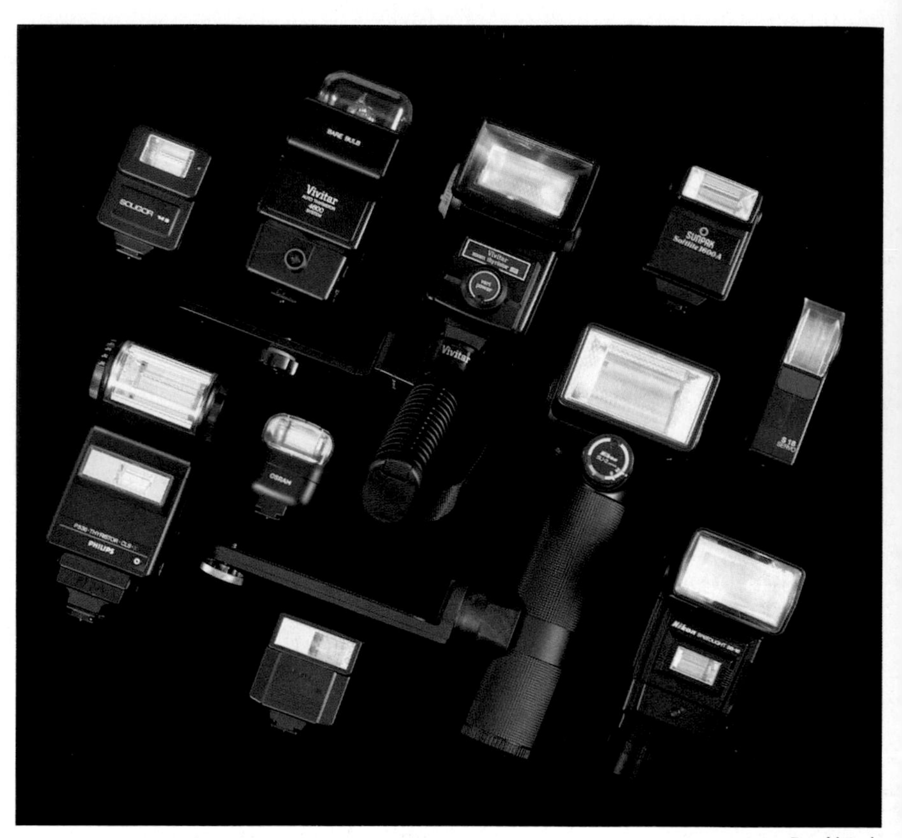

Donald Buck

To meet a variety of lighting needs, the commonly available electronic flashes range from units smaller than a cigarette pack to larger, more powerful and sophisticated units.

An electronic flash unit has a flash tube powered by a battery-fed capacitor. The capacitor stores energy from the battery and releases it to the tube for a brief instant to create the flash, which often lasts less than 1/1000 second. Most inexpensive flash units are powered by conventional batteries, which have to be replaced when their energy is exhausted. In addition to conventional batteries, advanced units usually offer other power options, including rechargeable cells and an adapter that lets you plug the unit into household current. Professional units carried on a belt or shoulder-strap can be powered with a high-voltage, longer-lived battery that needs a much shorter recycling time. These options offer greater economy and flexibility at a higher initial cost. But for occasional snapshots, conventional batteries are much more suitable.

In automatic rangefinders with built-in flash, one or two batteries power both camera and flash. This design saves you the inconvenience of carrying a separate unit around, and usually the camera alerts you when you need to use flash. But built-in units tend to be rather low-powered and can't be bounced or diffused to soften their light. On the other extreme, and at significantly higher cost, you can acquire electronic flash units with tilting heads for bounce light or "zoom" heads that match flash patterns to different lenses. Still other units offer variable power controls. But regardless of cost and power, most current units are automatic. A sensor reads the light reflected from the subject and cuts off the flash when enough light has been reflected for a well-exposed picture. "Dedicated" automatic flash units further automate flash photography, setting shutter speed and aperture for you. But most automatic units require that you set the camera initially.

Because of its ability to stop action within a fraction of a second, an electronic flash unit allows the photographer an enormous range of opportunities for taking creative pictures. Here, repeated firings of a high-speed flash unit have frozen the gymnast at various stages of his movement. The resulting multiple image conveys—almost as precisely as a moving picture would—the gymnast's graceful style and expertise.

John Zimmerman

Accessories

Synchronizing Flash

Because the duration of a flash is usually shorter than the fastest shutter speed on your camera, the length of the flash, rather than the shutter speed, is what determines the exposure time. Theoretically, this would mean that any shutter speed could be used with a flash. On rangefinder cameras with leaf-type shutters, this is generally true, although nearly all current rangefinders set flash shutter speeds automatically anyway. But because of the mechanical limitations of the focal plane shutters used on single-lens reflexes, the shutter speed must be set at 1/125 second, 1/60 second, or longer. (See "The Photographer's Most Common Problems," pages 148-149, for an explanation of the effect of using a shutter speed too high for flash photography.)

It is imperative that a flash be synchronized with the shutter—that is, that the light appear at exactly the right moment, when the shutter is open. Most modern cameras are already synchronized for electronic flash. Inserting a flash unit into the ***hot shoe*** (so called because it transmits the electrical signal that causes the flash to fire) or plugging in the flash cord automatically sets the synchronization. With most manual and automatic flash units, you must then set the shutter to the speed recommended for flash with your camera. With dedicated flash systems in which the camera and flash are designed to work together, attaching the flash to the camera usually also sets the proper shutter speed for flash operation. Older cameras have either a pair of flash-cord sockets—for bulb and electronic units—or a hot shoe that can be adjusted for the type of flash. The socket or setting for electronic flash is usually marked with an X; the other setting, labeled M or FP, works with flashbulbs. Your instruction manual should give full details about setting synchronization for your particular camera and flash unit.

Norman Kerr

Because flash duration determines the exposure time, your shutter speed will remain a constant, and you adjust only the lens's aperture to control exposure. The proper exposure for a subject is a function of its distance from the flash. As distance between subject and flash increases, the intensity of flash light striking the subject decreases. To determine exposure with the simpler, manually operated units, this distance is divided into a guide number (usually printed on the back of the unit) determined by the power of the flash and the speed of the film. The resulting number is the *f*-number you need to set on the aperture ring. Most flash units have a simple rotating calculator dial like the one shown in the picture above to help you determine the *f*-stop quickly. To find the subject-to-flash distance when using flash, just focus the lens on the subject and then use the distance indicated on the lens's distance scale. Otherwise, you must measure the distance.

The calculator dial on manually operated flash units is a simple rotary scale. Set the dial on the bottom to your film's ISO speed, then find the f-stop you will need opposite your subject-to-flash distance at top.

Donald Buck

The hot shoe on top of the camera is convenient to use, but not always the best place to put your flash, since it gives flat, even light with little modeling.

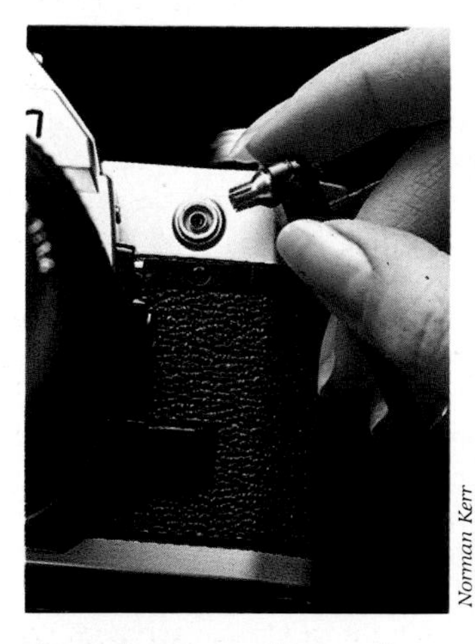

Norman Kerr

If you do not use the hot shoe on your camera, you must establish the electrical connection by plugging the flash cord into both the camera and the flash unit.

f/4 f/4–f/5.6 f/5.6 f/5.6–f/8 f/8

Jerry Antos

With a simple exposure test such as the one shown here, you can check the power output of your flash unit and, if necessary, adjust your guide number for correct exposure. The test can also be used to check the output of an automatic unit, or to determine what exposure adjustments are necessary for diffusing and bouncing techniques (see page 140).

The guide numbers for some electronic flash units may be somewhat optimistic about the unit's strength, so it's usually a good idea to run your own guide number test. One of the best ways to do this is to load your camera with a medium-speed (such as ISO 64) color slide film, attach the flash, and mount the camera on a tripod in a normal-size room. Have a person sit exactly ten feet from the camera.

Take your first flash picture using the aperture setting recommended by the flash unit's calculator dial for your combination of film speed and the ten-foot distance. Then bracket the recommended aperture at one-half stop increments, taking two or three shots at smaller apertures and the same number at larger ones. If the recommended aperture is *f*/5.6, your smaller apertures would be midway between *f*/5.6 and *f*/8; then *f*/8; and then midway between *f*/8 and *f*/11. Similarly, your larger openings would be midway between *f*/5.6 and *f*/4; *f*/4; and midway between *f*/4 and *f*/2.8. As in the example shown here, it is very helpful to have your subject hold cards showing the aperture setting for each shot.

After the roll is processed, compare the other slides with the one taken at the recommended exposure. If one of them looks better, tape a reminder to your flash unit to adjust the exposure. One easy way to make this change is to reset the film speed dial on the calculator to compensate. If you want to get a full stop more exposure, set half of your film's ISO number—32 for an ISO 64 film, for example. If you want one-half stop more, set a number that is 25 percent lower—150 for an ISO 200 film. To decrease exposure, double the film's ISO for a full stop, and set a number 50 percent higher for one-half stop.

Remember that this test is being done with slide film, which is more tolerant of (and often looks better with) some underexposure. An exposure that yields a slightly light result with slide film may be just right for negative film. If you do end up adjusting your meter based on this test, you may want to give a little extra exposure to negative film. This test can also be done with an automatic flash unit, discussed on the next two pages. If the unit consistently underexposes your film, set a lower ISO number on its dial; if it overexposes your film, set a higher ISO. You can also make these adjustments for any automatic flash system that does not have a light sensor at the film plane by changing the recommended aperture itself. In picking a subject to test an automatic unit, avoid including large areas of very light or very dark surfaces because these may throw the unit's automatic sensor off and you will be basing your adjustments on an atypical subject.

Automatic Electronic Flash

Many electronic flash units have automatic exposure control, which eliminates the need to work with guide numbers. A light-sensitive cell located on the front of the flash or behind the camera lens is pointed toward the subject. When the flash goes off, the cell almost instantaneously measures the light reflected from the subject and adjusts the duration of the flash. It gives a longer flash for a distant or dark subject and a shorter flash for a close or bright one, and because shorter flashes require less energy, the unit is able to recharge itself (recycle) more quickly than a manual model of comparable strength, which delivers the same amount of light with every flash. This also means that you generally get more flashes per battery. When you set your film's ISO number on an automatic flash, the unit's dial lets you choose from among several *f*-stops, each representing a different maximum flash-to-subject distance. Then, within that range, the flash makes all the exposure adjustments for you. Although your choice of aperture depends primarily on the farthest distance you expect your subject to be from the camera, there are other factors to consider. Because the flash unit will adjust its output for a close subject even at the wide apertures more distant subjects require, you can use a wide aperture to conserve the unit's power, since the lens will let in more of the flash's light. However, wider apertures make focusing more critical, which can be a problem in the dim light flash is generally used to overcome. The use of smaller apertures, provided your subject will fall within the shorter distance range they afford, will give you a little more latitude in focusing in dim light. The increased depth of field at smaller apertures is really only an issue with bounce flash (see next two pages) because the rapid fall-off of light from direct flash will make the background so dark that it won't matter if it's sharp or not.

Although generally providing reliable illumination, an automatic flash unit is prone to the same kind of exposure error that a camera's meter is because it averages the light reflected back to it. Just as a camera on automatic will overexpose a brightly spotlighted figure on a dark stage, an automatic flash may overexpose a subject without a fairly close, reflective background (as is the case outdoors at night), particularly if it's not filling the frame. The unit tries to illuminate the entire scene, sending out far too much light for proper exposure of the primary subject. However, this kind of adjustment can occsionally be helpful by compensating for an exceptionally dark or light subject. Just be wary of situations that may cause incorrect exposure and bracket your exposures if possible.

The customary place to attach an electronic flash unit is on the camera's hot shoe. (Be sure any unit you're considering purchasing fits your camera's hot shoe. Some adapters are available.) This location is a convenient one for a flash because it doesn't require a connecting cord. But when a flash is aimed directly at your subject from the camera position, the lighting can be flat and even, eliminating shadows and textures that give roundness and solidity to a subject. Lighting coming from the side and above the camera, on the other hand, makes most subjects look more three-dimensional—the effect is called modeling—and will be more flattering to people, provided it is softened in some way. Such a lighting angle also makes your subject more comfortable and eliminates the problem of red spots in your subject's eyes that are reflections off the retina itself.

There are several styles of brackets that attach to a camera and hold the flash to one side and at various heights above the lens. The pictures on these pages show some of the brackets you can use. To gain even more distance between the camera and the flash, hold the flash up in your hand, off to one side. If this proves awkward, you may need to place the flash on a stand.

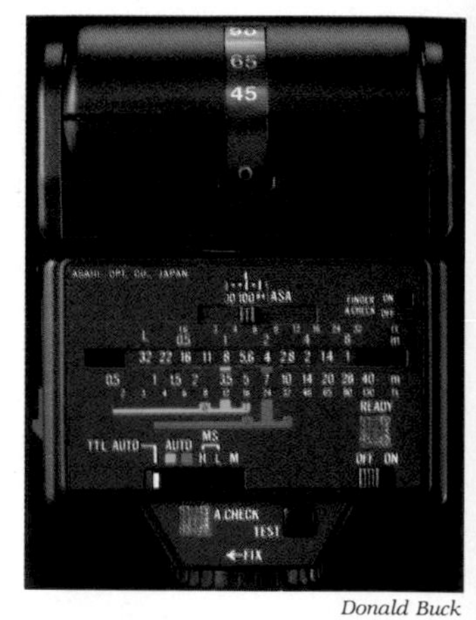

Donald Buck

Although the calculator dial on some automatic flash units is similar to that of a manual unit, many newer units look like the one above. With either variety, after you have set the ISO speed of the film you are using, you must choose from a selection of f-stops, and set your lens accordingly. Some units offer only a choice of two or three automatic shooting apertures; more sophisticated ones let you choose from a continuous range.

Jerry Antos

John Menihan

Flash attachments can be mounted directly on the camera's hot shoe (top left), but the light they provide may make some subjects look flat (bottom left). A variety of styles of flash bracket (center and right) allow you to change the angle of the lighting to create a more three-dimensional effect. You may also hand hold a flash away from the camera to achieve this effect if the two can be connected with a PC cord. The strong shadows that off-axis flash creates may be softened with the diffusion and bounce techniques described on the following pages.

Donald Buck

When an automatic flash unit is fired, a photosensitive cell on the front of the unit reads light reflected off subjects and regulates the duration of the flash, depending on the brightness of the subject and its distance from the flash. A "dedicated" flash unit, designed for a specific make or model of camera, is regulated by a sensor behind the lens itself.

Diffusing and Bouncing Flash

Light from a direct flash can be very harsh and create extreme contrast between highlighted and shadowed areas. Even from the side, direct flash can be too strong; it may wash out details and color in highlight areas and leave shadows completely empty. There are several techniques for softening light that will lower contrast. The most popular is known as ***diffusion.***

Many flash units are supplied with translucent plastic attachments that spread the angle of light so that wide-angle lenses can be used, but these also diffuse the light from the flash considerably and can be used for this purpose with normal or even longer-focal-length lenses. They will, however, reduce the output of the flash (and thus the light reaching the subject), so you should adjust your exposure calculations according to your unit's instruction manual. Although an automatic flash unit will take diffusion materials into account and put out more light to compensate for them, you may have to set a deeper distance range to give the unit extra capacity, especially if your subject is close to the outer limit of your chosen range. You can also diffuse a flash head by taping one or more layers of white tissue or matte acetate over the head of the flash. Increase your exposure by roughly one-half *f*-stop per layer of material, but for greater accuracy, it's best to run an exposure test (see page 137).

Another way to modify the harsh effects of direct flash is to bounce the flash off a nearby wall or ceiling. This technique produces a much more even kind of light, which is particularly useful in photographing a subject with a lot of depth. In a large group of people, direct flash will make more distant faces (than those you are exposing for) too dark and closer ones too light. Bouncing the flash off the ceiling will keep the light from dropping off so quickly. (See "Special Events," page 179, for an example of this technique.) You must, however, be sure that the angle of the bounce is such that it will cast light on your entire subject; if you aim the flash at an angle that isn't steep enough, closer parts of your subject may not receive enough light. With color film, avoid bouncing your flash off a colored surface, or your subject will be tinted by it. Some flash units have a tilting head that can be angled toward the ceiling while mounted on the hot shoe, and for other units you can buy special angling brackets. If your flash attaches with a cord, you can also simply hold the flash in your hand and point it at the surface.

Bouncing a flash, like diffusing one, requires an increase in exposure. The general rule is to add two *f*-stops to the exposure recommended for the flash-to-bounce surface-to-subject distance, but the results will vary depending on the brightness and distance of the reflecting surface. It's best to experiment until you get the feel for certain settings, and even then it's safest to bracket. If you do a lot of photography in one room, run an exposure test there. Some automatic flash units must be used in the manual mode for bounce, but units with tilting heads work on automatic, provided the sensor on the front is pointed at the subject. As with diffusion techniques, you may have to set a higher distance range (wider aperture); due to the absorption of light by the wall or ceiling, you should choose an aperture that gives an outside range greater than the total distance the light has to travel before and after it bounces.

A more controlled way to bounce flash is to use an umbrella or other reflector designed for photography. You can aim the umbrella or reflector where you want and adjust the light very carefully. These units differ in their reflective qualities, but most come with full instructions. You can make your own reflector by attaching a large sheet of white board to a lamp stand, but be sure to run an exposure test with it.

The effect on a subject of the flash techniques shown in the pictures at left is illustrated beneath them. Using a diffuser (top left) softens light without cutting too much of its brightness. The result of bouncing a flash off the ceiling or walls depends very much on how light the surface is and how close you are to it. Some units have movable flash heads (top right) that can be tilted upward to bounce the flash off the ceiling. When you use a white-card reflector (bottom left), the result will be more predictable and usually brighter than if you bounce the flash off the ceiling. A photographic umbrella (bottom right) gives a very pleasing soft light that can be aimed at the subject, somewhat like a parabolic reflector.

Jerry Antos

John Menihan

Flash Outdoors

Strangely enough, one of the best places to use flash is outdoors in bright sunshine. An electronic flash, which matches sunlight in color balance, is ideal for filling in the harsh shadows created by the sun on front- and sidelighted subjects and for making backlighted or shaded subjects stand out.

Many of the newer compact automatic rangefinders will provide automatic outdoor fill light with their built-in flash units. With manual rangefinders, the leaf-type shutter makes flash photography possible over the wide range of shutter speeds you are likely to use outdoors; all you need to do is set the aperture recommended by your flash's guide number and then use the camera's meter to determine the correct shutter speed for the sunlight. (Set your automatic flash on manual.) Theoretically, this combination would result in both light sources being of equal intensity in the final picture. Without reflective surfaces, however, some of the flash's light is lost outdoors, making its effect a stop or two weaker than for the indoor situations that the guide numbers are designed for. Thus the flash acts as fill-in light only, lightening shadow areas somewhat while preserving the directional character of the sunlight itself.

The focal-plane shutters of single-lens-reflex cameras, however, limit your choice of shutter speeds for flash photography. Many newer models permit speeds as high as 1/125 or 1/250 second, but sometimes this isn't fast enough for daylight situations. After you have set the recommended speed, set the aperture indicated by your camera's meter for the daylight in the scene. You then have to move back and forth to get a subject-to-flash distance that requires the same settings you've already chosen for the camera (see above) to ensure that the flash will be weaker than the sunlight. Because this will affect your composition, you may even have to switch lenses to accommodate the distance. Some flash units have a "power ratio" feature that allows you to reduce output by whole stops, so that you don't have to change your subject-to-flash distance to effect changes in balance. You can also reduce the output of your flash by using one or more layers of diffusing materials, such as facial tissue, estimating a half-stop change for each layer.

No flash

Fill-in flash

Neil Montanus

Although flash is subtly effective in filling in the deep shadows created by direct sunlight on a subject, it is more dramatic when used to balance a foreground in shadow with a brighter, sunlit background, as in the second picture of the yachtsman.

Jim Dow

To light the interior of this English pub, the photographer fired his flash unit over thirty times as he walked around the picture perimeter. The cumulative effect of the many flash bursts is a soft, shadowless light that is surprisingly inconspicuous; the available light in the scene would have otherwise produced an impossibly contrasty image. Because the lens's shutter was open the entire time the photographer was "painting" the scene, the dim ambient light sources were also recorded, and even contributed a subtle incandescent warmth to the image.

Open Flash

Once satisfied with your flash results in traditional applications, you will be enthusiastic about its many other creative uses. One such technique is called open flash and involves firing the flash unit independently of the camera with the test button on the back of most units. If you intend to fire the unit more than once, set an automatic flash unit on manual. Also, select a scene with fairly dim light, or the ambient illumination may cause overexposure while the shutter is open.

Set your camera's shutter speed on B, and lock open the shutter using a locking cable release. Fire the flash from your off-camera position, then return to the camera and close the shutter. If you are using the technique to achieve an unusual lighting angle or to increase the effective power of the flash by moving it closer to the subject, you will probably need to fire it only once, and the aperture you set on the camera will depend simply on the subject-to-flash distance. If you plan to side- or backlight the subject with flash, you may have to increase your exposure by one or two stops. If this compromises your depth of field too much, you can fire the flash more than once for extra exposure, making sure you allow it to recycle between flashes. One additional firing of the flash from the same point will give you double the amount of light, or one stop extra; a third flash will give you another half stop; a fourth flash, another third stop. A fifth flash will provide only 25 percent more light than the previous four have produced.

This technique works particularly well in illuminating a subject too large for a single flash burst, or in which a single burst would produce harsh, uneven light. To attempt it, you should determine how much area a single flash will cover and plan the sequence in which you will light your subject. Each firing of the flash should illuminate a different part of the subject, and you should try to maintain the same distance from the subject for all the flashes or give the more distant parts more light. Avoid overlapping the flashes, so that the exposure will be even. This technique, known as painting with light, was used to photograph the interior above, but works well on exteriors too.

Multi-Unit Flash

Studio photographers know that a careful balance of light from several sources gives the greatest amount of modeling and dimensionality to any subject. You can achieve this kind of lighting either with flash or photolamps. Two or three units will suffice, but with flash you must be sure that they will all fire simultaneously. With some flash units you can use standard extension cords to increase the range of your flash cords, and Y-shaped terminals to connect them all to your camera. But this can create a dangerous tangle of cords. It's much easier to attach "slave" photocells to all flash units except the one that is connected to the camera. When the flash unit attached to the camera is fired by the shutter, the slave photocells "see" the flash and fire their units in the same instant. The pictures at right show the effect of this technique on a portrait subject.

In photographing a portrait subject, the main light is usually placed about 45 degrees to the side of the camera, aimed downward at about a 20-degree angle. The fill light used to lighten the shadows created by the main light is close to the camera and near lens level to avoid more shadows. (It can serve as the camera-mounted unit that sets off the slaves on the other units.) If you keep in mind that the intensity of light decreases geometrically with increased distance (a light twice as far from a subject will provide only a quarter the illumination), you can use the position of the flashes to adjust their light levels. Assuming both units are equally powerful, and your fill light is about 50 percent farther from the subject than your main light, it will provide only half as much light. If the main flash casts two units of light on the principal features of the subject while the fill light provides one unit overall, the principal features receive a total of three units of light, while the shadows receive one—a 3:1 lighting ratio. You can also use the *f*-number relationships to position equally powerful units. For instance, just as an *f*/8 aperture transmits twice as much light as *f*/11, you can place the main flash eight feet from the subject and the fill light at eleven feet. Any equivalent combination will also work to achieve this 3:1 lighting ratio. Although this ratio is considered pleasing and flattering to a human subject, you can vary it. Moving the main light closer to the subject will give you greater contrast between highlighted and shadowed areas; moving it back will lessen the difference. You can also use a third light to backlight the subject or to brighten the background so that the subject stands out from it.

Bob Clemens

A tripod, background paper, photolamps or flash units, and a large room are all that are needed to do studio-quality work in your own home. The pictures at right show the effect of the traditional arrangement and balance of lights described on this page. Although this portrait was made with small portable flash units, as shown above, it could have been done as successfully with photolamps.

The Home Studio

Many photographers prefer the controlled setting of a studio for certain subjects—mainly people. A studio needn't be complicated. In fact, it can be entirely portable and still fit many applications. The main ingredients are light, background, and enough space to work in freedom.

For lighting, you'll need several light sources that can be moved around. Multiple flash (see facing page) is adaptable to the home studio, but photolamps are also popular. The chief advantage of the photolamps over flash is that you can see the effect of the lighting as you're arranging the shot. There's also no delay for recycling, and photolamps may be less expensive than flash. The disadvantage is that photolamps require films with special color balance (see page 96) or color correcting filters (see page 118). They are also hot and may make a subject uncomfortable during a long shooting session. Flash, on the other hand, is color balanced for daylight film, and quite cool. Whatever type of light you use, mount it on a steady support. Regular photographic light stands are widely available, and you can also attach both photolamps and flash units to clamps that can, in turn, be attached to almost anything.

For a background, a wall painted in a neutral color with matte finish is adequate, but a portable, changeable background is more flexible. Photo dealers sell tall, portable supports for a long roll of special studio background paper that can be pulled down to the floor for the background and out toward the camera as a foreground. Since there are no joints or separations in the material, it is called "seamless" or "no-seam" paper. It comes in rolls of standard widths and is available in many colors and textures for different subjects or effects. You can construct your own stand for seamless paper using two uprights with a pipe between them for the roll.

Main light

Main and fill light

Bob Clemens

Main and fill lights with backgound light

Almost any room can be converted into a temporary studio with a little imagination. Except for still lifes, however, space is important. Try to pick a room with a fairly high ceiling and some depth. This will give you enough room to use a variety of lighting positions and equipment, such as moderate telephoto lenses.

Accessories

There is a wide variety of photographic accessories. Some you may want to consider are discussed here.

For many photographers, a ***tripod*** is indispensable. It holds the camera steady when you're using slow shutter speeds or when you have a long telephoto lens attached. It assures that there will be a minimum of camera movement to blur a picture. To determine whether a certain tripod is steady enough for your purposes, extend it fully and place your hand on the camera-mounting surface. Rest some weight on that hand and try to move your hand in a circular fashion. If the tripod doesn't wobble or shift, it's steady enough for your camera. Make sure that the legs extend and contract easily and that the tripod raises to the height you want. Check to see that all adjustments lock securely. If you're going to photograph small subjects at ground level, be sure that the tripod center column reverses so that the camera can be mounted close to the ground. Make absolutely sure that the camera-mounting system, usually a plate with a screw that inserts into the bottom of the camera, is strong enough to hold a camera with a long telephoto lens. Last, test the tripod with your own camera and longest telephoto lens to made sure that you can move all the camera's controls while it is mounted on the tripod.

Cable releases, which screw into the camera's shutter button, provide an extra bit of steadiness when the camera is on a tripod by removing your hand from the shutter release. Most good cable releases have a lock to keep the shutter open for time exposures.

Remote releases free the photographer from the camera. The most common ones include old-fashioned air bulb releases and devices with photoelectric cells. Both can trigger a camera from many yards. More expensive units can fire the shutter by radio signals from miles away. Remote releases are most often used with wildlife, but they can also be handy in a home studio. Many late-model SLRs can be fitted with an automatic film advance device—an ***automatic winder*** or ***motor drive.*** Both incorporate a battery-driven electric motor that releases the shutter, advances the film, and cocks the shutter for the next exposure. Motor drives advance the film faster (three to five frames per second and faster) than auto winders and are usually a bit more rugged. Ideal for sports photography, informal portraits, and candid work, where scenes and subjects change rapidly, automatic film-advance mechanisms allow you to keep your eye to the viewfinder and concentrate on capturing the decisive moment without taking time to advance the film manually.

Camera manufacturers offer so-called ***ready cases*** that are designed to protect the camera from knocks, jolts, and moisture. Usually they are rigid and bulky, but the protection they afford more than makes up for loss of convenience. Soft cases are easier to handle but give less protection.

If you intend to use the ready case for storing the camera, but not for carrying it, you'll need a ***neck strap.*** A wide strap doesn't slip off your shoulder as easily as a thin one, and the increased surface area means less pressure on your neck or shoulder during long days with a camera.

For active photographers who don't want to have their cameras constantly swinging like a pendulum, there are special sports ***harnesses*** that make the camera ready and accessible but keep it flat against the chest when not in use. You can also find ***film canisters*** that connect to your camera strap.

All ***gadget bags*** serve the same purpose—to carry your gear safely and to make it

Jerry Antos

Tripods (upper left) range in size from small tabletop models to hefty studio supports. You will need a cable release to make most effective use of them. A flash unit may eliminate the need for a tripod, but for greater control you should consider mounting it on a light stand (upper right). If you travel with a lot of equipment, you will want to invest in a gadget bag (right), or, at minimum, protective cases for your lenses (lower left). A camera strap is further protection against accidentally dropping your camera. Finally, you should keep camera, filter, and lens-cleaning supplies (lower right) with you whenever you take pictures.

easily accessible. Some photographers prefer durable nylon bags with compartments for everything. Others use aluminum suitcases, and still others adapt backpacks, army surplus bags, or briefcases. Examine your own needs—the amount of equipment you own, the amount of protection it needs, whether you take long trips or short outings, and even your self-image. If you want to be inconspicuous, don't carry a bag that looks like the typical gadget bag. Try not to send photo equipment unguarded into airplane baggage compartments. It's usually better to get a bag that stows away under an airplane seat and keep your gear with you.

Both the lens and the body of your camera need periodic cleaning. In particular, you should watch for smudges and dust on the front and back elements of the lens. To remove smudges or dust, you need a soft brush (preferably camel's-hair), lens-cleaning tissue, and lens-cleaning fluid. Make sure that the tissue and cleaning fluid are not the kind for eyeglasses. First, carefully brush off all loose particles on the lens surface. Then place a small amount of fluid on a piece of lens-cleaning tissue, and wipe the glass gently in a spiral motion from the center out until it is clean. A final, gentle polish with dry tissue will help remove streaks and lint. Never rub too hard, or you may scratch the lens, particularly if any dirt or grit remains on it. Putting a UV or skylight filter on your lens will help protect the front element from dirt and scratches, but you should be sure that it is clean too. A dirty lens or filter can reduce the sharpness of your pictures greatly.

It's also simple to clean a camera body—both in the front where the lens is mounted and in the back where the film is loaded. All you need is a soft brush and a rubber air bulb or a can of compressed air. (If you use the latter, follow the instructions on the can. If misused, a compressed air container can spray propellant inside the camera, causing damage.) Look for any visible dirt or dust, remembering that cleaning must be as gentle as possible to avoid knocking delicate mechanisms out of adjustment. Clean the mirror only with the brush, and carefully. The mirror is precise and adjusted exactly—knocking it out of line can result in an expensive repair bill. Finally, give the viewfinder window the same treatment that you give the lens. (Dust visible in the viewfinder is on the ground-glass screen, not the lens, and will not affect your pictures. It is difficult to remove.) Clean cameras work better and spend less time in the repair shop. They also give better pictures.

The Photographer's Most Common Problems —and How to Solve Them

Every photographer—beginner or expert—is at times disappointed with the way pictures turn out. Sometimes it's just a matter of needing better timing or a steadier hand on the photographer's part. At other times a faulty camera may be to blame. In any case, it's helpful to study the unsuccessful elements of your pictures and learn to correct them. In the examples and the advice given here, you'll find over a dozen of the problems photographers most often encounter—and what you can do to solve them. The first list covers possible mechanical difficulties; the second concerns problems of technique.

Mechanical Problems

▶ ***Film jam:*** *If the film refuses to advance or rewind, take the camera to a dealer who is able to extract the film without ruining the pictures you have already taken. Don't force the controls, or you may turn a simple problem into a costly repair. The dealer should be able to determine whether the problem is with the camera, your loading technique, or with that particular roll of film.*

▶ ***Battery failure:*** *If the exposure meter starts to act erratically, or if it and the other battery-powered camera functions suddenly stop working, chances are that the battery needs to be changed. Replace it and see if proper operation is restored. If your electronic camera has a back-up mechanical shutter release, you can use it if no battery is immediately available. Refer to your manual to find out its speed, and extrapolate exposure from the suggestions in the film instructions.*

▶ ***Pictures consistently too dark or too light:*** *If your prints or slides always turn out underexposed (too dark) or overexposed (too light), make sure that you have set the correct ISO number on the camera's film-speed dial. Another cause of improperly exposed photos is a malfunctioning meter or shutter, for which you'll want to have the camera examined by a repair person. If your flash pictures are too light or too dark, make the exposure test detailed on page 137 to determine a corrected ISO setting or guide number for the film you use.*

Neil Montanus

▶ ***Flash failure:*** *If the flash fails to fire when you press the shutter release, check the connecting cord (if you use one) for a tight connection at both ends. If the connection is good and the flash does fire manually with the test button on the back, replace the connecting cord. If this doesn't solve the problem, have the flash unit and/or camera inspected by a technician.*

Neil Montanus

You can often minimize cluttered, distracting environments simply by moving close to your subject and changing the angle.

Technique problems

▶ ***Blurred pictures:*** *Many things can cause blurred pictures. Improper focus is usually blamed, but even if you don't focus correctly, part of the picture will usually be sharp—in front of or behind where you meant to focus. If nothing is sharp, the culprit may be camera movement, particularly if the blur has a directional quality. To prevent it, use a higher shutter speed, especially with telephoto lenses (see page 104 for specific recommendations), and brace your arms and the camera against your body. Use a tripod to prevent blur when your shutter speed must be slow, but if your main subject is blurred and the rest of the scene is sharp, your speed was too slow to freeze its motion (see page 182). Another common cause of blurred pictures is a smudged or dirty lens or filter (see page 147).*

▶ ***Poor composition:*** *Good composition is elusive and subjective. Try to be aware of all the elements inside the viewfinder frame and how they interact. Beyond this heightened sensitivity, you should consider some of the difficulties in making the transition from framed subject to finished print or slide. First, fill the frame with your subject or it will seem small and insignificant in the final photo —unless that's the effect you want. Next, although many focusing systems encourage centering the subject (a person's head for instance), this may leave part of the frame empty and thus make for a lackluster photo. After you focus, readjust the arrangement of additional elements in the frame for the most pleasing appearance. Lastly, don't be satisfied with your first effort; try other arrangements as well. Put your main subject at the top or bottom of the frame, right and left, and then turn the camera 90 degrees for a vertical and experiment in that format. Move closer and farther away and use different lenses. Composition can be as complex or as simple as you make it, but it is usually most successful when intentional.*

▶ ***Unattractive foregrounds and backgrounds:*** *In the heat of an exciting moment of picture-taking, it's easy to overlook distracting elements that surround the subject. Use a discriminating eye to look at the scene before you press the shutter release. If something's not quite right, change your position or move the offending object. Think about the subject's relationship to its environment. Don't, for example, let tree branches or telephone poles "grow" out of a subject's head.*

When you focus improperly, a subject takes on a soft, fuzzy blur. Camera movement, by contrast, can cause a streaky blur, although in its less dramatic forms it can appear as a simple lack of sharpness.

Neil Montanus

► ***Cropping part of the subject:*** *If you find that you consistently crop off some part of your subject—whether someone's head or the last person in a group shot—you need to practice aiming the camera. Carefully establish the locations of your subjects within the rectangular viewfinder frame. You should be able to see all sides of the frame at one time. Once you get a sense of how to control the way your subject fits the viewfinder frame, you can begin to experiment. Sophisticated photographers may even use seemingly arbitrarily cropped or tightly composed images to enhance their subject or emphasize a detail rather than the whole scene.*

► ***Contrasty scenes:*** *Your camera's meter is easily fooled by strong contrasts between bright and shadow areas. If your pictures look washed out in the lighter areas or too dark in the shadows, try taking close readings from the most important parts of the subject and then using a compromise exposure. If you have one, a photographic grey card (see page 90) is also handy for taking an accurate meter reading. When in doubt, with slide film, err on the side of underexposure to ensure highlight detail, and with negative film err on the side of overexposure to ensure shadow detail.*

Neil Montanus

Be conscious of reflective surfaces when you use flash, and keep them at an angle to the flash itself.

► ***Lens flare:*** *If a picture has an overall foggy or bleached-out quality, or if light, aperture-shaped patterns appear across it, direct light from your source struck the lens surface when you took the picture. A lens shade will help prevent this.*

► ***Dark shadows in indoor flash pictures:*** *Bounced, diffused, and multi-unit flash (see pages 140 and 144) will help eliminate deep shadows on your subject. (Outdoors, flash will soften shadows on a sunlit subject.) If you are shooting at wider apertures, it helps to turn on room lights so that the rest of the scene won't appear to be a dark void. (The wider the aperture, the more ambient light will be recorded in the shadows.) The difference in color balance on your subject will be negligible because the flash will overpower the tungsten or fluorescent light.*

► ***Partially exposed flash pictures:*** *If less than the full frame is exposed in your flash pictures, check to make sure you're using the correct shutter speed and synchronization setting for flash.*

► ***Glare spots in flash pictures:*** *Shiny surfaces will reflect light from a flash back to the camera. Be sure to take flash pictures at an angle to reflecting surfaces. If you are photographing people who wear glasses, have them turn their faces slightly to the side or tilt their heads down somewhat to avoid distracting reflections.*

► ***"Red-eye" in flash pictures:*** *Flash can create red reflections in a person's eyes. To lessen or eliminate this effect, hold the flash slightly away from the camera and turn on all the lights in the room to make the subject's pupils contract.*

► ***Bluish or reddish-orange pictures:*** *If you use film that is not balanced for the color of light in the scene, the color balance of the resulting pictures will be either bluish (for tungsten film used in daylight) or reddish-orange (for daylight film used in tungsten light). See pages 118 to 121. If your pictures have a greenish cast, you may have taken them under fluorescent or mercury-vapor lighting.*

► ***Unusual color balance:*** *If the film was outdated or exposed to extreme heat or humidity, the color balance and film speed may shift, giving unpredictable results.*

► ***Light streaks or spots on processed film:*** *Unexpected light spots or streaks may be the result of opening the camera before the film has been rewound into the cartridge. A light leak in the camera may also cause fogging, as can handling film in extremely bright light. Similar aberrations can be caused by processing errors.*

Dick Durrance/Woodfin Camp

Part III

The Image

People
Action
Nature
Landscapes
Still Lifes
Architecture
Photojournalism
Existing Light
Underwater
Inclement Weather
Special Effects

Photographing People

©Arnold Newman

Portrait photographer Arnold Newman is renowned for his images of eminent artists in settings that suggest their work. In this picture of composer Igor Stravinsky, the piano is a powerfully graphic shape as well as a symbol of Stravinsky's art.

Our mental images of people are kaleidoscopic. Their appearances, mannerisms, and relationships to us combine to create a distinct identity. Usually these impressions are gathered over a period of time. A portrait is a single, static image that must act as a metaphor for character and soul. It is an exciting challenge for the photographer.

To create a successful portrait, you must learn to isolate those characteristics that reveal a subject's distinctive personality and style. Sometimes the decisive element will be a fleeting facial expression. Other times it will be the way a person dresses or the pose a person strikes. Most often, several elements come together momentarily to provide a visual distillation of personality. Renowned portrait photographer Yousuf Karsh expressed it well when he said, "There is a brief moment when all that there is in a man's mind and soul and spirit may be reflected through his eyes, his hands, his attitude. This is the moment to record. This is the elusive 'moment of truth.'"

The background, setting, and props you select can play a significant role in the message you communicate. In the portraits here, for example, the ballet barre and piano not only suggest the subjects' professions, but produce striking compositions as well. Notice, too, how Newman has relegated Stravinsky to the far corner of the picture. Think about the position of the figure in the frame and try not to center it unless you feel that centering makes the most effective statement about your subject. Instead, you can focus attention on the subject by using simple backgrounds, such as sky, a plain wall, or seamless photographic paper (see page 145). You can minimize distracting backgrounds by shooting at close range, so

In his portrait of Martha Graham, one of the prime movers of modern dance, Newman uses a ballet barre to tell us about his subject. Like Stravinsky's piano, this bold background heightens the impact of the photograph and is a visual metaphor for the stark modernism that characterizes Graham's work.

that your subject fills the camera's frame, or by adjusting the depth of field so that only your subject is sharply focused.

When posing a subject, try to have the person relax as much as possible. Most people are self-conscious in front of a camera. You may need to reduce the tension with light conversation. If the person is seated, suggest that he or she lean slightly forward, a position that feels and looks more natural.

The direction the subject faces can also affect the mood of a portrait. Photographed straight on, people generally appear stiff and formal, especially if their expression is serious. Turned slightly to the side, for a three-quarters view, a subject usually looks more relaxed. This will also reduce facial distortion if you're using a normal or slightly wide-angle lens. Profiles, although frequently unflattering to the shape of the nose and chin, are nearly always dramatic.

A normal eye-level angle is best for most portraits. Too high an angle—often a problem in photographing children and seated subjects—can make the head loom and foreshorten the body. Too low an angle may result in an overly prominent nose or chin. But at reasonable distances, a slightly low or high angle can be used creatively. To dramatically isolate your subject, utilize a high angle. In a full-length portrait, an eye-level shot makes a subject look shorter. A picture taken from a squatting position indicates height more accurately; an even lower angle can make the subject seem taller.

Lighting is especially important in portraiture. Depending on its angle, intensity, and diffuseness, light can emphasize certain features and soften or obscure others. Light aimed directly at the subject tends to flatten facial and bodily contours and wash out details, although sometimes this can abstract the figure in interesting ways. For most portraits, light coming from an angle slightly above and to the side of the camera is preferable. This sidelighting brings out textures in the subject's skin, hair, and clothing that can be character-revealing. More important, it produces shadows, which give a rounded, three-dimensional appearance to a subject.

Too bright a light may create harsh shadows on one side of the subject's face. To compensate, use a reflector or a less-powerful diffused light to fill in the shadows produced by the main light. Just moving your subject closer to a light-colored wall or having someone hold up a large sheet of white paper may provide all the extra reflection you need. In general, however, the best way to lower the contrast between highlights and shadows is to avoid using intense, direct light. Most portraitists favor soft, indirect light that illuminates the subject more evenly.

People

Tools

A telephoto lens with a focal length between 75 and 135 mm, although useful for many other subjects, is often called a portrait lens. This is because it allows you to maintain a comfortable working distance from the subject and yet achieve a flattering, detailed likeness with a minimum of distortion. The short telephoto lens is particularly appropriate for close head shots in which even a normal lens might distort facial features. But the normal lens and sometimes a wide-angle lens are useful in showing a subject in natural surroundings, particularly if space is limited, as in Henri Cartier-Bresson's photograph of artist Henri Matisse at right. Whatever lens you choose, if you intend to photograph your subject in available indoor light you will need one with a relatively large maximum aperture, such as *f*/2.8 or larger.

If you plan to work with available light, a reflector should be considered basic equipment. A large white card produces a soft reflected light; crinkled foil pasted to a sheet of cardboard will give you a brighter, more directional reflection. Electronic flash is also helpful in supplementing existing light. Outdoors, you can use flash to fill in strong shadows caused by the sun in a side- or backlighted subject. Indoors, it can be bounced off walls, ceilings, reflectors, or umbrellas as a subtle supplement to light from a window. It can also serve as the main source of illumination.

Your choice of film will depend primarily on lighting conditions. A higher-speed film, from ISO 400 to 1000, may be necessary indoors, in dim light outdoors, or with restless subjects, such as children or pets. But the increased graininess typical in higher speed films (see page 98) may detract from some subjects. Lower speed films, ISO 25 to 125, produce a sharper, less grainy image, but to use them in dim light you will probably need a tripod, which permits slower shutter speeds. If your subject is fairly static, you can use exposures of 1/15, 1/8, and even 1/4 of a second with a tripod.

In addition to a tripod, certain other equipment can be useful to the portrait photographer. A skylight or 81 series filter will warm the bluish hue common to outdoor portraits taken in open shade (or indoor portraits taken by indirect window light on a clear day), and a diffusion filter will soften an image, minimizing wrinkles, freckles, and other blemishes. A vignetting lens attachment is useful for isolating a subject. Finally, an automatic winder or motor drive, which advances the film automatically, can help capture the quickly changing expressions of a subject's face—particularly the more relaxed, less self-conscious expression that inevitably appears once the shutter has clicked.

Doves were a favorite subject of artist Henri Matisse, and photographer Henri Cartier-Bresson's consummate portrait of the artist takes full advantage of their graceful presence. Because Cartier-Bresson wanted to show as much of the small, bird-filled room as possible, he used a slightly wide-angle 35 mm lens, not a customary lens in portraiture, but the perfect solution to this particular situation.

Henri Cartier-Bresson

Outdoor Portraits

Taking portraits outdoors has many great advantages. The light is far brighter than indoors, of course, and the number of potential settings is enormous. Mountains, parks, city streets, fields, beaches, and many other natural backdrops offer interesting portrait possibilities. But you should select an environment that will complement rather than compete with your subject. And, as always, you need to exercise careful judgment in choosing lighting.

Evenly diffused light is the best all-around illumination for photographing people, indoors or out. The gentle light of a misty morning, an overcast day, or a shaded setting all produce soft, flattering shadows. Usually subjects feel more comfortable in this type of lighting than they do in harsh, direct sunlight. And diffused light also permits wider apertures with medium-speed films, which reduces depth of field (see page 92) and allows you to emphasize your primary subject by softening the background. The picture of the shepherd shown here is a subtle example of this. It also illustrates the usefulness of a recognizable foreground or background in telling us what the subject does.

Although soft illumination is easiest to work with, bright, direct sunlight can also be used if you compensate for the deep shadows it creates. Try to pose your subject so that the light doesn't create unflattering hollows on the face, and take advantage of a natural reflector, such as the little girl's book in the picture on the opposite page. With color film, however, you must choose the reflector carefully, because it can give an unnatural tint to your subject's complexion.

Setting up your own reflectors outside the picture area is one way of avoiding this problem and doesn't force you to change your composition to control lighting. Flash can also be used on a sunny day to soften shadows (see page 143) or to fill in a backlighted subject or a subject posed against a bright background. In either case, be careful not to let it overpower the natural light, or your picture will look artificial.

A shaft of light singles out this girl on a rock from the surrounding deep shadow. The book she is reading acts as a very localized reflector, bouncing a softer light back onto her face.

Lawrence Fried/The Image Bank

Soft light enhances the pastoral feeling in this portrait of a shepherd. It has also allowed the photographer to use a wider aperture, reducing depth of field so that the shepherd is sharply defined against the distant but easily recognizable backdrop of his grazing herd.

Robert Kretzer

Mike Yamashita/Woodfin Camp

A real-life setting can be quite valuable in creating a successful portrait. The vibrancy of the fresh produce here seems to accentuate the confident stance and smile of this greengrocer.

People

Indoor Portraits

Portraits taken indoors present their own special problems. During the day, the best source of light is the natural illumination provided by windows and doors, but unless you're using strong supplemental lighting, avoid direct sunlight. The diffused light from an opening such as a window with a northern exposure or a doorway shaded by a porch will be more even and flattering. On an overcast day, any opening will provide even illumination. But because the light is considerably dimmer than on a sunny day, you will probably have to use a faster film, a tripod, or both.

If you pose a subject by a window, variations in brightness may fool your camera's meter. If you include the window in the shot, the meter may recommend underexposure. Even if you don't include the window, a dark or dimly lighted background may result in overexposure. To avoid these errors, move close and take your light reading from the primary subject. If you do include a window, remember that a proper exposure for your main subject will generally cause it to be overexposed and washed out. With an automatic rangefinder camera, use the exposure lock feature when determining exposure close to your subject. Non-SLR cameras with automatic focus, incidentally, can be very helpful when photographing indoors, because accurate manual focusing is difficult in dim light.

Indoors, even soft window light may be too directional, creating shadows that you might want to fill in. If you are shooting in color, add fill light that is compatible in color balance with the main illumination. Use a reflector, or bounce a flash off a neutral-colored ceiling or wall. In a pinch, tungsten room lighting can create a pleasant warmth in the shadows, provided it's not too overpowering. For black-and-white film, any light source is acceptable.

Daylight pouring through beachhouse windows and doors is the only illumination needed in this portrait of writer E.B. White. Jill Krementz's photograph of the author of* Charlotte's Web *has the spare, roughhewn quality of an Andrew Wyeth painting.

Charles Micaud

Diffused, almost nondirectional lighting enhances the deliberately soft and dreamlike quality of this indoor portrait of a young woman. Diffusion filters, which produce this effect, are described on page 130.

Indoor Portraits

At night indoors, or in a room with the shades drawn or without windows, artificial light may be adjusted to suit the needs of your subject. You can move a lamp to add light or even take off its shade if it's not a part of the scene. Or you can rig up a photolamp (see page 145) and bounce its light off walls, ceilings, or reflectors to soften shadows. You can even diffuse a photolamp with a suspended piece of white translucent shower curtain, or other neutral material, to approximate the quality of window light.

If you are shooting in color, use the film that is compatible with the predominant light source. With ordinary household bulbs or incandescent spots or floodlights, use tungsten film if possible. Daylight film will render subjects in this light more warmly, which may not be objectionable. Prints from color negative film can be partially corrected to tone down the warmer colors, but you may want to filter daylight-balanced slide film with 80 or 82 series color conversion filters (see page 118). An alternative is to use a blue photoflood lamp especially balanced for daylight film, but even this will produce warmer results than an electronic flash. One advantage of flash is that it will overpower other light sources in the scene.

Since both artificial lighting and indirect window light are far less intense than sunlight, you will usually need to use a high- or very high-speed film with a rating of ISO 400 or 1000, being sure to give it adequate exposure. Push-processing film gives you more exposure leeway if you are working in available light, but it will also reduce detail in shadows that may already be very deep. (KODAK EKTACHROME P800/1600 Professional Film (Daylight) for

David Hamilton/The Image Bank

To light this portrait of a young girl, the photographer used carefully diffused artificial light high above the camera to minimize shadows and give the image a felicitous softness. One advantage of artificial light is that it can be adjusted in an enormous variety of ways to suit the individual subject.

Timothy Eagan/Woodfin Camp

Although this is a posed photograph, the father's secure embrace and the direct gaze of both father and child give this portrait an exceptional intensity. To avoid distracting the viewer, the photographer has chosen a neutral background.

transparencies is especially designed for push processing.) If the scene is very dim, or if you want to use a medium-speed film for its greater descriptive power, the slower shutter speeds necessary may call for a tripod and cable release. These not only prevent blurring but can also elicit a more formal, considered response from a subject.

People

Babies

Babies and children are among the most rewarding and the most difficult of photographic subjects. On the one hand, their lack of self-consciousness can lend a special spontaneity to photographs. On the other, their attention span is short and their activity level high. Babies in particular tend to be uncooperative models, if only because they may not be able to understand your directions. The solution, in photographing either babies or children, is to avoid posing them, photographing them instead in the course of new or familiar activities.

But such active subjects also present a technical challenge, requiring a facility with the camera you may feel unprepared for. One way, though, to free yourself from continually having to set and reset the camera is to preadjust it, based on your light meter's recommendation. A relatively fast shutter speed, 1/250 or 1/500 second, is helpful in capturing a child's fleeting expressions or freezing an infant's squirming arms and legs. A small aperture, such as *f*/8, *f*/11, or *f*/16, will give you greater depth of field, so that even an active toddler will remain in focus.

Your choice of aperture is particularly important in photographing babies because of their small size and the need to get close to them to fill the frame. At such near working distances, depth of field is reduced, and you must focus even more carefully than when photographing older children. In particular, details of infants—pictures of hands, feet, and faces—can be very effective, especially when placed near an adult's for comparison, but compromise depth of field even further.

Technique aside, the tiny scale of a baby can be a great source of visual delight, and details are an interesting way to emphasize this scale. Place the baby on a larger object, such as a blanket or quilt, or try to include something of known size: an average-size

Sandra Lousada/Woodfin Camp

Gentle but defining light and a simple setting make this a particularly pleasing portrait of a sleeping baby.

Donald R. Wilhite

Joanne Leonard/Woodfin Camp

In this lovely portrayal of an adoring grandmother and her grandchild, the proximity of their faces invites us to compare them—one smooth, rounded, and unblemished, the other weathered and more angular. In offering this contrast, the image becomes more than just a cherished moment in this particular relationship.

B. Jacques

Dramatic backlighting has given this angelic little girl a halo, but the photographer has exposed for the gentler light filling in the front of her face. In photographing backlighted subjects (see page 48) be sure to adjust your exposure for the most important part of your subject.

The diminutive stature of this young Chinese boy at the Great Wall is reinforced by the inclusion of an adult's shoulder bag in the picture. And the vast setting behind him makes the toddler's seeming bewilderment all the more charming.

teddy bear serves this purpose in the full-length photograph of a sleeping baby shown here. This kind of imagery conveys not only size but the endearing vulnerability of an infant. By including toys, pets, or other playmates, you may often elicit those wonderful expressions that amuse and enchant us—a yawn, a frown, a tremulous smile. And in the rich interaction between child and adult, delightfully displayed in the photograph of a grandmother and grandchild above, is often the most evocative statement of the love and pride a child inspires. Don't forget that your pictures of your own child are a visual record of growing up. The changes in the first year are especially dramatic, so photograph both routine events and the special occasions that serve as milestones, such as your baby's first steps or your toddler's first haircut. The moments they capture will become an indelible part of family history.

People

Gary Whelpley

Children

As children grow older, the uninhibited enthusiasm of babyhood sometimes gives way to shyness and the beginnings of adolescent self-consciousness. Children are also more easily bored, and posing them for pictures may make them restless. So it's best to photograph children when they are otherwise occupied—in fascinating new surroundings or playing with a new toy in the midst of a spirited game. Engage them in lively conversation for a more direct image, or have someone else talk to them so that you can concentrate on taking pictures.

Even when involved in play, a child may be more relaxed if you aren't intrusive with your camera. But because children are small, your inclination may be to move in close to capture their facial expressions. A good solution to this problem is to use a medium telephoto lens (see page 104), which will allow you to stand back and still get a full-frame image of your child, or even a close-up of his or her face. The lens should have a relatively wide maximum aperture, though, if you plan to use it indoors in available light. A high- or very high-speed film, ISO 400 or 1000, will give you the extra speed needed to use the higher shutter speeds a longer lens requires. But if indoor light levels are too low to make this practical, you can always use flash, bouncing or diffusing it to eliminate its harsh effects.

Automatic rangefinders can be particularly useful in photographing children or babies. The autofocus feature saves you the constant manual refocusing an active child or infant requires. And the automatic film advance allows you to keep your eye glued to the viewfinder and your attention on the subject. These features can sometimes save pictures whose moments might otherwise have been lost to fumblings with the camera.

The joy of children is often unpredictable, and you need quick reflexes to capture it, as the photographer did in this picture of Eskimo youngsters. The photographer realized that he had to kneel down to keep the image friendly and not condescending. Avoid pictures of children from your own eye level unless you want to emphasize their smaller stature.

Timothy Eagan/Woodfin Camp

The classic moods of childhood—carefree, inquisitive—are all expressed in this idyllic scene of a favorite summer activity.

In this photograph of children playing, the statue of a young couple in the background not only echoes the children's activity, but is also a harbinger of experiences to come.

Ulrike Welsch/Courtesy of the Boston Globe

People

Elders

If a child's mood is immediately reflected in the face, an older person's is often revealed by more subtle nuances of facial expression. Frequently, details such as skin texture can suggest the richness of experience. Successful portraits of older people require a particular sensitivity to the commentary created by a lined face, worn hands, or energetic stance.

As in other kinds of portraiture, you should think carefully about how light describes the unique skin of an older person. If you want to disclose skin surface—wrinkles, lines, subtle variations in hue—without overdramatizing it, use a soft light from the side as your main source of illumination, filling in shadows with a reflector. Direct light from the side will make skin texture stand out sharply, but tends to be uncomplimentary and minimizes color variations as well.

Nondirectional diffused light, such as that created by overcast skies, shady settings, or bounced flash indoors, is flattering and can further enhance the subtle coloration of an older person's complexion. But an older person's paler skin may take on a bluish tinge if illuminated by open sky, such as indirect window light on a clear day. The slight warming effect of a skylight filter may correct this, but an 81 or 81A filter will do so more effectively, often adding an attractive warmth to your portrait. And if you want to minimize skin texture even more than light alone can, a diffusing attachment (see page 130) or a neutral filter smeared with a light coating of petroleum jelly may be used, but it will also reduce the clarity with which features are rendered.

Larry Daniels

The beautiful close-up of an American Indian woman above captures both the weathered texture of her skin and the warm directness of her eyes.

Far from showing a loss of motivation, these two men have taken on a new challenge in their later years. Photographs of older people can be inspirational as well as reflective, providing role models for us all.

Ulrike Welsch

More important than any technique is your attitude in photographing older people. Be wary of stereotyping them; balance the contemplative portrait with more active depictions, such as the photograph of senior marathoners above. And don't always portray older persons as solitary figures—show them in groups, with their peers as well as younger friends and family. Finally, don't forget that older people are still full of creative energy; try to choose situations that will portray this.

A lifetime of sharing is conveyed as these musicians accompany one another in concert. The strong, warm light lends a vibrancy and richness to the image that seems to suit the couple's own vitality.

Martin Rogers/Woodfin Camp

Figure Studies

The interpretive possibilities of figure photography are wide-ranging. On one extreme, a photograph of a nude can be a study in subtleties; on the other it can reduce the human body to bold, abstract shapes. In either case, the body becomes a medium in and of itself, which the photographer uses to celebrate the sheer beauty of form, color, and texture, or even to suggest an idea, such as innocence or sensuality. Eadweard Muybridge used sequential figure photographs to examine human and animal motion before the advent of moving pictures. His study of a nude woman's movements, shown here, was a technical feat in its day, involving three rows of eight cameras that were tripped automatically by a time-clock device. But with modern technologies, photographers have since turned to more purely artistic approaches to the nude, such as those shown on the following pages.

Muybridge's photographs captured the grace and fluidity of the human body in motion. Most figure photography, however, focuses on a single, static form. When the subject's face is shown, the expression must be treated with as much sensitivity as in a portrait. When the face is obscured, the nude becomes more impersonal, yet often more dramatic in its sculptural qualities. Many of the world's greatest photographers have photographed nudes this way, including Edward Weston and Bill Brandt. But even their approaches were different: Weston produced full-toned, exquisitely rendered images, while Brandt used the distorting effect of a wide-angle lens and high-contrast printing techniques to produce startling abstractions.

Careful lighting is probably the most effective way to reduce the human body to abstract forms. Bright light coming from the direction of the camera flattens features and bleaches out skin texture, but if carefully focused and controlled can emphasize the receding curve of parts of the body. From the side, the same intense light highlights skin texture and creates deep shadows that emphasize contours. These effects can be moderated by filling in shadows with a reflector or by using softer lighting. Strong light coming from behind the subject, whether directly or bounced off a backdrop, produces a silhouette effect that can be striking if its shape is strong. A backlighted figure can be filled in from the front to produce more detail. In thinking about light, be aware of the different qualities of the male and female physique; lighting appropriate to the more angular character of male anatomy could be too harsh for the softer contours of the female body.

As with portraits, diffused light is generally the best choice for figure photography. If it is completely even and nondirectional, it will soften shapes and make the skin look smoother without sacrificing nuances of color or tone. Diffused light coming from one direction, such as through a window, is even more effective. It is gentle, yet it brings out contours. The shadows it creates, while less severe than those created by direct light, can be filled in with a reflector or additional lighting.

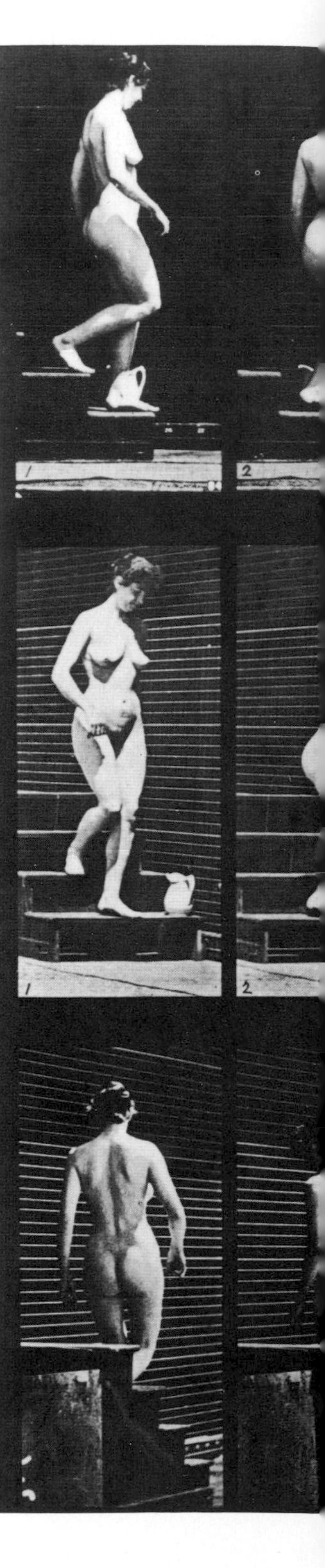

In 1878 Eadweard Muybridge used photographs to settle a famous bet, proving that all four of a trotting horse's hooves are off the ground at one time. His success led him to study motion at the University of Pennsylvania, where he recorded the movement of hundreds of different subjects, including this woman on stairs.

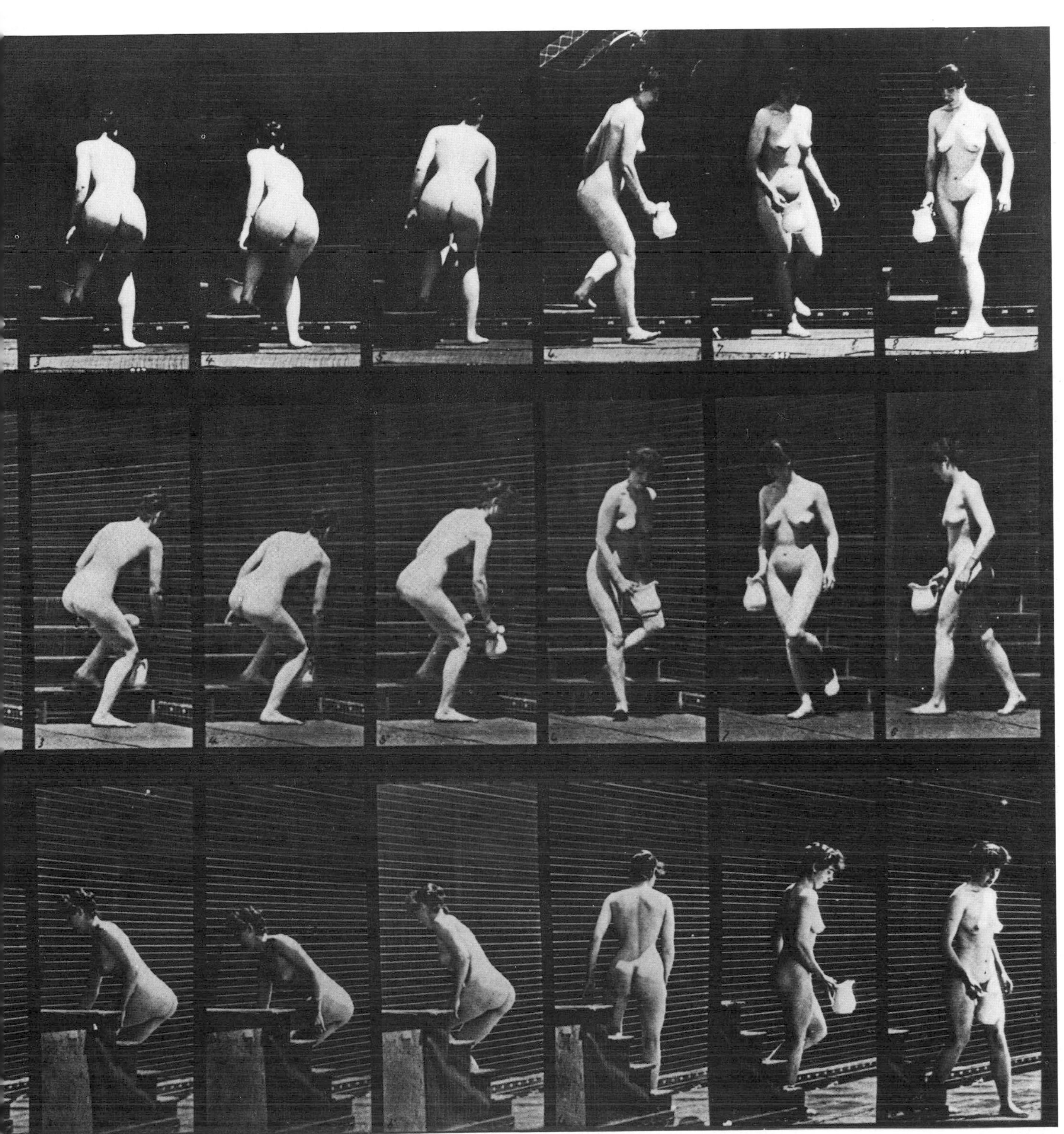

Eadweard Muybridge

Figure Studies

Your choice of film for a figure study is also important. The finer grain and greater sharpness of a low- or medium-speed film, for example, will emphasize textural detail and individual features. But if you want to stress broad shapes, you might elect to use a higher-speed film, letting its graininess overpower the finer details of body surfaces. Depending on the light level, a higher-speed film might also let you use smaller apertures for increased depth of field, a potential advantage given the closer working distances many figure studies require.

In posing the model for figure photography, keep in mind that a model who is relaxed without being too casual will give you a more natural-looking image than one who assumes a stiff, artificial pose. Often, it helps to ask your model to perform some imaginary task, like reaching up to take a book off a shelf. Some posing techniques can be used to idealize the figure or to achieve certain effects. For example, the neck appears longer when the head is thrown back. The structure and shape of legs is more apparent from the side or when the model is sitting or kneeling. When the model lies down, the stomach flattens. With a female model, the breasts lift and the upper arms look thinner when the model reaches upward.

Robert Farber/The Image Bank

Warm, directional light and deep shadows give the photograph at left an almost painterly quality, as if centuries of varnish have yellowed and darkened the image. It accents the curves and lines of the body in a very graceful, romantic manner.

Paolo Curto/The Image Bank

A natural outdoor setting can be a very dramatic backdrop for photographing the nude. In the absence of more familiar surroundings, we feel free to examine the figure in an objective way, and appreciate its relationship to its environment as well as its intrinsic sculptural qualities.

Your distance from and perspective on the figure should also be considered. A short, standing model will appear taller when shot at knee level or below. Moving closer may allow you to capture a striking detail. From certain angles, a telephoto lens will foreshorten the body and thicken the limbs, while a wide-angle lens will attenuate the body. And by using a wider aperture, you can keep one part of the body sharply focused while the rest is softly blurred.

People

Everyday Events

Candids: To effectively photograph the routines of human interaction in our daily lives the photographer must remain unobtrusive and ever-ready. The 35 mm camera's small size and sophistication make it the ideal instrument for such an approach, but to produce truly candid pictures—pictures that show people at their most relaxed and natural—you need to understand how to use it in a discreet but effective way. The early photojournalist Erich Salomon, for whose work the term "candid" was coined, hid his camera in a hollowed-out book to take pictures inside a Monte Carlo gambling casino. Usually, such extreme methods aren't necessary to get good unposed photos. As you take more and more pictures, frequent subjects will begin to accept the camera as part of your presence and go about their activities in an unself-conscious way.

In addition to maintaining a low profile, in candid photography it's important to shoot frequently and rapidly because only a small number of your pictures will successfully capture those moments that typify everyday life. For every picture such as the one of the little girl at right, which epitomizes the shivery thrill of running through a sprinkler, there may be three missed shots. For this reason, editing is very important in candid work. But as your skills develop, and you learn not only to catch the fleeting gesture or the telling expression but also to be conscious of light, composition, and all the other ingredients of a photograph, more and more of your pictures will be on the mark.

Of course, there are techniques that will help you get good results. Outdoors during

Jill Krementz's candid photograph of playwright Tennessee Williams invites us to share a casual yet intimate moment of good humor. This lends a vitality not always found in the more typically formal portraits of famous people.

the day, you can take a light reading and preset a fast shutter speed (such as 1/125 or 1/250 second) that will stop most normal action. Similarly, you can preselect a small aperture (such as *f*/8, *f*/11, or even *f*/16) that will give you good depth of field. Everything you snap within the given range of that depth of field will be sharp. Provided the lighting conditions remain constant, you can continue to shoot many pictures within that range without changing the setting.

Indoors, and in dim light, you won't have such latitude, although an ISO 1000 film or higher-speed transparency film pushed two stops will certainly help. You can still preadjust the camera's aperture and shutter speed for the prevailing light, so that you only have to focus and shoot. By keeping the same distance from your subjects, you can sometimes also avoid refocusing. If the light is so dim that you must use a slow shutter speed, one that won't freeze motion (such as 1/30 second), learn to look for momentary lulls in the action. A person talking, for example, will often pause in midgesture to make a point, and if you are alert, you can utilize that moment.

Adam Woolfitt/Woodfin Camp

The bleakness of the landscape in this image of a boy and his dog reinforces its classic theme and makes the bond between the two even more powerfully felt. The simple, centered treatment draws us inevitably toward the pair.

enes, high- or
400 to 1600 if
ou the greatest
ler apertures and
s, tripods, and
hinder the
n optional motor
s the film to the
ay make an SLR
work.

Russell Hart

In this touching image of an older woman and her cat, we sense a significant relationship between them. This sense of interdependence is reinforced by the desk crowded with items that suggest sentiment and the passage of time.

Derek Doeffinger

Set against the calm of the water's surface and spotlighted by the sun, this dog's eager expression invites —begs—for just one more stick to retrieve.

People

Special Events

Celebrations vary from family to family and from country to country, but the desire to record special occasions seems almost universal. Gatherings of family and friends generally provide lots of picture opportunities—images that in later years help us to relive the events.

A good starting point is to review the information about candid photography in the preceding sections. Remember that friends and relatives are much more likely to be relaxed around your clicking shutter than are strangers. You will want to take pictures that capture the emotional essence of the occasion as well as its rhythm. But pay attention to the props as well. You may want to pose some pictures before the activity—holiday dinner, anniversary, class reunion—begins. Once the celebration is underway, that beautifully set table may become distractingly chaotic. However, the tired aftermath of a toddler's birthday party can be equally precious, so try to take pictures before, during, and after to get a good representation.

If you choose to pose people in groups, arrange them in interesting configurations rather than simply lining them up. Take advantage of natural settings, posing people on steps or on the slope of a hill if the event is outside. In this way the subjects' heads won't be hidden behind one another. If such a setting is unavailable, consider taking a shot from a high angle—a second-story window, a balcony, or even a stepladder—so that everyone's face is clearly visible. If you have to photograph large groups at their level, put the taller individuals at back, shorter people in front.

Kasia Gruda

Bounce flash (see page 140) is an effective way to light a large group of people evenly, as it does in this picture of a children's birthday party. The limited range of direct flash can cause more distant faces to darken significantly.

R.S. Uzzell III/Woodfin Camp

The happy expression on this boy's face says more about the occasion than a formal portrait might. The photographer has chosen to single him out against the busy background of adult preparations, thus giving the image an immediacy not always found in a posed group portrait.

In this jovial photograph of members of a fire department, the photographer has used the traditional staging technique of having the front row kneel. The side of the truck serves as a bright and simplifying background, reinforcing their colorful costumes as well as boldly identifying what binds them together.

Tools: Any 35 mm camera can be used for photographing special events. If you have an SLR, you may find it helpful to purchase a wide-angle lens with a focal length of 35 mm or less. This will enable you to photograph a large group or smaller groups within a crowd without the need to back away so far that other people obstruct your view. If you will be shooting indoors, your lens should have a large maximum aperture, *f*/2.8 or wider. For the same reason, you will probably want to use a high- or very high-speed film, ISO 400 or 1000. If you need supplemental lighting, a flash is handier in congested rooms than are photolamps or other spots and floods. Bouncing the flash off the ceiling or a wall will usually give you good, even illumination. Be careful, however, about mixing flash with incandescent lights, since the latter produce warmer colors. If you want to include yourself in a scene, you'll need a tripod or some other firm support and a camera with a self-timer.

Nathan Benn/Woodfin Camp

People

Weddings

Few special events are as frequently or extensively photographed as weddings. Colorful, sentimental, and symbolic, weddings can provide many wonderful photographic opportunities. If the wedding is large, a professional photographer may have been hired to cover the main event. However, as a friend or relative of the bride or groom, you can work comfortably behind the scenes at home, at the ceremony, or at the reception. The couple is likely to feel more at ease with you and look more relaxed in your pictures.

If the bride and groom can be pried away from well-wishers for a few minutes, you may want to take some photos that express their mood on this special occasion and reflect their personality as a couple. Since you are not likely to have much time, you should scout a location in advance and plan the kinds of photos you want to take. Choose a simple, scenic setting, and encourage the couple to be playful. Your pictures will be a refreshing addition to the traditionally formal and static wedding album photograph.

If the official photographer is arranging group portraits, take advantage of his or her staging skills. But try shooting before or after the formal sessions to catch people in a more relaxed and interactive state. If you're on your own, remember that even lighting is particularly important in photographing a large group. Outdoors, an overcast sky or open shade on a sunny day will provide it; indoors, if you're using flash, arrange the group so that all the faces are roughly the same distance from the flash, and bounce the flash if possible. Flash is most effective, though, in freezing the often animated activity of a wedding, whether it be dancing or the throwing of the bridal bouquet.

A wedding has a certain rhythm to it, and if you follow it through photographically, your pictures will be as interesting in the story they tell as they are individually. Of course you will want to photograph the guests as well as the bride and groom; they can be as memorable and expressive of the event as the couple. People are tense and expectant at the beginning of a wedding, and your pictures will probably reveal this; by mid-celebration, they're more at ease; and they're positively uninhibited after the bride and groom have been safely seen off.

Nancy Rome

The quieter moments of a wedding can be evocative. In this picture, the photographer has turned his attention away from the bride and groom to catch a pensive flower girl on a love seat, perhaps dreaming of her own wedding day.

Because a wedding is such a long affair, you will need a lot of film. Pack a variety of films, too, including higher-speed types such as ISO 1000, so that you can shoot by available light as well as with flash. The equipment useful in wedding photography is basically the same as for other candid picture taking (see page 174) or other special events (see page 178). In a group portrait, for example, a medium telephoto lens will make those faces in the back seem closer and thus more in proportion with faces in the foreground.

Perhaps more than other celebrations, weddings tend to bring the generations together. This emotional embrace in the bright sunlight perfectly expresses the joyous mood of the occasion, enhanced by the bride's exuberant smile and bountiful bouquet.

Elizabeth Hamlin/Stock Boston

In this overview of a wedding ceremony, the elegant shapes and curves of a small church lend a sense of harmony to the happy occasion. The wide angle lens has enabled the photographer to capture the complete scene.

Mike Mazzaschi/Stock Boston

Photographing Action

Freezing Movement

One of the greatest challenges in photography is to convey with a still image the dynamic movement that is so much a part of our daily lives. As we will see, a feeling of motion and a sense of the thrust of an action can often be suggested by techniques that blur either the subject or the background. Other kinds of action are best expressed by freezing their peak moments.

With the fast shutter speeds on today's 35 mm cameras, stopping action is not a technical problem—especially in bright daylight. A setting of 1/1000 second will produce a sharp image of most rapidly moving objects, provided you have focused correctly. Some SLRs offer an even more motion-stopping 1/2000 second. An automatic rangefinder's highest shutter speed is usually 1/500 second, making it less useful in photographing high-speed action.

A sense of timing is invaluable. If you wait until you see the event to push the button, it will usually be over by the time the shutter clicks. You must be ready to push the button an instant *before* the action reaches a peak—in effect, predicting the moment you seek to record. Follow the movement through your viewfinder, keeping in mind that at very fast shutter speeds camera motion won't affect the sharpness of your picture. And try to think about how the background relates to the subject, making sure it won't distract from it.

Sometimes your subjects will appear to be suspended in midaction. Ironically, such seeming lulls are often the most expressive of the event, perhaps because we can anticipate the movement to come. If you plan for these moments, you can use an even slower shutter speed, such as 1/125 or 1/250, to stop most of the action—an advantage if you are working in dim light or need to use a smaller aperture for better depth of field.

John Vaeth

Two other techniques permit you to freeze action yet still use a slower shutter speed in less-than-perfect lighting. The first involves the direction of an action relative to the camera. If a subject is crossing your camera's field of vision at a right angle to the axis of the lens, the subject will appear to be moving faster than if it is moving toward you or away from you. Thus, you don't need as high a shutter speed to freeze a subject approaching you head on as you would to freeze the same subject approaching from the side. If you don't want a head-on shot, even changing your position so that your sight line is at a diagonal to the direction of the subject's movement will help reduce the possibility of blur.

Your distance from a moving subject also has an effect on your ability to stop its motion photographically. To freeze a runner passing twenty feet away, for example, you can use a much slower shutter speed than would be needed to photograph the runner from five feet away. However, if you use a longer lens to make the subject fill the frame as it did when you were close, the blur will be the same.

In the picture of acrobats at left, the photographer exploited the happy coincidence that the most important part of the action was also its least active part. A spotlight provided enough illumination to permit a relatively fast shutter speed, but the same speed would have been ineffective in freezing the performers in the midst of a somersault.

Alain Courtois

In order to be able to use a shutter speed fast enough to freeze these swimmers in mid-dive, the photographer had to use a wide aperture, which reduced his depth of field considerably. This is a typical trade-off in photographing action in dim available light. But the fact that the more distant divers are out-of-focus doesn't bother us because they are part of a pattern established by the sharply defined diver in the foreground.

Neil Montanus

Tools: To stop action with shutter speeds of 1/500 or 1/1000 second, you will usually need a lens with a large maximum aperture. A fast zoom lens can be useful, if your mobility is limited, in making the action fill the frame. High- or very high- speed film, ISO 400 to 1000, and push-processing when possible for additional speed, will make better use of the available light during the extremely short period the shutter is open. A motor drive, which can take several shots a second, will increase your chances of capturing the exact moment desired. Indoors, when the action is fairly close, an electronic flash with a fast recycling time is often necessary. A higher-speed film and the use of wider apertures will facilitate faster recycling times.

Action

Blurring Movement

In the early days of photography, when the precise record-keeping capabilities of a photograph were still a wonder, subjects were cautioned to remain perfectly still so that the photographer could produce a sharp image. Today, however, modern films no longer require long exposures because of their increased sensitivity. As more creative uses of photography have become common, the blur created by deliberately long exposures is accepted as a way to convey motion. A blurred picture can re-create the way fast-moving objects appear to us, or it may be expressionistic, giving the viewer a sensation rather than information.

In this approach, action is usually most effectively suggested by a blurred subject that contrasts with sharp or recognizable surroundings. How much blurring you allow affects the quality of motion the photograph conveys. Certainly this is true in the picture opposite, where the speeding bicyclist is almost unrecognizable while the rest of the scene is sharply in focus. However, a softer, more languid sense of motion prevails in the photograph of the ballerina, at right.

The shutter speed you select will depend in good part on how fast your subject is moving. In the photograph of the dancer, a speed of 1/8 or 1/15 second allowed for considerable blurring of her arms and costume. A more rapid subject, such as a speeding car, may blur at a relatively fast shutter speed of 1/125 second. In general, the slower the shutter speed, the more blur you will get. Speeds below 1/30 second can blur motion dramatically but usually require the use of a tripod to keep the surroundings sharp. At 1/8 second and less, most or all of a moving subject will be blurred. With a compact non-SLR camera, you may find that your options for such speeds are limited. Check your camera manual to see what capabilities your particular model offers.

Tom Beelmann

By blurring the dancer's arms and swirling dress the photographer has effectively captured a sense of fluid and graceful motion. The colorful aura—created by using a Harris shutter (see page 128) —further enhances her loveliness.

Good timing on the photographer's part accounts for the success of this image, rather than a particularly slow shutter speed. Not only does the stop sign provide a sharp detail to contrast with the bicyclist's blur, but it also adds a touch of ironic humor, as its authoritative command goes unheeded by the speeding bicycle rider.

In planning a shot, keep in mind that the closer you are to your subjects, the more likely they are to blur. The same is true of subjects moving across your field of vision rather than approaching you head-on. Also remember that the fastest-moving parts of a subject will be most blurred.

Tools: Other than a tripod for long exposure, no special equipment is required to blur a moving subject. When working at slow shutter speeds, which let in a lot of light, you may need relatively low-speed films, such as ISO 32 or 25, especially in bright daylight. If you prefer to use medium- or high-speed films, you can cut down on the light entering the camera with neutral-density and polarizing filters. (See pages 116 and 129.)

John Kush

Action

Panning

A relatively sharp subject against a blurred background also effectively conveys the impression of speed. To produce this effect, you must follow the subject with your camera during the exposure, a technique called *panning*. As the photographs of the horseman and the skater here show, panning focuses attention on the subject, de-emphasizing its surroundings. It is one of the trickiest techniques in photography, and the results are not always predictable. The camera movement must be smooth and the subject must be held in the same location in the viewfinder as long as the shutter is open.

When panning, prefocus on the spot directly in front of you where your subject will be when you start the exposure. Then stand firmly with the camera to your eye and slightly twist the upper part of your body in the direction from which the subject will come. Begin following the subject as soon as it appears in the viewfinder. When your subject reaches the spot you have selected, release the shutter and continue following it in one smooth movement. With practice, you will be able to release the shutter smoothly and avoid jarring the camera.

The combined techniques of panning and blurring here create an impressionistic image of pure motion that makes action—rather than detail—the essence of the shot.

Donald Maggio

Guy Samoyault

A good panning shot does not necessarily have to show a perfectly sharp subject against a totally blurred background. In the picture above of an Arabian horseman, the blurred movement of the animal's legs and the recognizable setting of a stucco house and palm trees are important elements.

When photographing repeating action, such as a child on a carousel, follow the action several times without releasing the shutter just to get the rhythm of the motion. Once you start shooting, make several exposures to be assured of at least one successful image.

Panning requires a relatively slow shutter speed, but the exact speed will depend on the situation and the subject. You will learn to judge these variables as you gain experience with the technique. A very fast-moving subject, such as the Arabian horseman above, may allow you to blur the background at a speed of 1/60 second. In general, though, it is very difficult to obtain this effect at 1/125 second or faster. At the other limit, it is virtually impossible to avoid some vertical camera movement with speeds less than 1/15 second. As a basic rule of thumb, the slower the subject is moving, the longer the exposure you will need.

Tools: At slow shutter speeds, a carefully leveled tripod with the head loosened can be used to lessen the possibility of jarring the camera vertically. Unless the light is dim, longer exposures may also require low-speed film—ISO 32 or 25—or filters to reduce light. Although most people may not be aware of it, the viewfinder on an SLR blacks out the instant you push the shutter release. If you find this disorienting, consider using an auxiliary viewfinder in order to follow the action.

Outdoor Sports

It is fortuitous that so many sporting events take place outdoors, where bright natural light gives the photographer more flexibility in choosing shutter speed and aperture. Whether the subject is the explosive spring of a high-diver or a jumping horse clearing a fence, the key to getting good action shots is in presetting your camera to suit the particular event. Many sports photographers favor fast film so that they can use both small apertures for good depth of field and the higher shutter speeds that freezing action requires. Generally, such a combination will give you the most freedom.

When the action you want to shoot is confined to one spot, however, a wider aperture may be more appropriate. This will enable you to focus selectively on the main point of interest and to blur a distracting background, as the photographer at right has done in the shot of the horse jumping a fence. Again, preset your camera and focus on the spot before the action begins. It may help to scout the playing field or arena in advance to determine the most advantageous position. For night sports, take exposure readings from the lighted field because darker surrounding areas will cause the meter to indicate too much exposure. Flash is ineffective unless you're very close to the action, and its use may result in underexposed pictures. Since artificial light requires larger apertures and slower shutter speeds, it may be difficult to freeze fast-moving action.

Tools: Although any camera can capture action close at hand, a telephoto lens is needed to cover action at a distance. Depending on how far away you are from the activity, the focal length of the lens can range from 85 mm upwards. Lenses over 200 mm are difficult to handhold, so a tripod or a unipod (the tripod's one-legged counterpart, favored by some professionals for its greater portability and ease of use)

F.P. Foltz

In the photo above, the shallow depth of field of a powerful telephoto lens blurs the background, keeping our attention on the force of the jump.

John Zimmerman

Tensed musculature combines with formal grace to produce a striking photograph of Olympic highdiver Greg Louganis. With virtually no background to distract us, we can feel the awesome power of his extended arms and feet, and anticipate the moment of impact with the water below.

may be necessary. A zoom lens with a range of 80 to 200 mm is also very handy. The combination of a fast shutter speed and small aperture usually requires a relatively high-speed film, ISO 400 or higher, depending on the brightness of the scene. A motor drive, which permits several rapid sequential shots of fast-changing action, is especially helpful when photographing fast-paced sports events.

Action

Indoor Sports

Good indoor action pictures demand much from both the photographer and the equipment used. The larger apertures required in dimmer light reduce depth of field, while slower shutter speeds make stopping action far more difficult. In these circumstances, timing and technique are crucial. In a sporting event with wide-ranging action, such as basketball, choose locations that are likely to be the scene of peak activity—the basket, for example—then prefocus your camera, preset your exposure, and wait for the action to come into view. If you are forced to use slower shutter speeds, be on the lookout for moments in which movement hesitates briefly.

Tools: Unless you are close to the action, you'll need a telephoto lens. Since relatively dim light will require a large maximum aperture, *f*/2.8 or wider, the lens should probably be a telephoto with a focal length between 80 and 135 mm. With their generally smaller maximum apertures, long lenses of 200 mm or more and zoom lenses are not very effective in stopping indoor action. High- or very high-speed film, ISO 400 or 1000, is advisable, but be careful to balance color film for the light source. If flash is permitted, it can be effective in stopping motion, but you'll need a fairly powerful unit. Higher-speed films will give you more range and/or faster recycling times with automatic electronic flash. Finally, if you're shooting with existing light, a motor drive can be helpful in catching peak moments.

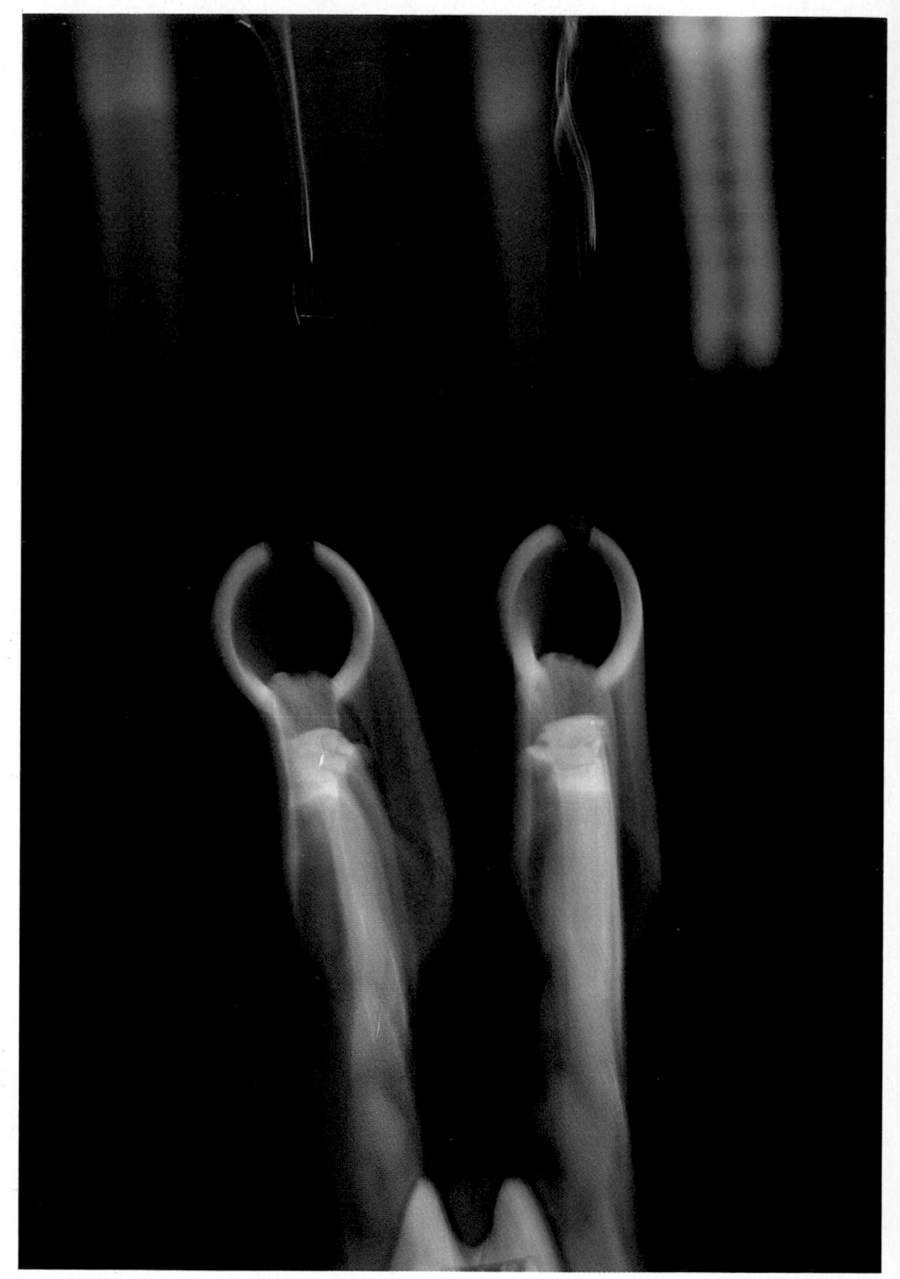

Bill Ross/Woodfin Camp

Four exposures on a single piece of film produced this image of a young gymnast's somersault on a balance beam. Such unconventional approaches to sports photography can often be more revealing about the skill and prowess of the athlete than a straightforward recording.

Bill Ross/Woodfin Camp

Careful use of flash units mounted above the backboard gives an available-light look to this professional shot of basketball players rising to the hoop. Only flash can freeze movement with such clarity in dim indoor light, although you must be careful to check whether flash is permitted.

Recognizing that the light illuminating this gymnast on the rings was too low to permit a shutter speed fast enough to freeze his movement, the photographer used a deliberately slow shutter speed to blur it instead. The effect is as suggestive of the intense effort involved as any sharp picture would have been. In this instance, the photographer moved the camera during the exposure to enhance the blur.

John Zimmerman

Photographing Nature

Tight head shots of predators nearly always have to be taken in zoos. Even with a long lens, a photographer is rarely able to get this close in the animal's natural habitat.

Derek Doeffinger

Distinctive light often separates a good nature photograph from a bland one. Here, bare branches strongly highlighted against a deep background dazzle the viewer's eye.

In photographing nature, you will inevitably encounter active subjects, such as this trotting mare and her colt. Mother with offspring is a perennial theme of nature photography.

James Mascarella

Capturing plant and animal life on film is one of the most fascinating areas of photography. Perhaps no other subject matter has as much inherent grace and symmetry. The nature photographer is an interpreter of nature's forces—its beauty, mystery, immensity, power, and brilliance. When we respond with delight, awe, or curiosity to a photograph of the natural world, we are sharing the photographer's perception and echoing his or her response. The skilled eye of a nature photographer can isolate the spectacular in what may appear to be the merely ordinary.

Sometimes detail is paramount—a single bloom or an insect's wing can be more impressive than an entire field of flowers or a swarm of bees. For such pictures you will need to move in very close and perhaps use special close-up equipment (see page 196). At other times, the larger view will be more expressive—perhaps a herd of deer grazing on a hillside or a beautifully sculpted rock formation. In such instances, you may need to use equipment that will allow you to stand a distance from the subject (see page 102) in order to get the proper perspective or to photograph a shy or skittish animal.

You needn't travel to exotic places for interesting and appealing subjects. You can find them in the flora and fauna of city parks, forest preserves, zoos, and even your own backyard. Take pictures of the geraniums in your windowsill planter or the robin splashing in your birdbath. Photographing close subjects and distant wildlife both require patience, good technique, and practice, but the photographer who masters the necessary skills will be richly rewarded. New and unexpected aspects of nature's apparently random hand will be revealed as patterns and textures, shapes and colors. The artistic possibilities for the creative photographer are endless.

Neil Montanus

Nature

Close-Ups

To photograph the diminutive aspects of nature, you need to learn to handle two special conditions. First, the closer your camera gets to a subject, the shallower the depth of field becomes. The zone of sharpness can be as narrow as a fraction of an inch. Using a small aperture alleviates the problem somewhat, but even then you must be sure that the most important parts of the subject are at the same distance from the lens. Movement is also greatly exaggerated at close range, whether it's in the subject or the camera. A faint breeze can cause a flower to flutter in and out of focus, while an insect can scurry out of view in less than a second. Even at your usual shutter speeds, handholding the camera may result in a loss of sharpness. In addition, the vibration set off by the mirror in an SLR can become significant at close range, so you may want to lock it in its "up" position if your camera has a mechanism for doing so. (Unfortunately, this will block the viewfinder, a problem if your subject is active.) These problems are compounded if you are using a low- or medium-speed film (ISO 25 to 200) to capture fine detail and a small aperture to get greater depth of field. This is because in natural light, the combination requires slower shutter speeds.

Patience, planning, and ingenuity can help you overcome some of these difficulties. A plant can be stilled by constructing a simple windscreen with stakes and a plastic bag. Don't be afraid to manipulate your subject matter, and try to anticipate its activity. In a garden full of bees, prefocus on a flower and wait for it to be patronized.

Just as with a landscape, lighting can make a nature close-up magical or mundane. Follow the general guidelines about the angle of light and light at different times of the day (see pages 48 to 57). Use a piece of white cardboard as a reflector or drape a piece of translucent material on broomsticks for a diffusing canopy. You can use flash in close-ups either as the main light source or for fill light. To soften it, you can diffuse it or bounce it off a reflector. Mount the flash off the camera and determine flash-to-subject distance based on the aperture that gives you the appropriate depth of field. Most automatic units must be set on the manual mode to give you proper exposure at such close distances. If you can't mount a powerful flash unit far enough away from the subject for correct exposure, cut flash output with a tissue or handkerchief.

Derek Doeffinger

Nature's elegance is often best revealed in close-ups, as in this shot of graceful new branches and brilliantly backlighted leaves.

In a close-up photograph, the zone of sharpness can be a matter of millimetres, as shown in the way the stem of this dewy wild pansy falls out of focus while its petals remain sharply defined.

Joyce Connor

A close-up of a shy nocturnal subject, such as the owl at left, requires great stealth and usually a flash unit.

Donald Maggio

Close-Up Tools

The best camera for close-ups is the single-lens reflex. Unlike a rangefinder, the SLR allows you to see your image through the lens and usually to preview the depth of field at your chosen aperture. In addition, while there is only one way to obtain close-ups with most rangefinder cameras, the SLR offers several possibilities.

The close-up tools that can be used with either type of camera are the filterlike attachments known as close-up lenses. When attached to your camera's lens, they increase subject size by decreasing minimum focusing distance. With an SLR, the change can be seen through the lens; with a rangefinder, you must measure and calculate distance and area following the lens's instruction sheet. Close-up lenses are commonly sold in sets of three, rated +1, +2, and +3 diopters, according to their degree of effectiveness. The greater the number, the closer you will be able to focus on the subject. Close-up lenses can be combined to allow the camera lens to focus even closer, thus increasing the image size (magnification) on the film. They are compact and inexpensive and do not require exposure adjustments in a camera with a through-the-lens meter. Sharpness may be reduced, however, especially with all three lenses attached.

If you own an SLR, a better choice might be extension tubes or a bellows attachment. Both fit between the camera and its lens to permit close focusing. Extension tubes can be used singly or in combination and are available in several lengths—the longer the tube, the closer the lens can focus on the subject. Some extension tubes require that you stop the lens down manually before taking your picture, causing the viewfinder to become dim at smaller apertures. If you're waiting for an active subject such as an insect to position itself, this might be a problem.

Derek Doeffinger

Shallow depth of field, usually a disadvantage of close-up work, has effectively separated this moth from a confusing background. But because the insect isn't shown full frame, the few sections of blades of grass are important in the way they give the image a framework and establish the setting.

William Ratcliffe

The delicate tracings of frost on these autumn leaves and grass appear almost luminescent. The photographer has used a close-focusing lens to come in close without distorting the shapes of the leaves.

Derek Doeffinger

After a rainstorm, the combination of wet surfaces and brightening overcast skies makes nature's colors especially vibrant, as in this study of leaves and flower petals.

Bellows, although costly and somewhat cumbersome, are more versatile and permit you to get an image that is life-size or larger. Both extension tubes and bellows reduce the amount of light reaching the film in proportion to their length. As a result, you usually need to correct exposure according to their instruction sheets and your camera manual. Also, any such extension of the lens will further reduce depth of field at a given aperture.

For the more serious SLR user, a close-focusing, or macro lens (see page 111), may be a wise investment, despite its somewhat high price tag. Specially designed to work at close distances, these lenses are unsurpassed in ease of use and optical performance. Most stop down to an aperture of *f*/32 (longer focal lengths to *f*/45), the use of which can increase your depth of field considerably at close distances. Macro lenses are available in normal to medium telephoto focal lengths and focus smoothly from infinity to just a few inches in front of the lens. They can be used with bellows or extension tubes for greater image magnifications. Many newer zoom lenses have similar close-focusing capabilities and in effect can replace three or four macro lenses (as well as three or four telephotos). They are somewhat more awkward to use, though.

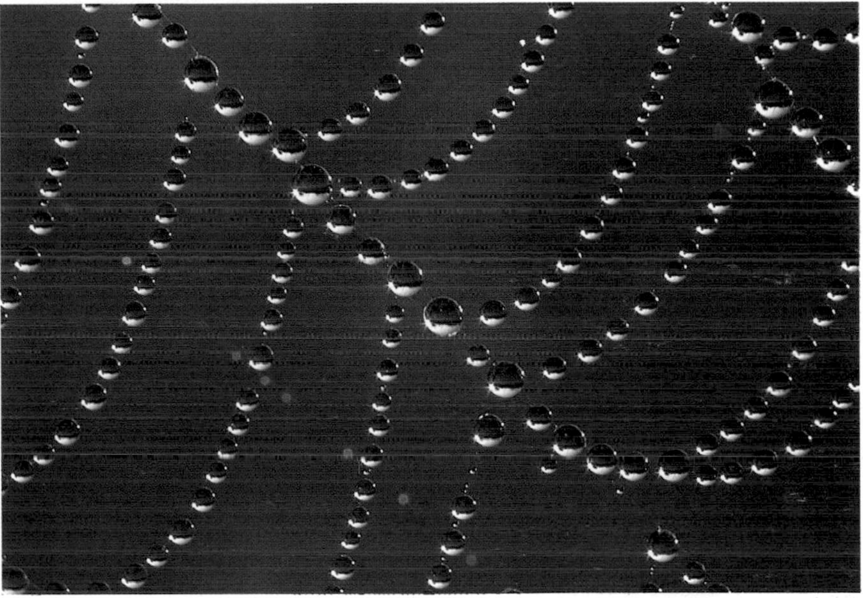

Derek Doeffinger

As perfect as a string of pearls, water droplets define a spider's web so fine it's almost invisible in the picture above. We can't help but be impressed by the enormous strength of the web. Close-ups are often more effective in revealing the exquisitely functional designs of nature than broad views.

A tripod is almost indispensable in close-up work to guard against camera movement, particularly during long exposures. Ideally, the tripod should have a reversible center post for low-level subjects. Small, inexpensive electronic flash units are also useful, and many avid nature photographers use two or three for complete control over a scene. Low- or medium-speed film (ISO 25 to 200) is best for rendering details.

Nature

Wildlife

For many of us, the mere mention of "wildlife photography" conjures up rather exotic images: stalking lions across Africa's Serengeti Plain or capturing the rainbow plumage of exotic birds on a trip up the Amazon. Yet wildlife subjects abound everywhere. National parks and game preserves offer spectacular glimpses of animal life, like the herd in the picture at right. And you can find subjects for your camera even closer to home. Local woods and fields are filled with small mammals, birds, and snakes; marshes provide a haven for migrating or native waterfowl; and even a local park or your own backyard has its squirrel and bird populations.

Since nearly all wild creatures are both timid and fast, capturing them on film requires a combination of quick reflexes, planning and perseverance. You can learn much about the animals in a particular area from field guides. Especially note the animals' behavior patterns—their feeding and nesting habits, the time of day they are active, their modes of defense. Thus informed, you will know where to look for animals and what reactions to expect from them. The ability to predict animal behavior is an invaluable skill for the wildlife photographer. As a general rule, most animals venture out early in the morning or late in the afternoon rather than at midday. Consider taking along food or seed to attract them to the spot you want.

When you are stalking animals, remember that many wild creatures will accept your presence if you don't appear too threatening. A powerful telephoto lens will help you keep your distance, but it is equally important to keep your movements to a minimum. When you do move, proceed slowly and carefully. Nothing frightens an animal faster than an abrupt action. Seek out some natural cover that still gives you good visibility. Remember that the senses of hearing and smell in many animals are much keener than ours.

A snapping twig, a rustling bush, or a downwind whiff of you may be disruptive. If possible, set your camera up on a tripod in a location that gives you maximum advantage—clear visibility, a safe distance from any real danger, and some natural cover. It is sometimes a good idea to wrap the camera in dark cloth to muffle the sound of the shutter and prevent reflections.

Less elaborate procedures are needed to photograph the more exotic and accessible subjects at zoos. Captive animals photographed in natural-looking environs or parklike settings often appear as authentic as their counterparts in the wild. Carefully select your camera angle to exclude moats, railings, and other signs of captivity. The best kind of picture to take in a zoo is a close portrait with a telephoto lens, including as little intruding surroundings as possible.

Like portraits of people, close-ups of animals will be most flattering when the illumination is the soft, even light of an overcast day. The low, raking light of morning or afternoon effectively emphasizes an animal's contours and the texture of its fur or feathers. In strong daylight, you should be able to use the fast shutter speeds necessary to capture a moving subject. The shallow depth of field that results from large apertures can subdue foliage interference between you and your subject or effectively separate the animal from an intentionally blurred background. Panning (see page 186) can also help you isolate a moving animal from a nondescript setting.

As caribou travel rapidly across a snowy plain, they are struck by the long shadows of late afternoon. A mountain bluff or another unusally high vantage point is often the only place to get such pictures of fast-moving migratory herds.

Y. Shirakawa

Nature

Wildlife Tools

Since wild animals instinctively keep their distance from humans—and you'll want to keep your distance from them if they are dangerous—an SLR equipped with a long telephoto lens is by far the best choice for wildlife photography. A lens with a focal length between 200 and 400 mm will pull most subjects close enough to fill the frame, yet will not be too cumbersome or difficult to use. Lenses of mirror-telephoto design (see page 104) are available in 300 mm focal lengths and beyond and offer more compactness at a price, both monetary and optical. Any lens in this range of focal lengths, however, must be used conscientiously. Depth of field is extremely shallow, particularly with the wide apertures required to compensate for the higher shutter speeds needed to photograph moving animals, so careful focusing is essential in keeping your subject sharp. And because of the degree of magnification of these lenses, they can emphasize even slight camera movement.

Given these conditions, it helps to use medium- or high-speed film, ISO 200, 400, or 1000. Pushing film is another possibility. But it is also essential to steady the camera. Depending on the circumstances, a long lens can be supported on a tree stump or the hood of a car with a folded jacket under the camera. Some nature photographers even carry a small bag filled with beans or Styrofoam pellets for such shots. You should carry a tripod or a unipod, however, as basic wildlife equipment, and you might also want to consider using a gunstock support.

If you have more than a passing interest in wildlife photography, you may want to consider two other helpful devices. The first is a blind, a small tentlike construction with a hole in the side for your camera lens. A blind is especially useful in open areas where there are no trees or bushes for cover. You can purchase one from a hunting supply store or you can construct one using canvas and a light wooden frame. Many animals, most notably birds, quickly become accustomed to a blind and return to their normal activities in its presence.

A remote release, which allows you to trip the shutter at a distance from the camera, is also useful for dangerous or extremely shy

Robert Bastard

subjects, or for tricky situations such as photographing a bird's nest from a nearby branch. A simple bulb-and-air-hose release allows you to take a picture up to twenty feet away. Another kind of remote release has a battery-powered electromagnetic plunger that can push the shutter button from an even greater distance. And an expensive radio-controlled release can trip the shutter from more than a mile away. You can also arrange to have your subject unwittingly trip the shutter with a cord attached to a lever that depresses the shutter button. A more sophisticated trip device uses photoelectric cells to actuate a plunger. To take more than one shot of a subject with a remote release, you need an automatic winder or motor drive.

This picture of strolling penguins illustrates the shallow depth of field characteristic of long telephoto lenses. The birds are sharp only because they are all about the same distance from the lens. From a side angle or straight on, some of them would probably be out of focus.

In this tranquil image of African elephants cooling themselves in Tanzania's Lake Manyara, the photographer used the shallow depth of

field of a telephoto lens to obliterate the distinction between sky and water, giving the image a primeval simplicity.

Alvin Cohen

Photographing Landscapes

As a photographic genre, the landscape has uniquely diverse possibilities. It may be a swatch of sky or the reflection of a city skyline in a puddle; an endless chain of mountains or a flat abstraction of sand dunes with no horizon. A landscape can be a straightforward recording of a magnificent vista, or a challenge that confounds our notions of scale and perspective.

Unlike a human subject, a mountain can't be told to move a little to the left, and beginning photographers may be frustrated by what seems to be a lack of control over the elements of the landscape. Moreover, the descriptive power of the 35 mm format may appear limited compared to the clarity of master landscape photographers' prints from large negatives. For this reason, when working in 35 mm, you must rely on the raw power of light to reveal textures and define shapes. Create an image with form and dynamic composition so dominant that you don't need to distinguish every tree trunk on the mountain.

Landscapes need not always be vistas with elements of equal interest. Emphasize an aspect such as a waterfall or a windmill by choosing a distinctive angle and the appropriate lens. Try to convey a sense of depth and balance by including things that relate to the subject in the foreground, such as a boat in a marine view. This treatment is most effective with a slightly wide-angle lens. Experiment, too, with your position and with the position of the horizon line. A low point of view can make a close object seem larger, or even make it loom, but it also tends to flatten out the picture space because it eliminates the middle ground. A high vantage point (perhaps even from the roof of your car) tends to separate the foreground from the background and creates more of a continuous, receding space. The vanishing ribbon of a highway or river would enhance this effect, as would a high horizon line. A low horizon emphasizes the sky and its less defined spaciousness.

Don't be afraid to distort scale and perspective or to abstract the landscape by isolating parts of it. In this way a landscape photograph can transcend simple recording. We tend to preconceive landscapes as "natural," yet sometimes the most interesting scene is one in which civilization and nature meet. We also make the mistake of thinking that bright, sunny conditions are most flattering to a landscape, and yet sometimes the worst weather conditions yield the most exciting picture.

In fact, the broad, flat light of midday sun can be detrimental to a landscape image. Early and late in the day, the long, dark shadows cast by the sun can emphasize the three-dimensionality of a scene, and the light's raking angle can enhance textures dramatically. Colors, too, are made more interesting by atmospheric diffusion, as in the pale yellow of a spring dawn or the rosy palette of a winter sunset. Many professional photographers plan their shots weeks in advance, to coincide with these times of day or year. A little scouting ahead often leads to a better landscape image.

The light in a landscape varies tremendously in brightness. The supremely sensitive human eye adjusts instantaneously for these extreme variations. But photographic film is sometimes incapable of recording both shadows and highlights. You may have to expose for one and sacrifice the other. More often, you will want to determine an intermediate exposure by taking a close-up reading of a middle value in the scene or by metering both light and dark areas and splitting the difference. Particularly if you second-guess your meter, it's a good idea to bracket your exposures with two shots that overexpose by a half and a full stop and two more that underexpose by a half and a full

Herb Jones

Time of day is often the key to a good landscape photograph. An ordinary scene can be given extraordinary drama by the right combination of light and cloud patterns, as in this image taken at dusk. The beginning and end of the day often offer the most interesting lighting possibilities.

stop. With color slide film, when in doubt err on the side of underexposure to avoid washed-out highlights.

Nothing is more baffling to your camera's built in meter than a landscape. Although the trend toward computerized analysis of lighting may one day improve this, the averaging meter in most cameras assumes that the values of every scene averages to a middle grey. This characteristic allows it to be easily misled by certain conditions typical of landscapes—often aesthetically desirable ones. A large area of sky in your picture, for example, can fool your camera's meter to recommend an exposure that is inadequate to obtain good land detail on the film. White snow or sand can also make the meter recommend settings that will underexpose the scene. One way to keep the meter honest is to position a photographic grey card so that it reflects scene illumination the same way major subject elements reflect. Take a close-up meter reading of the card and use the suggested settings. Lacking a grey card, you can also use the palm of your hand—give one stop more exposure than recommended. Be sure to lock in the reading of an automatic camera; otherwise it will return to the previous setting when you readjust your composition. If it has no exposure lock, but has an exposure override on its film speed dial, you can compensate by adjusting toward "plus." When in doubt, bracket.

Sunsets and sunrises can be particularly appealing but rather tricky unless you are willing to let the meter take its normal course. You'll probably get acceptable results over a short range of exposures. It's likely that foreground subjects will be silhouettes, unless you give an additional two or more stops exposure. Beware of lens flare—bright spots and a washed-out appearance—caused by internal lens reflections that can intrude any time the sun is in the scene. When the sun is bright, you may want to conceal it behind something or wait for a handy cloud.

The soft light of an overcast day intensifies the warm hues of a lakeside village in the Austrian Alps. Atmospheric haze lightens and

softens the sheer cliff in the background, emphasizing the church's sleek steeple.

Norman Kerr

Landscapes

Three superimposed views of Half Dome in California's Yosemite National Park

Tools

The 50 mm lens on most SLRs is a useful lens for general landscape photography because it reproduces the true size relationships in a scene. But other lenses can alter these relationships in interesting and effective ways.

Because of its ability to encompass a broad view, a wide-angle lens with a focal length of 20 to 35 mm is well suited to landscape photography. (Many present-day rangefinder models come with fixed lenses of 35 to 40 mm.) The wide-angle lens can also include a fairly close foreground without sacrificing any of the overall scene, and its good depth of field ensures that both will be in focus, at a small aperture.

A telephoto lens is useful if you want to enlarge a portion of the landscape but are unable to get closer to it, or if getting closer would mean sacrificing your vantage point. It can also bring widely separated picture elements closer together, but your aperture must be small enough to get both in focus (see page 92). Remember that the longer a lens, the shallower its apparent depth of field at a given aperture. A zoom lens lets you play with the angle of view and spatial relationships of the scene.

Filters are almost indispensable in landscape work. An ultraviolet or haze filter can reduce atmospheric haze, which can result in photographs with lackluster skies. A polarizing filter has a stronger effect, and it can add definition to clouds. With black-and-white film, a yellow, orange, or red filter will darken the sky and highlight clouds. (See pages 112 to 133 for more information on filters.)

Low- or medium-speed film, ISO 25 to 200, renders detail with the greatest sharpness, which may be preferable in shooting landscapes. At small apertures and slow shutter speeds, a tripod may be necessary.

Herb Jones

illustrate the effects of a wide-angle lens (upper left), a normal lens (middle), and a telephoto lens (lower right) on a landscape.

Landscapes

The Countryside

Shinzo Maeda/The Image Bank

The gentle and usually pleasing order imposed by agriculture on the seemingly chaotic wilderness has inspired artists for centuries. What makes each new interpretation refreshing and interesting is the eye of the individual artist. Although these two photographs show fields under cultivation, each portrays not only geography but a distinctive culture. At left, the use of a telephoto lens accentuates the steepness of the subtly monochromatic farming hamlet of Hiroshimo, echoing the tradition of the vertical Japanese scroll. The bright French vineyards below drift slowly away from the viewer through emphasis on aerial and linear perspective, reflecting the Western approach to the depiction of size and space.

The towering expanse of river, mountains, and sky is emphasized by the panoramic format (produced with a special camera) and the inclusion of the diminutive and seemingly insignificant vessel in the foreground. Because the composition echoes art typical of the dignified and structured Oriental culture it portrays, it implies a strong sense of China.

Sébastien Marmounier

In the rural Vermont landscape at right, a curving road and the framing bough of a tree together establish a feeling of depth, and the receding planes formed by the houses, trees, and hills further heighten this effect. Again, an overcast sky contributes to the scene's rich, vibrant color.

Norman Kerr

John Paul Murphy

Landscapes

The City

By taking this photograph of the New York City skyline in the half-light of dusk, the photographer was able to maintain detail in the buildings yet preserve the jewel-like glitter of their windows. The long-distance perspective of a telephoto lens makes the moon seem much larger than life.

Grafton Marshall/The Image Bank

Mike Yamashita/Woodfin Camp

The use of a warming filter enhances the old-world feeling in this view of the northern Italian hill town of Assisi. The position of the bell tower—against the part of the sky where the sun was breaking through—emphasizes its contours and at the same time keeps direct light from entering the lens. A photograph is particularly satisfying when it combines technical and aesthetic solutions in this way.

Derek Doeffinger

City landscapes are as much vertical as they are horizontal, and their vertical surfaces can provide the same element of pattern afforded by horizontal surfaces in natural landscapes. In this image of an old building under restoration, a man painting windows interrupts the pattern they form and gives the image a needed focus.

Photographing Still Lifes

For this still life of cut flowers, the photographer chose to depart from the traditional approach of flowers in a vase. The result is far more decorative, reducing the flowers, leaves, and stems to flat, colorful shapes.

Derek Doeffinger

For centuries, painters have used still life both as a visual exercise and as a way of exploring the symbolism of objects. The earliest photographers found similar virtues in still lifes. Whether approached as an experiment with light, shape, color, and composition, as a study in meaning, or as a combination of the two, still life offers the novice photographer both a learning experience and a vehicle for his or her imagination.

Every day we are bombarded with seductive still life images—of tantalizing foods, gleaming appliances, and other tempting products. The professionals who produce these advertising images spend hours, and often days, setting up each shot. As a result, much can be learned simply by studying the ones that you find most striking and original. Notice how these photographers use repeating shapes and lines to create patterns, and subordinate secondary subjects as well as combine harmonious or clashing colors to make a statement about the product. Any object or group of objects can be the subject of a still life. But because of their intriguing shapes and inherent beauty, flowers, fruits, and vegetables, as shown here and on the following pages, have traditionally served as still-life materials. Such natural items are easy to obtain; they offer countless possibilities for arrangements and color combinations; and they can be used to achieve effects ranging from the lushly exotic to the cooly abstract.

However, many other objects, including very functional and ordinary ones, are suitable for still lifes. They can be familiar or unfamiliar, of obvious or uncertain purpose, but you shouldn't feel bound by conventional thematic associations between them. The juxtaposition or isolation of objects can create very different kinds of images. A delicate piece of lace, for example, will have a different meaning when paired with opera glasses and a swatch of velvet, than if placed next to a grimy piece of machinery or the gleaming surface of stainless steel. Still lifes can exist as combinations of "found" objects in the world outside the studio, or even as single objects that offer pleasing studies of shape or line. And a still life can be utilized as a kind of three-dimensional collage. Photographer Frederick Sommer, for example, has produced a group of finely detailed pictures of his own assemblages of disparate objects, photographing them after allowing them to weather for years outside his Arizona home.

But most professional photographers use studio set-ups for their still lifes, and it is fairly easy to do this yourself on a smaller, simpler scale with a few photolamps and suitable background material. Together with reflectors and diffusers, photolamps offer an almost infinite variety of lighting possibilities: soft, even light to enrich hues; backlighting to create a dramatic silhouette; strong sidelighting to heighten textures; and more diffuse sidelighting to stress contours. Natural lighting, especially the soft light of a window with a northern exposure, can also be used and supplemented with reflectors. Professional seamless background paper (see page 145) provides an easy-to-use neutral setting for a still life. For small objects, however, you should consider using a smooth illustration paper or board because the texture of background paper may become visible when close to it. If you use other backgrounds—such as a wooden tabletop or a surface draped with fabric—be sure they are appropriate in some way to the objects you are photographing. Although you have less control over light outdoors, natural settings may make more sense for some objects, such as shells on a sandy beach.

Still Lifes

Tools

Professional photographers have traditionally used large-format cameras to photograph still lifes because of their ability to record intricate detail. But with a good lens and effective lighting and design, the 35 mm SLR is an equally versatile tool. A medium telephoto lens, or a zoom lens at a comparable setting, will let you back away from your subject to minimize the distortion common at close range, but its closest focusing distance may not be close enough for your setup. Using the macro feature on many zoom lenses will solve this problem, as will close-up lenses and other close-up devices (see page 196). Otherwise, a macro lens of medium telephoto length, such as 105 mm, should be used.

A tripod lets you check the composition of your still life through the camera viewfinder as you arrange it. It also permits slower shutter speeds, particularly important when you use smaller apertures to compensate for the shallow depth of field of longer lenses and closer distances. A tripod also makes possible the use of low- or medium-speed films, ISO 25 to 64, which you may prefer in shooting still lifes for their finer grain and higher sharpness. To further assure sharpness, use a cable release or your camera's self-timer for exposures longer than 1/60 second.

Photolamps, reflectors, diffusers, seamless background paper, and other equipment useful for still-life work are detailed on pages 140 to 145. Most of this equipment is easily adapted to the tabletops you will probably be using for still lifes. With photolamps, use film of compatible color balance (or one of the filters noted on page 118), and be sure the lights don't stray into the lens, which could cause flare and loss of

Bill Strode/Woodfin Camp

Natural window light gives a powerful sense of volume to this kitchen counter scene. Still lifes needn't be arranged; in everyday life, objects often present themselves in a pleasing way, and all you need to do is isolate them.

Herb Jones

Your repertory of still-life objects should by no means be limited to fruits and flowers. In the photograph above, patent medicine bottles are lined up as if on an apothecary shelf, their strong, simple shapes and richly translucent colors sustaining the image.

contrast. With black-and-white film, filters can be used to change the relative lightness and darkness of objects (see pages 122 to 123). Also helpful are a photographic grey card for determining exposure (see page 265) and a polarizing filter to tone down reflections from nonmetallic surfaces. If your camera's reflection shows up in a shiny surface, such as a dark ceramic vase, try shielding the camera behind a large black card with a small hole in it for the lens.

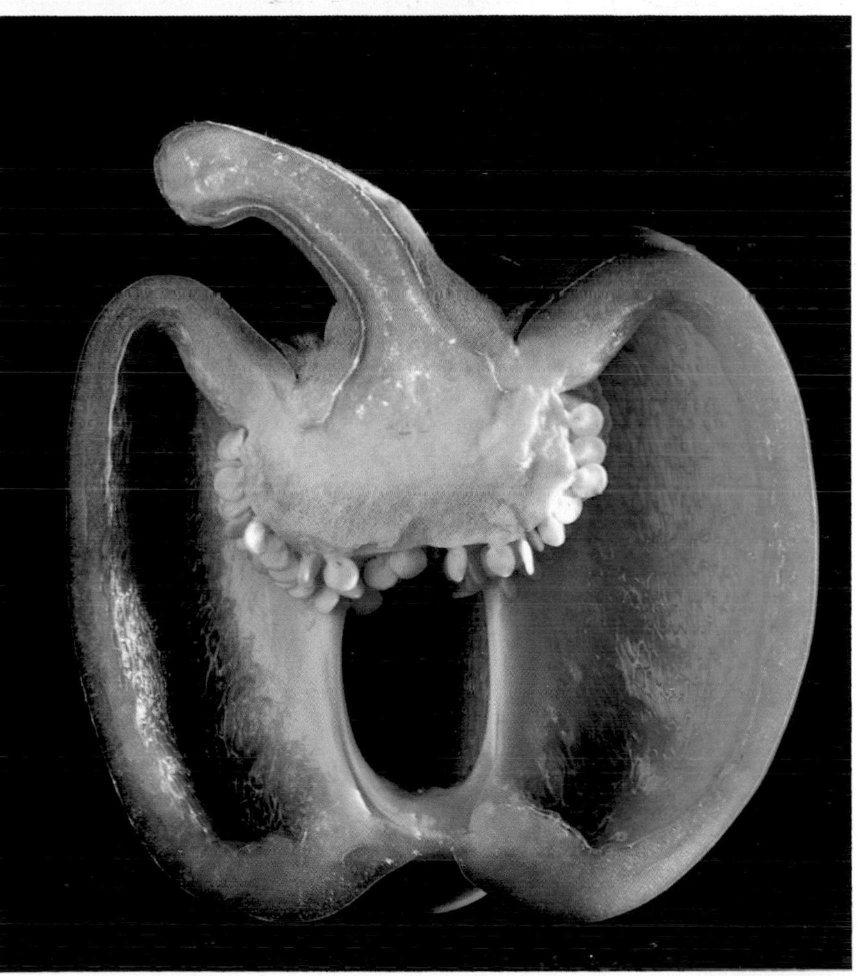

Although it may seem difficult to improve on nature, natural still-life objects such as vegetables can be made even more photogenic. Glossiness can be accentuated with a thin coat of mineral oil, for example, and surfaces made more vibrant with a quick spray from a misting bottle.

Eastman Kodak Co.

Photographing Architecture

An architect exploits on a grand scale many of the same elements central to photography—shape, line, texture, and pattern. When you photograph a building, try to remember the features that first caught your eye—the elements that you found visually exciting from the start. Perhaps it was a repeating row of arches or windows, a steeply pitched roof, or a coarsely textured concrete wall. Or it may have been a series of tiered terraces, the low lines of a sprawling ranch house, or the vertical lines of a skyscraper.

The way you choose to interpret and emphasize these features will largely determine the vantage point and camera angle you select. You may decide to shoot straight on to show only a façade, from an angle to show both the front and a side, or even from the back, like the adobe church below, or you may want to squat down to get a very low-angled view of the building or climb a nearby rise to shoot downward. A low angle is especially useful for singling out a building and for enhancing its height

Master photographer Ansel Adams took this picture of an adobe church in the American Southwest. Its stark, massive shape is accented by shadows caused by the sidelighting of the afternoon sun.

Ansel Adams

Ezra Stoller © 1979 ESTO

Although built many years later, the Art Museum of South Texas in Corpus Christ (above) is conceptually similar to the adobe structure at left in its clean, strong shapes and lines. It also has been photographed straight on to emphasize its harsh planes and ponderous solidity.

and massiveness, while a high angle draws attention to its layout and relationship to the environment.

The lighting you select should also stress a building's unique features. If possible, study a structure at different times of day to see how it is affected by the sun. Depending on when the sun hits the desired side of the building, the angular light of midmorning or midafternoon is the first choice of most architectural photographers. At these times, the sun provides good illumination while creating shadows that define structural details. If your subject has an intriguing shape, like many factories and other industrial structures, it may look best dramatically backlighted by a rising or setting sun or by a low-lying winter sun at noon. Other buildings take on a glow when washed with the warm light of dawn or dusk—from certain angles, windows may even seem to be ablaze. Some structures assume a solitary splendor when floodlit at night, others appear best when the soft light of overcast skies enriches their subtle colors. And, of course, fog, snow, and rain (see pages 236 to 241) all have great potential for enhancing the appearance of any edifice—especially one with majestic proportions, such as a cathedral, a castle, or a skyscraper.

In composing an architectural photograph, you should carefully consider a building's setting. A flower bed, a reflecting pond, or a driveway can lead the viewer's eye to the structure. A tree, a fountain, or a statue in the foreground can be used to frame the building or to provide a sense of scale. You can also manipulate the sky to your advantage by changing your camera's angle to increase or diminish the sky's prominence. If a building has a glass façade, you may want to experiment with reflections in the windows; images of neighboring buildings, clouds, or the setting sun can add great visual interest.

Architecture

Tools

For the single-lens-reflex camera owner, a wide-angle lens with a focal length between 35 and 24 mm, or even less, is a great asset in photographing buildings and other structures because of its greater angle of view—a real advantage when shooting in the close quarters of urban architecture. Keep in mind, of course, that extreme distortion can occur with these lenses.

The phenomenon known as keystoning—the convergence of a building's vertical lines as you tilt a camera upward—is especially exaggerated by a wide-angle lens. One way to overcome this difficulty is to find a vantage point—a nearby hill, if possible, or another building, as in the picture below—that brings you more in line with the center of the building you are shooting. Another alternative is to photograph the building from a distance with a telephoto lens, although obstructions may limit your vantage point. To a limited extent, keystoning can also be corrected by careful printing in the darkroom. But a perspective control lens, available in focal lengths of 35 or 28 mm, lets you shift the position of the lens while keeping the camera level. Because this keeps the film itself parallel to the plane of the subject, it keeps straight those vertical lines that would otherwise converge, as shown in the two shots of an old mansion at right. The only disadvantage of this lens, which is described more fully on page 110, is that the aperture ring is usually not keyed automatically to the camera meter or body and must be stopped down manually before you snap the shutter.

Low- or medium-speed film, ISO 25 to 200, renders subtle architectural details more sharply than do faster films. These films, together with the smaller apertures often needed to attain greater depth of field, may necessitate shutter speeds slow enough to require a tripod and a cable release. In any event, the customarily tight composition of

For this striking view of New York's Brooklyn Bridge and World Trade Center, the photographer used a 200 mm telephoto lens which permitted an unusual vantage point and the compressed perspective necessary to create the image.

Norman Kerr

George Hall/Woodfin Camp

In this richly detailed image of a galleria in Milan, the photographer's high vantage point enabled him to keep vertical lines from converging, in spite of the fact that he was using a wide-angle lens to encompass more of the scene. With careful use, the wide-angle lens often used for architectural shots needn't cause obvious distortion.

much architectural photography makes a tripod particularly useful. And it may be almost essential in using a perspective control lens because stopping the lens down manually before taking your picture usually darkens the viewfinder, making hand holding the camera difficult. And, a tripod will allow precise adjustment for wayward lines and angles.

Because buildings present broad areas of a single tone, be aware of how your camera's light meter might be fooled. A bright building may cause your meter to recommend extreme underexposure, but if you take a reading off a photographic grey card (see page 90), you may choose to deliberately underexpose the same subject by half a stop to keep it from looking washed out. The opposite would be true for a very dark building. Remember, too, that the proportion of sky in your image will also affect the exposure (see page 205).

With black-and-white film, yellow, orange, and red filters will darken a blue sky, making the shape of a lighter building stand out dramatically. A polarizing filter will do the same thing with color or black-and-white film and will also minimize glare from glass. When photographing a modern, all-glass building, however, you may want to use it cautiously in order to preserve the reflective character of the building.

The two pictures below of an ornate, nineteenth-century gothic revival mansion taken from the same ground-level vantage point illustrate the value of a perspective control lens. In the shot at left, taken with a regular 35 mm lens, the structure's vertical lines converge toward the top. In the photograph at right, a 35 mm perspective control lens was used to straighten the lines. The result is a more accurate representation of the way our eyes perceive buildings.

Martin L. Taylor

Architecture

When photographing stained glass, such as these panels in the spiraling ceiling of Thanksgiving Square in Dallas, Texas, remember to expose for the light of the window, not the dim interior light, and use daylight color film. If you are shooting glass lighted from the inside at night, switch to tungsten film.

Interiors

Photographing a building's interior is very different from shooting its exterior. Light is usually dimmer indoors, and there is less room to maneuver. Even in an ample space, you may have trouble positioning yourself so as to give a true idea of the structure's shape and size. The task becomes much more difficult in the average-size room.

One common solution is to shoot toward a corner to show parts of two walls and the floor. You may wish to include the ceiling if it is low to convey the room's cozy, intimate —or even confining—character. A room will look most airy and spacious if you stop just short of the ceiling, creating the impression that the vertical lines of the walls continue upward. If stairs or landings overlook the area, try shooting downward to give a better sense of the layout. Most of these treatments will result in some distortion of perspective lines with the wide-angle lens usually needed to photograph interiors. Keeping the camera level will prevent convergence or divergence of vertical lines, but this can limit your composition, forcing you to include a disproportionate amount of floor or ceiling. A perspective control lens can solve these problems.

Existing light, either natural or artificial, is often sufficient to photograph an interior (see pages 230 to 232). If not, use an electronic flash to supplement daylight. Depending on the size of the room and the amount of light you want, use a single flash, a series of flashes, or photolamps as the chief source of illumination. The soft light provided by bounced or diffused flashes and photolamps is generally best for interiors. To achieve even, overall illumination in a large area, many professional photographers use a technique known as painting with light (see page 143).

Tools: Wide-angle lenses from 18 mm to 35 mm are very helpful in shooting interiors. A tripod and cable release are indispensable for the slow shutter speeds required with smaller apertures and for the low- or medium-speed film you'll need to achieve the most detailed images. In dim interiors where flash and tripods aren't convenient or permitted, such as in a museum or church, a high- or very high-speed film, ISO 400 or 1000, is a better choice.

Anna Marchese

Beams of light from the windows in the dome suggest a heavenly presence in the majestic interior of St. Peter's Basilica in Rome, while the visitors below give a good indication of the church's immense proportions.

John Rogers

Photojournalism

In its most obvious sense, photojournalism means news photography—the informational pictures we see in our daily paper. News photographers record events just as reporters do. But since the heyday of the big picture magazines such as *Life* and *Look,* which gave the public a real sense of the social power of the photographic medium, photojournalism has come to mean more than being first on the scene. It has come to represent an attitude and commitment, a willingness to involve oneself in an unfamiliar situation and take chances in order to comprehend it, document it, and, in doing so, create images far more eloquent than words or statistics. From Mathew Brady's magnificent Civil War portraits to Lewis Hine's poignant depictions of young mill workers (later used to support the passage of child labor protection laws), from the unforgettable faces and places seen in the work of Walker Evans and Dorothea Lange in the 1930s to the startling immediacy of Vietnam combat photos, photojournalism has profoundly influenced our world view. Whether recording a celebration or a tragedy, a famous ruler or an impoverished worker, photojournalism provides a sensitivity to the meaning of human events.

The Bettmann Archive

Good photojournalism does not merely record a specific event but often evokes emotions, even memories. The image of a soldier celebrating V-E day with a jubilant kiss has become a symbol of the optimism of post–WW II America.

A series of photographs often tells a story more effectively than any single image. In this sequence, a despairing elderly widow is rescued from a suicide attempt from a fourth-floor window in Boston's Chinatown.

Hank Walker/Life Magazine © 1960 Time Inc.

Sometimes photojournalism concerns itself with drama; at other times it shows us a private world, as in this picture of the Kennedy brothers conferring during the 1960 Democratic convention.

As the pictures here show, photography's ability to isolate a moment in time has a lot to do with its power as a journalistic tool. These images elicit strong feelings in us as we look at them. And although many photojournalistic images are timeless, needing no historical context to be understood, others, such as the picture of the Kennedy brothers, become emotionally charged by their context or by our hindsight and knowledge of things to come.

The methods and techniques of photojournalists are as varied as their subject matter, making it difficult to provide general guidelines here. It's safe to say that sometimes they use unorthodox techniques to cope with the volatile and unpredictable nature of their subject matter: shooting from the hip to avoid a confrontation, holding the camera overhead in a crowd to get an otherwise impossible shot.

Sometimes the specific information a photograph provides is as important as the strength of the image itself. Effectively capturing the intensity of a runner's effort, this photograph also records an historic event: the breaking of the four-minute mile record by Englishman Roger Bannister in 1954.

AP/Wide World Photos

Stanley Forman

Photojournalism

The Photo Essay

In a photo essay, a series of pictures is organized to give a deeper understanding of a topic than one picture alone ever could. In establishing the photo essay form, the European and American picture magazines of the 1920s and 30s created a new kind of journalism in which words were secondary to the photographs themselves. As the 1955 *Life* magazine essay on Irish country life shown on these pages demonstrates, much of the impact of a photo essay comes from the size, arrangement, and sequence of the pictures, as well as their individual content. In this essay, Dorothea Lange, who is known for her Depression-era photographs of the American dustbowl, turned her eye on the more permanent poverty of western Ireland. Her pictures show a people cheerful in the face of adversity and sustained by faith. The pictures work on two levels—as a document of a specific human environment and as a testament to human indomitability.

But the photo essay is by no means the exclusive domain of the magazine world. Many of your own photographs will be strengthened by conceiving and presenting them as part of a larger group. The organization of a photo essay can be thematic or chronological, but, before you actually begin photographing, it is important to determine what kinds of pictures you will need. Plan images that can be used to introduce your subject, establishing a mood or setting. Shoot others to be used in a larger size to develop the central theme or story, and relate major events. Other photos can be used in smaller sizes to supplement

Dorothea Lange

Irish Country People

SERENELY THEY LIVE IN AGE-OLD PATTERNS

A wild and rugged country tests

a man's best

Dorothea Lange

Dorothea Lange

the main images or provide transitions. Finally, you should take pictures that will provide a sense of completion to use at the end of the essay.

Professional photographers often shoot hundreds of images on an assignment—often taking many shots of the same scene using different lighting, exposures, lenses, and camera angles. You need not be so extravagant, but plan to shoot at least several rolls of film to get a large enough number of pictures with which to plan your essay. Most people edit their pictures with contact sheets—proofs of an entire roll of film on a single sheet (see page 251)—or in the case of slides, by sorting them on a lightbox. You can organize, size, and crop the pictures you have chosen on a rough pencil layout before having the images enlarged and placed in position in an album or wall display.

Dorothea Lange

Photographing in Existing Light

Outdoors at Night

Some very striking photographs can be taken in less than ideal lighting conditions—outdoors at night or indoors using only the illumination from windows or light bulbs. But "existing" or "available" light, as such marginal illumination is usually called, demands much from the photographer—in planning and taking a shot as well as in judging the quality of the light. Besides being dim, available light usually varies greatly in intensity from one part of a scene to another. If no precautions are taken, some parts may end up blank from overexposure while others are impenetrably dark.

When shooting outdoors at night, one way to circumvent this contrast problem is to photograph in the early evening, up to an hour after sunset, when the lingering light provides even, overall illumination. Street scenes and nature shots benefit from twilight, but, as the pictures here show, it helps if any artificial light is evenly distributed throughout a scene.

The relatively even lighting of this Indonesian street scene made it an ideal subject for a night picture. Since longer-than-usual exposures are often needed for such scenes, you may have to accept as inevitable some blurring of people in motion.

Donald Maggio

Neil Montanus

Even though the lingering light of day provided fill illumination for this shot of a town nestled in a snowy valley, a time exposure was necessary. The longer exposure had the added effect of transforming the car headlights into luminous streaks of light. Note the green cast created by mercury vapor streetlamps.

High-speed film is indispensable for handheld nocturnal photography. Black-and-white film, such as KODAK TRI-X Pan Film, rated at ISO 400, can be push-processed to 800 with a gain in contrast and some loss of shadow detail or to ISO 1600 or 3200 with a noticeable increase in graininess. KODAK EKTACHROME P800/1600 Professional Slide Film (Daylight), on the other hand, is especially designed for this application, and its daylight color balance matches that of twilight. It can also be used for late-night street scenes, although it will probably need to be color-corrected with a filter (see pages 118 to 121). A better choice might be tungsten-balanced slide film such as KODAK EKTACHROME 160 Slide Film (Tungsten), which is rated at a slower ISO 160, although it can be push-processed to 320. Because photographing at night is often better done with a tripod, the slower shutter speeds tungsten film will require shouldn't be a problem unless your subject is very active. In fact, when you photograph still subjects with your camera mounted on a tripod you may prefer to use slower films for their better detail and less pronounced grain. Exposures of several seconds or longer, however, can cause color shifts. This often makes high- or very high-speed color negative film, ISO 400 to 1000, preferable because its color can be adjusted in printing.

Some SLRs now offer very long shutter speeds—eight, sixteen, or even thirty seconds—and can be useful in low-light photography, although a watch with a second hand and the "B" setting work just as well. The wider maximum aperture of fast lenses permits faster shutter speeds, which in turn can minimize color shifts, but sometimes the color discrepancies between different light sources can produce interesting results.

Existing Light

Natural Light Indoors

Direct sunlight cascading through an open window may be a joy to behold, but it is also pretty tricky to photograph. This is because sunlight is directional and much more intense than the room's ambient light, so the scene presents a range of brightnesses that photographic film is unable to encompass. Hazy sunlight may reduce this range slightly, but the best advice is either to avoid photographing directly sunlit interiors or be prepared to supplement the light in some way.

When shooting inside use windows or doors that receive reflected light from the sky as your source of illumination. The light from them will be directional but softer and less intense, as in the picture at right of the baby. If direct sunlight is unavoidable, blinds or translucent shades can moderate it considerably. Sometimes the best place to photograph a subject is at the opposite end of the room, where the light is more uniform, if dimmer.

Contrast can also be reduced by secondary lighting. Use light-colored walls as reflectors to fill in shadows, or open a door or curtains to let in softer natural light from another direction. With black-and-white film, use artificial lighting or flash to reduce contrast. If you are shooting daylight color

Momatiuk/Eastcott/Woodfin Camp

Light is bounced into this baby's face by the magazine she is looking at, filling in the shadows created by soft window light. In the absence of such natural reflectors, white cards or cloth carefully positioned outside the image area are very effective in controlling contrast.

Chuck O'Rear/Woodfin Camp

In the deep, dark interior typical of a bar, natural light quickly diminishes. But even indirect illumination, such as in this scene of a poker game, creates a powerful composition of light and dark values, in this case singling out faces and hands very effectively.

film, improvise a simple reflector by having someone hold up a large piece of white paper or cloth, or use bounce flash. High- or very high-speed film, ISO 400 or 1000, will give you the greatest flexibility. Avoid pushing film under these circumstances because it will only exaggerate the already strong separation between light and dark areas. Black-and-white negative film can actually be given extra exposure and underdeveloped to reduce contrast, and permits further control of contrast in printing (see pages 278 to 279). Even in a color print, areas can be burned in and dodged (see page 280) to maintain detail. Finally, since your camera's meter is easily tricked by direct light from a window, be sure to take a close-up reading of your subject.

Existing Light

Arthur Field

Photographing figures on a lighted stage can be especially tricky because a camera's averaging meter overcompensates for the dark, unlighted background, resulting in overexposure of the figures. In such situations, try to get a light reading with the figures filling the frame, either by getting closer to the stage or using a longer lens, then return to your original vantage point or lens, if you prefer. In this picture, a medium telephoto lens has effectively isolated rock star Bruce Springsteen by cutting out the rest of the stage, giving the image a presence unusual in live concert photographs.

Artificial Light Indoors

Working with existing artificial light indoors is a challenge. The chief problem is the unevenness of the illumination, which results in images with severe contrast. Indoors at home, you can reduce this contrast by turning on all lamps and overhead lights. If the lamps are not included in the photograph, remove their shades to further increase overall brightness.

In public places, pose your subjects in locations where they will be evenly lighted. Or look for scenes in which the main light is balanced by softer illumination from other sources. Whenever you are working with existing light, be sure to take a close-up reading of your subject.

With color film, especially slide film, be careful to match the film with the main light source. Most indoor artificial lighting requires tungsten film or daylight film with a filter (see page 118) to compensate for the warmer color of the light. Daylight film can sometimes be exposed unfiltered under tungsten light to produce a warmer-than-normal rendition of a scene. Even a patch of daylight, on the other hand, will appear as a strong bluish color on tungsten film, usually an unpleasant effect, so be wary of its presence in an artificially lighted interior. Unlike other common artificial light sources, fluorescent light is deficient in red and so is better rendered by daylight film, although it must be filtered nonetheless (see page 120). Color negative film, because it is balanced for daylight, will produce a more natural-looking print if filtered for tungsten or fluorescent light sources, although any color imbalance may be corrected somewhat in printing.

Tungsten film, ISO 160, can be push-processed to 320 to make it more versatile in dim light, but this treatment will increase contrast, which may be a problem given the unevenness of artificially lit interiors. Fast daylight-balanced film, even when filtered for tungsten light, will yield good speed without affecting contrast. An ISO 1000 film will have an effective speed of ISO 250; EKTACHROME P800/1600 Film will become ISO 400 if given Push-2 processing. High-speed black-and-white film, ISO 400, may also be push-processed for greater film speed and, thus, more versatility in dim-light conditions.

Votive candles clustered together below provide an even and intimate light source, as well as an unusual environment for the subject. Because it contains even more red than incandescent light, candlelight will always be rendered more warmly when photographed with color film than it is in reality.

John Sabo

Tools: For nearly all existing-light pictures, a lens with a large maximum aperture, *f*/2 or wider, is preferable because it allows relatively short exposure times in dim light and produces a brighter viewfinder image, which makes composing and focusing easier. Also, since many dimly lit scenes will require exposures longer than 1/30 second, a tripod and cable release are often necessary. If your camera's meter doesn't function in very low light, use a more sensitive auxiliary meter or follow the suggested existing-light exposures in the film instructions.

Although the light in work interiors is generally more even than that found in the home, it also tends to be more mixed, combining daylight, tungsten, and fluorescent sources. Existing-light photographs taken in these conditions, such as the shot at right of the Harvard University School of Education Library, usually need careful corrective filtration (see pages 118 to 121).

Ezra Stoller © 1979 ESTO

Photographing Underwater

Recording the beautiful world of the deep on film is less difficult than you might think. With the proper equipment, including a special camera housing, it is simply a matter of learning the unique characteristics of light in water. For example, because of water's magnifying properties, both your eye and the camera's lens interpret underwater subjects to be about one-fourth closer than they really are. If your housing permits focusing through-the-lens, this will be taken into account; if not, you should set the distance scale on your lens for three-quarters of the actual distance.

Visibility is often limited underwater, so get as close to your subject as is practical. And because the amount of light is severely reduced, the best time to shoot is when the sun is high and the water calm. Setting exposure for underwater conditions depends on the kind of camera and watertight housing you use. Some housings permit you to operate your camera in the usual way; less expensive housings may require you to set the exposure above the surface. The typical exposure adjustments needed for various underwater depths are given in the chart on the next page. The data are based on average lighting conditions between 10 A.M. and 2 P.M. on a bright sunny day with slight winds and an underwater visibility of fifty feet. Since it is difficult to steady a camera underwater, try to use the fastest shutter speed lighting permits—1/60 and 1/125 are common.

Given the rapidly decreasing level of natural illumination underwater, flash is very useful below the first few feet of surface water. And because water absorbs red light, creating an almost totally blue-green world below ten feet, flash is particularly necessary in shooting color. To calculate flash exposure, divide the above-water guide number by three when based on the actual (measured) distance and by four if based on the focused distance. For best color, stay within five feet of the subject because beyond this even the light from the flash will become blue-green.

Tools: Serious underwater photographers usually own special waterproof 35 mm cameras, but any camera with a watertight housing can be used below the surface. Such housings are made of metal or plastic with glass ports and are often designed to accommodate specific cameras. The best housings offer external controls connected directly to the camera, but even on some better housings the use of the camera's viewfinder is limited or impossible. If this is the case, you need an auxiliary frame viewfinder mounted on top of the housing. Because of the parallax problem, you'll also need a special wire framing device that projects out in front of the lens for close-ups. In general, metal housings are preferable to plastic: they are more durable, require less ballast, and are less prone to such problems as reflections and condensation on the lens. Special underwater flash units and housings for some regular flash units are also available.

Because of low light levels underwater, a lens with a large maximum aperture, *f*/2.8

Underwater you need to work as close to your subject as possible to get sharp images. If accurate color rendition is important, flash at close distances will overcome the progressive red deficiency that accompanies greater depth—you can see the difference between the flash-lighted fish and the naturally lighted diver in the picture at right. Tight shots such as the flash-illuminated picture of the anemone may require close-up equipment (see page 196) and a wire framing device.

Robert Cranston

S. Harold Reuter

or wider, is necessary. A wide-angle lens, 35, 24, or even 21 mm, will let you move closer to your subject to reduce the water's blue-green cast. The magnifying effect of water increases effective focal length, so that a 35 mm lens has an angle of view equivalent to that of a 50 mm lens on dry ground. Available-light work will require a high-speed film balanced for daylight. KODAK EKTACHROME P800/1600 Film may be particularly useful, and other slide films can be push-processed for additional speed. ISO 400 or 1000 speed color negative films offer more exposure latitude and some correction of the blue-green cast in printing. Especially with slide film, a color correction 30 red filter should be used with natural light down to thirty feet. With natural light at depths below thirty feet, however, the filter is useless because the light has lost all its red. The filter requires additional exposure of about two-thirds of a stop. Be sure to use rolls of thirty-six exposures, so you won't have to surface as often to change film.

Underwater Exposure Settings

Depth of Subject	***Number of f-stops to increase lens opening over normal above-water exposure***
Just under surface	$1\frac{1}{2}$
6 feet	2
20 feet	$2\frac{1}{2}$
30 feet	3
50 feet	4

Photographing in Inclement Weather

Rain and Lightning

Rain, snow, fog and other inclement conditions can literally add atmosphere to a photograph, especially to a landscape or an architectural shot. If you are willing to brave the elements, you will be amply rewarded.

Rainfall imparts a gleaming, glassy appearance to hard surfaces and adds a more subtle sheen to grass and foliage. Like a coat of varnish on wood, the wetness enhances the richness of the colors: bright hues especially stand out in the dim light created by heavily overcast skies. Shots taken from porches, under street canopies and overhangs, and through windows can also be very effective—a rain-blurred window may even enhance an ordinary image. Immediately after a rain, surfaces will still be wet and shining, and often the light will be brighter. Look for reflections in puddles, mist rising from the ground, and subjects splattered with droplets. Watch the sky, too, for as a storm approaches or leaves, cloud formations can be unusually dramatic.

Capture rain itself with a fast shutter speed, 1/125 second or less, and try to get the drops sidelighted against a dark

François Botton

Storm clouds loom dramatically over the stubble of a harvested field in the graphic shot at left. To record such cloud formations on black-and-white film, use yellow, orange, or red filters (see page 122). With both black-and-white and color film, a polarizing filter helps to define clouds.

Hans Wendler/The Image Bank

In this extraordinary image of lightning and a breaking sun, the photographer has caught the weather in an instant of transition. Repeated exposures were probably necessary to capture this unique juxtaposition.

background. Freeze ripples in a puddle with a short exposure. You can even photograph lightning. Mount your camera with a normal or wide-angle lens on a tripod and aim in the direction of the storm. Select an angle that excludes any nearby light sources. In daylight, use the smallest aperture and the slowest shutter speed the scene lighting permits to capture the biggest spread of lightning. To get even slower shutter speeds, reduce the amount of light reaching the film with a neutral density or polarizing filter (see pages 128 and 116) or use a slower film. Snap the shutter the instant lightning appears. At night, with no other light in the scene, you can make a time exposure (see page 244) and record several flashes of lightning on the same frame. (Don't use your camera on automatic.) Look for interesting foreground objects, such as a windmill or a tree, that will be silhouetted when lightning strikes. Beware the hazards of lightning and choose a safe vantage point. Indoors, shooting through a window or a door is best.

Tools: For rainy, overcast days, use a lens with a wide maximum aperture, *f*/2.8 or larger; high- or very high-speed film, such as ISO 400 or 1000; and even a tripod and a cable release. But with less formidable cloud covers, you can use smaller apertures and medium-speed film, ISO 64 to 125.

If you actually go out into the rain, it is essential to protect your camera. Keep it under your raincoat or umbrella. For additional protection, attach an umbrella to your tripod or put your camera in a plastic bag with a hole for the lens. If you have an underwater housing (see page 234), use it in the rain. You should also have a lens shade to help keep droplets off the lens and a soft, absorbent cloth handy to wipe them off if they do accumulate. Don't load or unload the camera when your hands are wet. Store your camera and film in plastic bags along with packets of moisture-absorbing silica gel crystals.

Inclement Weather

Fog

Millions of tiny water molecules are suspended in the air during fog. Objects take on a gauzy quality in its even, diffused light, and hues become muted and subtle. Fog simplifies, making distant shapes merge into a milky white backdrop.

Fog can range from a mild morning mist to a dense atmospheric cloak, and its effect on a scene depends on its density. In a slight fog, light shapes may take on a gentle, impressionistic quality; in heavier fog, the reduction of contrast may call for darker, more distinct shapes that will stand out against the background. The lightening effect of fog can deceive your camera's meter, often requiring an increase in the recommended exposure of a stop or more. Bracket several half-stops in either direction, if possible.

Vicki Armour

Mist can give an ordinary scene the quality of an impressionist painting. In this picture, the angular shed is softened by its dreamy reflection in the placid water. The two horses accent a sense of pastoral romanticism.

John Pearson

Rising in silhouette out of a low-lying fog, San Francisco's skyline resembles a fairy tale image of a kingdom in the clouds. Large bodies of water, such as those that surround this peninsular city, are the best places to look for mist.

Tools: Since mists are most common in the reduced light of morning and evening, it is helpful to have a lens with a large maximum aperture, *f*/2.8 or wider, and to use high-speed film—ISO 400 for example. Because fog minimizes the surface textures of objects, higher-speed films can impart a particularly pronounced graininess to a scene, which can in turn enhance the impressionistic character of the fog itself. Keep in mind that longer lenses will compress the fog and make it appear denser. A wider-angle lens, by contrast, will reduce the fog's effect.

Similarly, an ultraviolet or haze filter slightly reduces the effect of fog, whereas a diffusion filter enhances it. And color filters can add a surrealistic quality to a foggy scene. Though less noticeably so, fog, like rain, is wet and potentially harmful to your camera and film. In heavy mists, follow the suggestions on the preceding pages for protecting your camera.

Inclement Weather

Snow and Cold

Low temperatures and snow conspire to make one of the most photographically challenging of all weather situations. A snowfall may impart an overall gauziness to a scene, similar to that of fog, although (as with rain) at faster shutter speeds the individual flakes will be more apparent. In such conditions, you may favor scenes with stronger forms.

Snow on the ground can isolate objects and smoothe their contours. But its high degree of reflectance will fool your camera's light meter into underexposing by as much as several stops. The solution is to take your reading from a known value such as a photographic grey card. For an important shot, especially in color, bracket that exposure by a half, one, and two full stops in both directions.

Frigid temperatures may cause the lubricants in your camera's shutter to thicken, slowing it down enough to overexpose your film. Also, film can become brittle and break or in dry air generate static electricity that causes streaks and fogging. In addition, ice can form on the lens or viewfinder if you breathe on them or if they come in contact with snow. On a cold day, the camera's battery may lose power, causing the meter to give erratic readings and making an electronic camera inoperative. Most problems can be avoided by keeping the camera well-protected until you want to take a picture. If your camera does get cold, don't attempt to warm it up too quickly indoors. A rapid temperature rise can cause condensation to form within the lens or on the film. Instead, let it warm up slowly in a cooler place.

Martin L. Taylor

The bright snowsuits of these two siblings are useful contrasts to their snow-covered surroundings. The lower angle also helps to emphasize their importance to the scene.

© N. Jay Jaffee

This picture powerfully expresses snow's less pacific side. The use of black-and-white suggests the bleak violence of a storm.

Shinzo Maeda/The Image Bank

Tools: In snowy landscapes, low- or medium-speed films will give better definition. Although our eyes adjust somewhat for it, film will register the blue skylight reflected by snow on a clear day. A skylight filter may reduce excessive bluishness, but some should be expected and even desired, particularly in the shadows. If snow is actually falling while you are taking pictures, follow the suggestions on page 237 for protecting your camera from moisture.

When photographing in freezing weather, you may find it useful to wear two pairs of gloves—thin silk or polypropylene ones under heavier ones. When you take the outer layer off to operate the camera, your hands will still be protected and responsive.

Snow on the distant mountains and the overhead branches echoes the luminous whiteness of the swans in this photograph, producing an almost monochromatic study in white and blue. Steam from the lake acts as a natural simplifier, giving the image the extraordinary tranquility and beautiful sparseness of a Japanese scroll.

Photographing Special Effects

Multiple Exposures

While your camera is adept at recording the real world, you can also use it to create fantasy images that will baffle and delight your viewers. Among the most notable of these special effects is multiple exposure—two or more images superimposed or juxtaposed on the same frame of film.

The mechanics of taking a multiple exposure vary from camera to camera, so you should consult your instruction booklet. Some newer models have a control for multiple exposures that enables you to cock the shutter without advancing the film. On many SLRs, you can do the same thing by depressing the rewind button while operating the advance lever.

On any camera with a B or T setting, you can make multiple exposures by leaving the shutter open and covering the lens with a dark card between exposures, but you won't be able to register the following exposures precisely because the viewfinder is blocked by the mirror. Prevent overexposure with slower films, smaller apertures, and dim lighting. It is possible to use flash successfully in a darkened room.

In some multiple exposures, much of the superimposed images will overlap. Try to make the images complement each other, and distribute their tones so as to avoid too much exposure in one area and not enough in another. After taking the first shot, make a rough sketch of the scene on paper to position the next scene for the best effect. To prevent overexposure, give each shot in a montage less exposure than it would need by itself. Calculate the correct reduced exposure by multiplying your film speed by the number of shots in the montage. Set that number on your camera's film speed dial. For example, for three images on ISO 100 film, set the dial at ISO 300. The guidelines given in the chart will also serve as a good starting point. You can also adjust exposure to emphasize one image in a montage. In general, in this approach you should favor scenes with a normal range of tonalities. The image of the Brooklyn Bridge at right is a good example of this.

Montage Exposure Settings

Number of images in montage	*Number of f-stops to decrease exposure*
2	*1*
3	*$1\frac{1}{2}$*
4	*2*
5	*$2\frac{1}{4}$*
6	*$2\frac{1}{2}$*
7	*$2\frac{3}{4}$*
8	*3*

Michael DeCamp/The Image Bank

Multiple exposure offers a facility for commentary on our surroundings. This "Vacancy" sign hovers in ironic confirmation of the desolate scene beyond.

© N. Jay Jaffee

Four exposures of the Brooklyn Bridge on a single piece of film produced this dazzling montage of cabling and buildings. The result also gives the impression of a much denser skyline. The method for producing such multiple exposures varies from camera to camera.

Another type of multiple exposure involves images of subjects that do not overlap, such as three views of an object in the same picture. To do this, you must use a very dark background (a soft, unreflective black cloth is most common) and strong lighting on the subject—flash or photolamps are ideal. Since the film is recording only the brightly lighted subjects and not the dark background, use a full exposure for each shot. To emphasize one image more than the others, give it a full exposure and the others less. Usually, multiple exposures combine both effects described here, and you should adjust your exposures accordingly.

Tools: In general, you'll find it easiest to use low- or medium-speed films, ISO 25 to 200. In a montage, they reduce the chances of overexposure, and in a multiple exposure with separate views, they are less likely to pick up stray light bouncing off your dark background. For careful juxtaposition of images, a tripod is essential.

Special Effects

Time Exposures

In a sense, every photograph is a time exposure. When you slow your shutter to 1/8 second, however, to record a moving subject, the result can be quite striking or even dazzling. A person a few feet away strolling across your camera's field of view will be recorded as an almost unrecognizable series of streaks during a half-second exposure. Similarly, a speeding car given this same exposure will appear on film only as the bright traces of its headlights, and a pirouetting ballerina will resemble a madly spinning top. Using an even longer exposure, perhaps one of several seconds, you can create scenes with ghostly figures and other provocative images.

To avoid overexposing the image, time exposures usually require a combination of low-speed film, a small aperture, and a relatively low level of lighting. In very dim light, even the best camera light meters are not sensitive enough to respond, so you'll have to determine the length of exposure through trial and error. When you first start taking time exposures, experiment with several different exposure times for each scene. In this way, you can become familiar with the various special effects available.

Rapidly moving water becomes almost ethereal in appearance with only a very brief time exposure. For the best effect, it is important to keep a part of the scene sharp, as in the well-defined slope surrounding the water in the image here. Experiment with different exposure times because the speed of moving water varies tremendously.

Herb Jones

Charles Harbutt/Archive Pictures Inc.

Photographing fireworks is very much like photographing lightning (see page 237). You can't predict what part of the sky they're going to appear in, so it's best to mount your camera on a tripod, set the shutter for a time exposure, and wait for the right configurations. Keep the shutter open as long as necessary. You can even make multiple exposures, covering the lens between bursts to prevent overexposing other parts of the image, as described on the previous pages. In this spectacular image, the photographer has included rooftop shapes as a reference point.

When you're using color film and accurate color rendition is important, it is usually best to keep time exposures to less than one second. With longer exposures in dim light, the film sensitivity decreases and the color balance shifts. For many long exposures, however, correct color rendition may not be important. Lengthy time exposures on black-and-white film are not a problem. Since there are no colors to change, the film's lowered sensitivity makes it possible to take even more extended exposures. With low- or medium-speed black-and-white film and a small aperture, for example, you may expose for several minutes to record the dimly lit interior of a building. With that long an exposure, a person walking through the scene would not register on the film.

In planning a time exposure, try to balance still and moving elements, paying special attention to the patterns that will be created by bright and light-colored moving subjects. Consider firing an electronic flash during the exposure, so that your subject will be sharp and well exposed in one spot and soft and streaked in others. You can also make a subject appear ghostlike or surreal by including the person for only half the exposure time. Cover your lens while the person moves out of the scene or make a multiple exposure.

Tools: Even with small apertures and ISO 25 or 32 film, you may need neutral density filters (see page 128) to cut down on the amount of light reaching the film during a long exposure. A tripod and cable release are absolutely essential, and the cable release should have a lock. A stopwatch or a watch with a large second hand is useful for timing the exposure.

1
26
25
1
22
21
13
24
23
19
30
27
HYPO CLEARING AGENT
FIXER
STOP BATH
29
31
28
20
32
21
33
28
34
30

Part IV

The Process

Darkroom Principles
Processing Color Film
Making Color Prints
Processing Black-and-White Film
Making Black-and-White Prints
Basic Printing Controls
Creative Darkroom Techniques

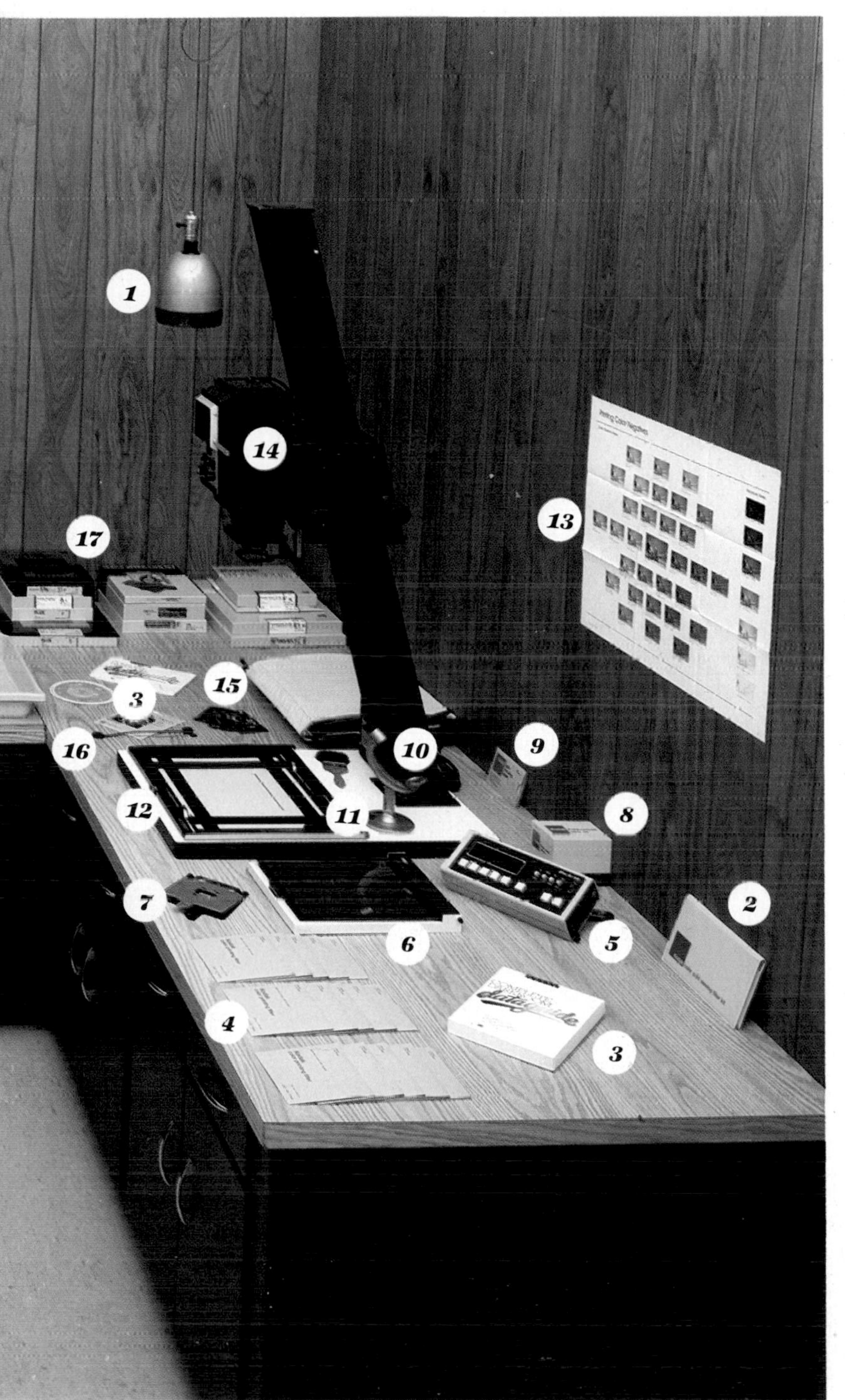

Michele Hallen Infantino

1. *Safelights*
2. *Color print viewing filters*
3. *Darkroom reference guide*
4. *Color printing filters*
5. *Enlarging timer*
6. *Contact printing frame*
7. *35 mm negative carrier for enlarger*
8. *Variable contrast filters for black-and-white printing*
9. *Lens cleaning tissue*
10. *Grain magnifier for focusing enlarger*
11. *Camel's hair brush*
12. *Enlarging easel*
13. *Color printing filtration guides*
14. *Enlarger*
15. *Print dryer for fiber-base papers*
16. *Dodging tools*
17. *Black-and-white and color printing papers*
18. *Darkroom timer*
19. *KODAK EKTAFLEX Printmaker*
20. *Print processing trays*
21. *Darkroom graduates*
22. *Eye protection*
23. *Processing chemicals for color*
24. *Chemical storage containers*
25. *Rubber gloves*
26. *Film drying clips*
27. *Chemical mixing container*
28. *Chemical stirring paddle*
29. *Print washing tray*
30. *Film developing tanks*
31. *Chemicals for black and white*
32. *Rubber squeegee for drying prints*
33. *Photographic thermometers*
34. *Deep print tray*

Darkroom Principles

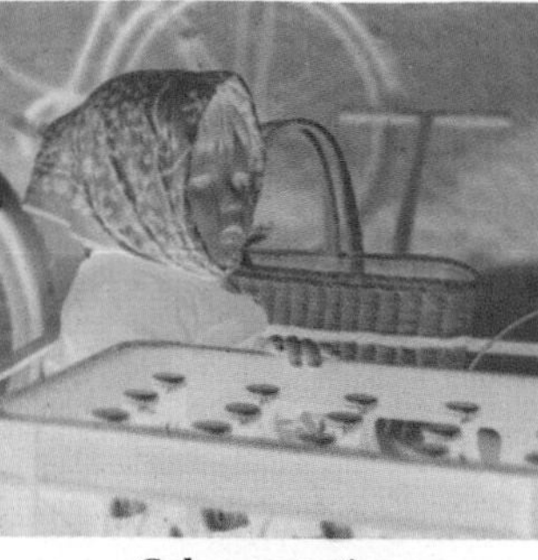

Color negative

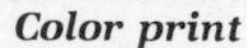

Color print

Color transparency

Black-and-white negative

Susan King

Black-and-white print

Many photographers feel that snapping the shutter only begins the photographic process. By using techniques in the darkroom that allow you to control both film development and the character of the print itself, you can exercise considerable control over the final image. Ansel Adams, whose darkroom skills are legendary, compared the photographic negative to a musical score and the positive print to a performance. His analogy suggests how much one depends on the other. By recognizing this relationship you can produce images that express your personal viewpoint more accurately.

With some equipment and a permanent or temporary darkroom, virtually any photographer can process black-and-white or color film (negative or transparency) and make prints. The procedures are precise but not difficult. This section provides an overview of darkroom fundamentals—processing and printing and the equipment and techniques involved—giving enough detail to help you decide whether or not to put together your own darkroom. You'll want to talk with your photo dealer before setting up. He or she will be able to provide specific information, as well as ideas and sources for supplies.

When you take a black-and-white picture, light coming through the camera lens produces an invisible image on the film's emulsion, a layer of gelatin containing suspended light-sensitive silver halide crystals. This "latent" image is made visible with chemical processing, which converts the silver halide crystals to black metallic silver. Because more metallic silver is created where more light strikes the film, light areas in your subject will appear dark in the negative. Darker areas in the subject will be more transparent in the negative because lesser amounts of silver will reveal more of the clear plastic base of the film.

Black-and-white photographic paper also has an emulsion that contains silver halide crystals. When light is projected through the negative onto the paper, the silver halides react the same way that they did in the film. The more transparent an area on the film, the more light it transmits to the paper, thus creating a darker tone. Areas of the negative with a lot of silver density transmit lesser amounts of light, which leave the corresponding areas in the paper light grey or even white. The end result is an image with a full range of tones, from white, to grey, to black.

Black-and-white and color photographic materials and techniques are similar, but color films and papers contain several layers of color receptors as well as silver halides. Different layers are sensitive to different colors of light—some to red, some to green, and some to blue. While one chemical reaction converts the silver halides, others create complementary hues in the color reception layers during processing. Red areas in the subject appear as cyan in the negative, green areas as magenta, and blue ones as yellow-orange. As with black-and-white photographs, dark and light areas in the original scene are reversed in the color negative, which is printed on color photographic paper through a combination of colored filters. Processing makes the color information visible in the different layers of the paper, reversing the complementary colors of the negative so that the original subject color is reproduced. The silver halide layer ensures that the colors will appear in their correct tonal relationships. Color transparency (slide) film is constructed differently and processing reverses both tones and hues to duplicate the original scene.

Black-and-white technique is somewhat more flexible as well as more forgiving than color, and for this reason it may be a good

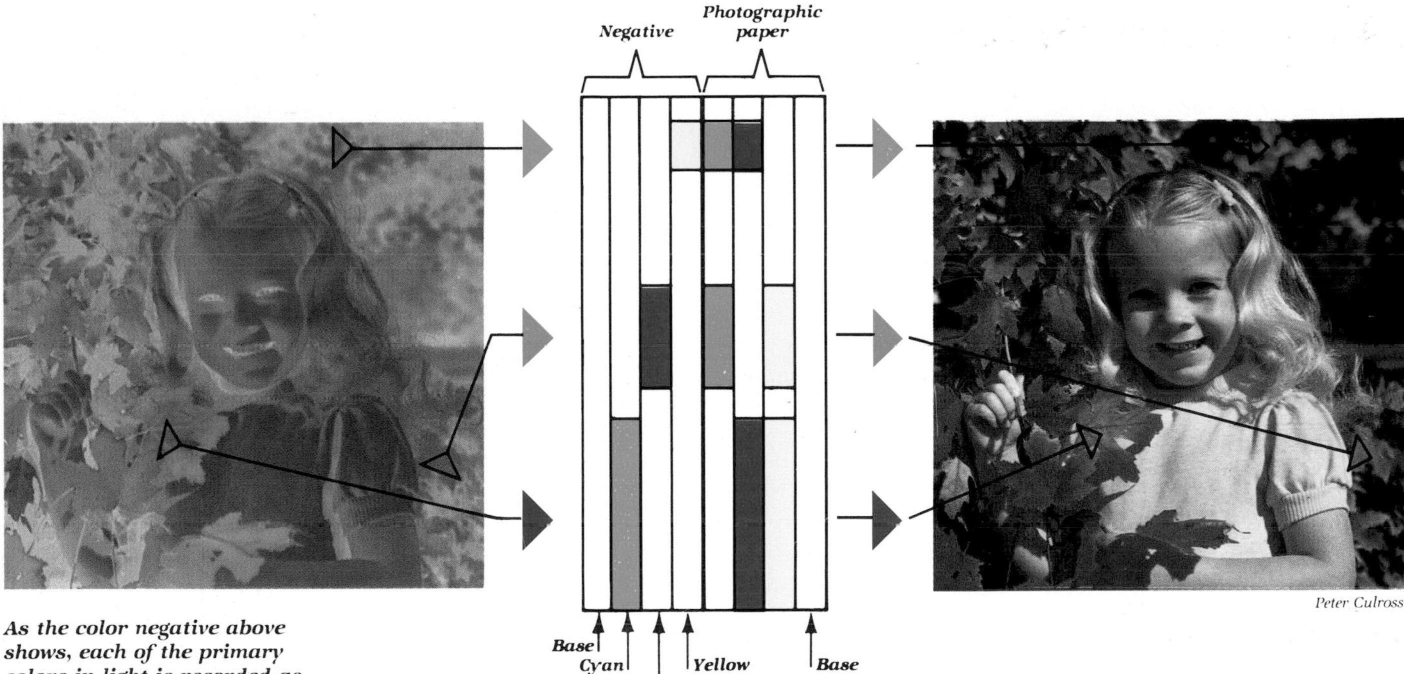

As the color negative above shows, each of the primary colors in light is recorded as its complementary on one or several of the film's layers. Blue is recorded as yellow, green as magenta, and red as cyan. Photographic paper has similarly sensitive layers. During printing, each dye layer in the negative controls the amount of complementary light that reaches the paper. Colors complementary to the light from the negative are formed in the dye layers of the paper. After processing, those colors give the same appearance as the original scene—the original primaries.

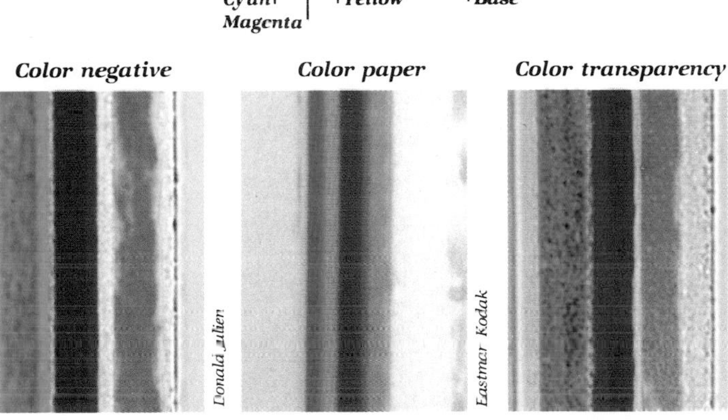

The cross-sections at left show, under extreme magnification, the three color layers in an exposed and processed color negative (far left), in a piece of color printing paper (middle), and in a color transparency (left). All three types of materials produce the three complementary colors—yellow, magenta, and cyan. The order of the colors on photographic paper is different from that of film to provide better definition.

The types of images produced by 35 mm film are shown at left. The first image is a color negative, used to produce a color print (second). A color transparency, or slide (third), can be either viewed with a handviewer or projected; it can also be used to produce a print. A black-and-white negative (fourth) is used to produce a print (last).

starting place for the darkroom novice. The materials are usually less expensive, and black-and-white paper can be handled under a fairly bright safelight. However, you should not feel that color printing is too complex to attempt; KODAK EKTAFLEX PCT products provide a simple and flexible alternative to conventional color systems. They are described in detail in this section.

With the right equipment and a little practice, doing your own darkroom work is not only easy, but rewarding, because of the control you have over the final image.

Principles

The photo at right shows the gradual overall darkening—or fogging—of paper placed too close to a safelight. Safelights must be kept at least four feet from sensitized materials.

Total darkness **1 minute**

Tools

For processing and printing film, you don't need an elaborate ***darkroom***, but a lighttight room is necessary. You can darken any room by covering the windows with opaque black material (sheet plastic for this purpose is available commercially) and sealing light leaks with black masking tape. Spend five minutes in the darkened room, and if you can still see a piece of white paper, look for other light leaks. Darkrooms need counter space and electrical outlets, and they should be fairly dust-free. Running water is handy but not a necessity if it is nearby. Kitchens and large bathrooms make excellent temporary facilities. For permanent darkrooms, you can organize a basement area or closet.

One or two ***safelights*** will illuminate a small darkroom without exposing (fogging) photographic paper; a larger area may need more light. Most good safelights have filters that can be changed for black-and-white printing or color negative printing. Make sure the filter you use is right for your materials; some safelights and filters that claim to be all-purpose for black-and-white work, for example, may transmit too much light for certain rapid (more light sensitive) emulsions. You must also be careful to use the correct wattage bulb and keep your safelights at reasonable distances from your work areas—four feet is typical.

Many darkroom process ***timers*** work like kitchen timers, and can be set to buzz or jingle when the given time expires. A second hand or digital display (often calibrated in tenths of seconds) is imperative for accurate control.

For processing film, you'll need a ***developing tank*** with a ***loading reel.*** Tanks come in many shapes, sizes, and materials; some process more than one roll at a time. Your photo dealer can help you assess your needs and choose the right tank. After processing a roll, you may want to wipe off water drops with a ***photo sponge*** or ***chamois*** to speed drying. You'll also need ***film clips*** or spring clothespins for hanging the film to dry.

To make prints from your negatives (or slides), you need an ***enlarger***, which doesn't have to be expensive or cumbersome. For 35 mm film, it should have a 50 mm lens. For color prints, you need an enlarger with a color head or one that can hold color filters. An ***enlarging timer*** will shut off the enlarger light automatically when the determined exposure time has passed; some timers can be used for both processing and enlarging. For removing dust from the negative before putting it into the enlarger, you need a ***camel's-hair brush*** or a can of compressed air.

A photographic ***easel*** holds the paper flat so that the projected image will be uniformly sharp. Less expensive easels are fixed-size or have two moving blades, but the better ones have four adjustable blades that allow you to crop the image to any shape or size and that give an even border all around the image. Make sure the easel is solid enough so that it doesn't shift when opened or bumped. You can also get a ***printing frame*** for making contact prints, as shown in the series at far right, but a piece of plate glass and a smooth board will also work.

A ***focusing aid*** will help you make sharper prints than if you focus by eye alone. Models that allow you to focus on the film's grain structure make accurate focusing easier to achieve.

Trays are required to process black-and-white paper (and may also be used for some color processes). They are available in the same sizes as the paper itself—5 × 7, 8 × 10, 11 × 14—for most efficient use of chemicals, but you may want to save

The layouts and picture below and to the right illustrate some typical permanent darkroom arrangements. Plan D shows how to adapt a large laundry room. Note that the dry areas, where you enlarge, should be kept separate from wet areas, where you process film and paper.

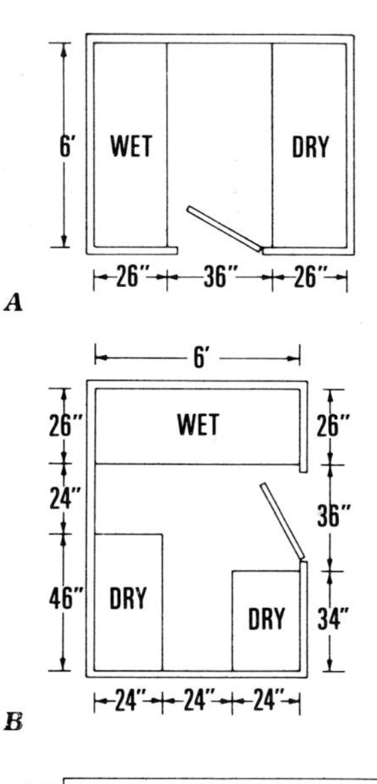

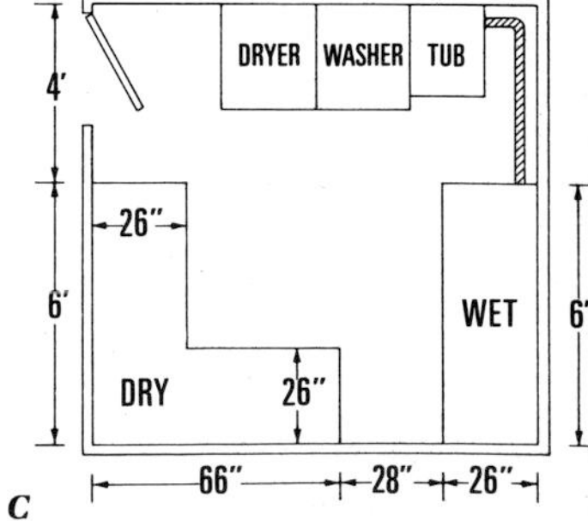

Keith Boas

3 minutes **7 minutes**

yourself the cost of an extra set by purchasing them for the largest-size paper you're likely to be using. A larger tray also makes it easier to process a number of smaller prints simultaneously. You'll need at least four trays, plus a large, deep tray for a water bath to bring smaller containers of chemicals to the required temperature. Since color processing must be done in total darkness or under extremely dim safelights with fairly expensive chemicals, ***rotating drums, tubes, "canoes,"*** and other devices are often used instead of trays. They require smaller quantities of the solutions for greater economy, and most let you work in room light once the exposed print is loaded into the processing apparatus. Finally, if you're using trays, you may want to purchase ***tongs***—a pair for each chemical—to transfer prints from one tray to the next. Although you can also do this by hand, you must wash your hands thoroughly after each processing sequence. (Some people may have skin allergies to chemicals.)

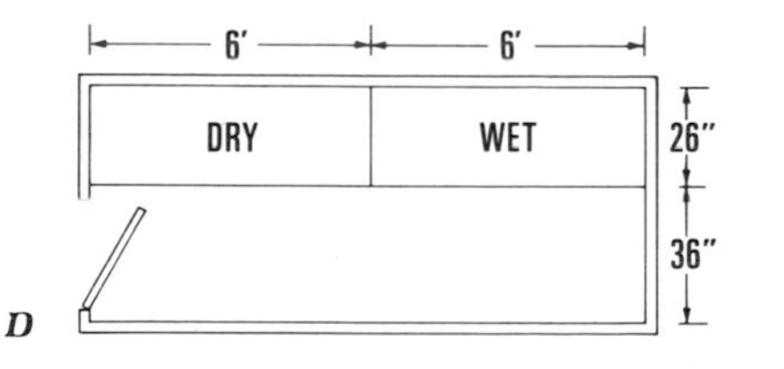

Michele Hallen Infantino

Processing chemicals are widely available—some as powders and others as liquid concentrates. If you do a lot of processing, buy large, economical batches. Otherwise, buy smaller quantities to avoid spoilage from aging. You will need a chemical-resistant container big enough to mix chemicals in and plastic or glass ***storage containers***. You will also need ***darkroom graduates*** to measure chemicals in preparation for processing. ***Rubber gloves*** are also a good idea, particularly for anyone with allergies or sensitive skin.

For black-and-white film or paper you need a ***developer*** to bring out the image, a ***stop bath*** to halt development, and a ***fixer*** to make the image stable. There are many developers to choose from. Some are strong, for rapid action; others are less active, for the sharpest possible image. Two other chemicals for black-and-white work are a ***clearing agent*** to reduce washing time and a ***wetting solution*** to prevent water beads from leaving spots when the film is hung up to dry.

Chemicals for color processing are matched to the particular film or paper, since each process is specific. Processing EKTAFLEX PCT Printmaking Materials requires one ready-to-use chemical. For other processes, several manufacturers offer kits. Depending on what you are processing, you may need a developer, a ***bleach***, a fixer, a ***stabilizer***, a ***reversal bath***, a ***conditioner***, a ***bleach-fix (blix)***, or a ***potassium iodide wash.***

Black-and-white and color prints are made on light-sensitive ***photographic paper***. Black-and-white papers, either fiber-base or resin-coated (RC), come in a variety of sizes, weights, textures, sensitivities, and tones. They also come in different contrast grades (see page 279). Start with a smooth, medium-weight variable-contrast paper that is of neutral tone and fairly sensitive. (The shorter processing times of RC paper will speed the learning process.) Then go on to experiment with other papers.

It's easier to choose color printing material because there's less variety. There are two groups of conventional color paper—one for negatives and one for slides. Both kinds are resin-coated and medium-weight, with some choice in size and surface texture. KODAK EKTAFLEX PCT Printmaking Materials offer films for printing slides and negatives and image transfer paper in two surfaces.

Raymond Miller

Most photographers preview a roll of negatives by making a "contact sheet." As illustrated in the series above, the negative strips (top) and a sheet of photographic paper (second) are placed in a printing frame, emulsion sides together. Then the frame is tightly closed and exposed to light, usually from an enlarger (third). The paper is processed normally (bottom).

Processing Color Film

Color Negative Film

Tools:
Totally dark room
Film tank and reel for 35 mm film
Thermometer accurate to ¼°F (0.15°C)
Timer
Graduated beakers (4)
Chemical solutions
Water-bath tray
Clips
Negative-storage envelopes (see page 288)
Hook-type bottle opener
Scissors

You can process most color negative films with a minimum of equipment, but be sure to use only the recommended chemicals—the wrong ones can ruin your film. Chemicals usually come with complete instructions, which you should follow exactly; and since the life of color chemicals is rather short, mix them just before you start. They'll last a little longer if you keep them in tightly closed bottles. Keep processing solutions separate from one another and in clean storage containers. When chemicals are contaminated by dirt or other chemicals, your results will suffer.

For accurate processing, the chemicals *must* be at the correct temperature. Place the beakers in a tray of running water at the recommended temperature to stabilize their temperatures, checking frequently with the thermometer. (Clean it after each immersion.) The developer temperature is most critical, so be sure to check it just before starting. Although there is some leeway with the succeeding chemicals, try to keep their temperatures as consistent as possible for best results.

The procedure for loading film into the processing tank is shown in the series above. Since this must be done in total darkness, it's best to try it several times in room lighting, using outdated film, before attempting it in the dark. Place everything you need in front of you, where it can be easily reached. After seeing the procedure, try it with your eyes closed.

1

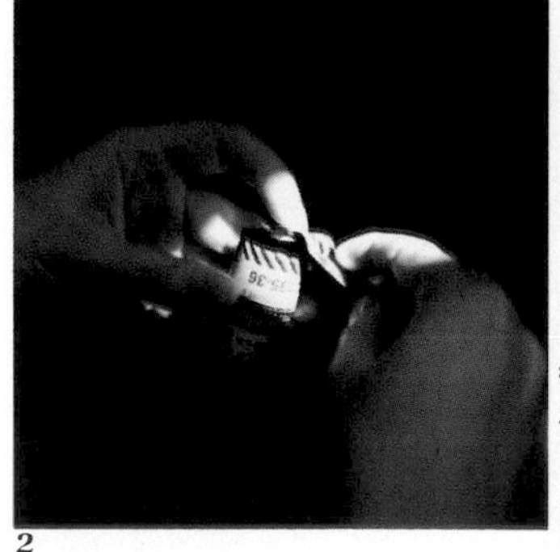

2

Raymond Miller

The basic steps for preparing to process color negative film are shown in the series above. Start by placing the empty processing tank and premeasured quantities of the chemical solutions you will need in a water bath (1) to bring them to the recommended temperature. Then, working in total darkness, hold the film magazine in your hand with the projecting end of the spool downward, and open the upper end using a hook-type opener (2). Remove the film from the magazine, and clip off the half-width leader at the beginning of the film (3). Wind the film, holding it by the edges, onto the tank's spiral

Michele Hallen Infantino

For color printing on an enlarger without a color head, you will need a set of filters such as the one shown above, available from several different manufacturers. They are made in different densities in the three primary and three complementary colors.

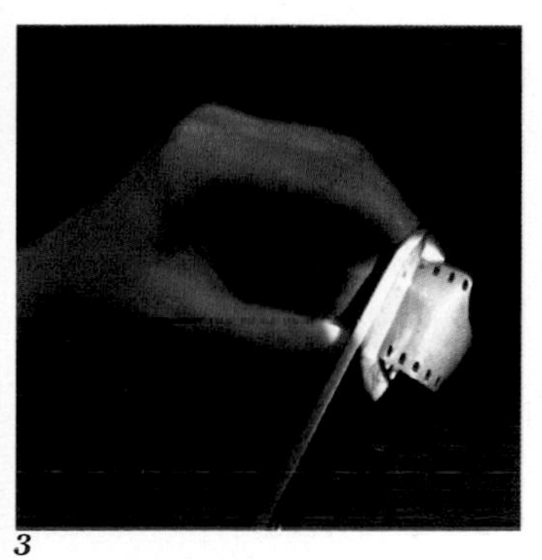
3

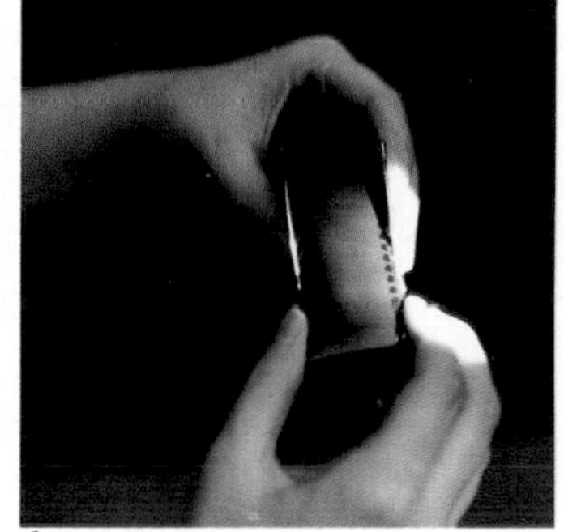
4

5

6

Raymond Miller

reel following the directions for your type of tank (4). When most of the film is on the reel, clip off the film's spool and finish winding the film onto the reel (5). Finally, place the reel in the tank and put on the lid (6). You can now turn the room lights back on for processing.

A comprehensive, quick-reference guide that gives exposure times and processing information is an invaluable aid in the darkroom.

Michele Hallen Infantino

Photographic paper comes in many different forms. For black-and-white work in particular, it is available in various sensitivities, surfaces, and contrasts. The 8 × 10-inch size is most popular, but many photographers make 11 × 14 prints (bottom three packages) for their extra impact.

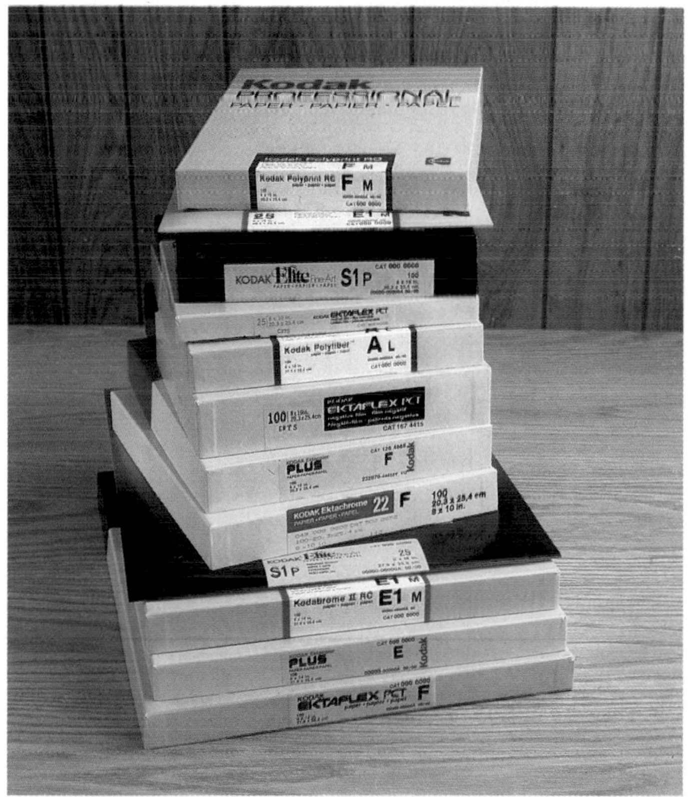

Michele Hallen Infantino

Processing Color Film

Color Negative Film

The color negative process shown in the table below has seven steps that take a total of about twenty-five minutes. The number of steps and the timing will vary with the film and chemicals you use. Chemicals can be purchased in a kit or separately in various quantities.

Start timing when you pour each solution into the tank. The time for each step includes about ten seconds for draining, but different tanks drain at different rates. Make sure the solution has completely drained before you start the next step.

The developer temperature of this process is critical—it must be accurate to within ¼°F. Other solutions and the wash water can be between 75° and 105°F (24° and 41°C), although it's best to keep their temperatures as close as possible. Fifteen minutes before you start, put the beakers of solutions and the empty processing tank in a water bath that registers 100°F (38°C). Make sure the water is high enough to cover the solution levels. Check the temperature of the developer frequently until it is correct. You may use a brief plain water presoak (also at 100°F) before development to prevent possible lowering of the developer temperature on contact with cooler film or tank. During processing, keep the tank in the water except when agitating. Again, load the film in *complete darkness*. The film must not be exposed to light during the first two steps in processing. Most film tanks are lighttight, so you can turn on the light after loading the film. When the developer and bleach steps are complete, you can open the tank for greater convenience and more efficient washing.

Agitate the tank at the intervals specified in the table by inverting, rotating, and tumbling it to ensure that the developer circulates freely around the film. Because repeated agitation patterns can create currents in the developer that might cause uneven development, agitation technique should be irregular, combining different kinds of movement. It should be neither sluggish nor violent, but brisk. At the end of each agitation, rap the tank squarely on a counter to dislodge any air bubbles that may cling to the film surface and prevent complete development.

Michele Hallen Infantino

Follow instructions for mixing solutions.

▶ Use a water bath to control temperature.

When the last step is complete, hang the film to dry in a dust-free place with adequate circulation. (Depending on the humidity, it will take one or two hours to dry completely.) Use a clip or clothespin at the bottom of the film to prevent curling. To prevent water spots, use a wetting agent or a stabilizer as your final step, diluting them according to instructions for drip drying, or wipe the film with a photo sponge or chamois moistened with stabilizer solution. Be gentle—when wet, the emulsion is soft enough to be scratched easily.

▶ Rap tank squarely on counter.

The series of pictures here shows the steps involved in processing color negative film.
Photos by Raymond Miller except where noted.

The table below shows the times and temperatures for Process C-41 with the Kodak Hobby-Pac Color Negative Kit. There are other similar kits, and for each one you should follow the manufacturer's detailed instructions.

Processing KODACOLOR in the KODAK HOBBY-PAC Color Negative Kit, Process C-41

Processing step	Minutes*	°F	°C	Agitation (seconds) Initial	Rest	Agitation
1. Developer	3¼	100 ±¼	37.8 ±0.15	30	13	2
2. Bleach	6½	75–105	24–41	30	25	5
Remaining steps can be done in normal room light						
3. Wash	3¼	75–105	24–41			
4. Fixer	6½	75–105	24–41	30	25	5
5. Wash	3¼	75–105	24–41			
6. Stabilizer	1½	75–105	24–41	30		
7. Drying	10–20	75–110	23–43			

**Includes 10 second drain time in each step*

1. Add developer to loaded tank.

► Set developing time on timer.

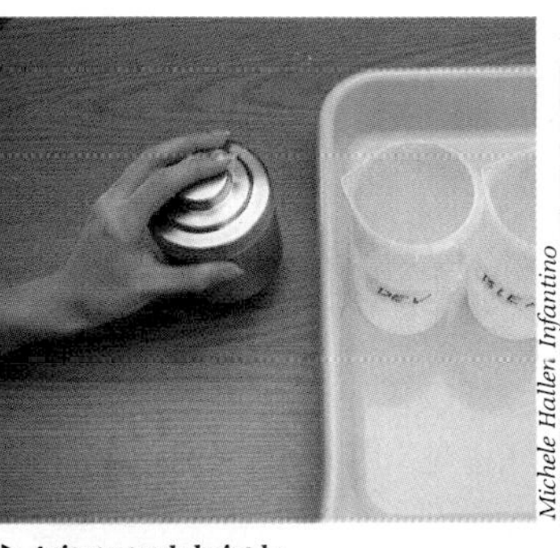

Michele Hallen Infantino

► Agitate tank briskly . . .

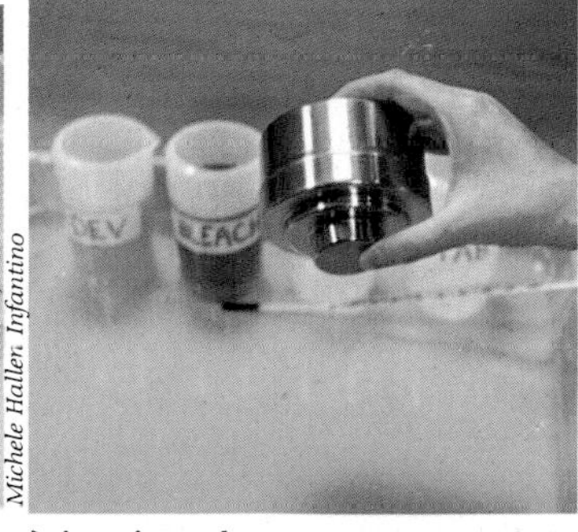

► inverting tank too.

► Drain developer at correct time.

2. Add bleach, set timer, and agitate.

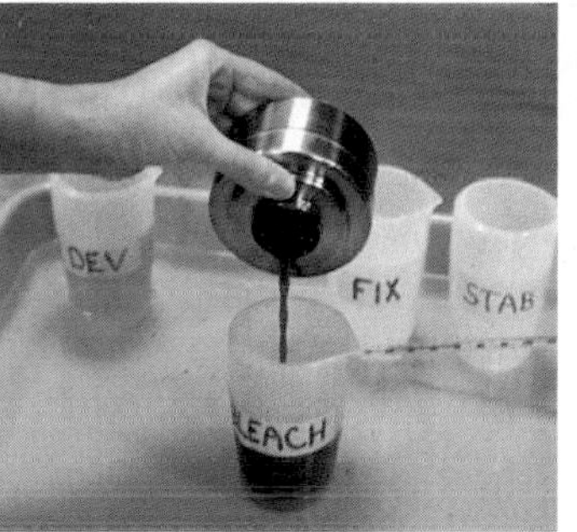

► Drain bleach. You may open tank.

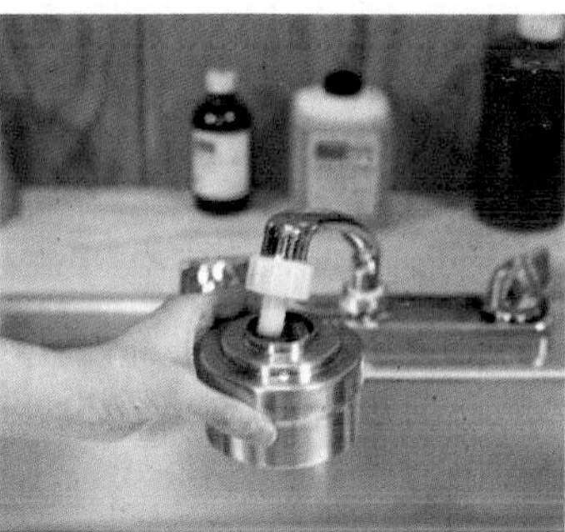
3. Wash film in running water.

► Drain wash water at correct time.

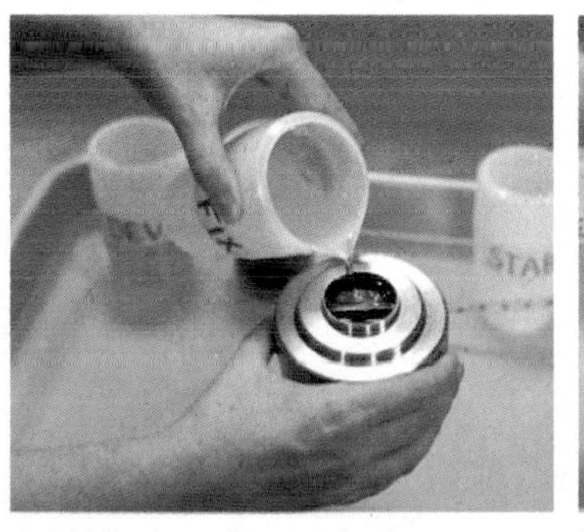

4. Add fixer, set timer, and agitate.

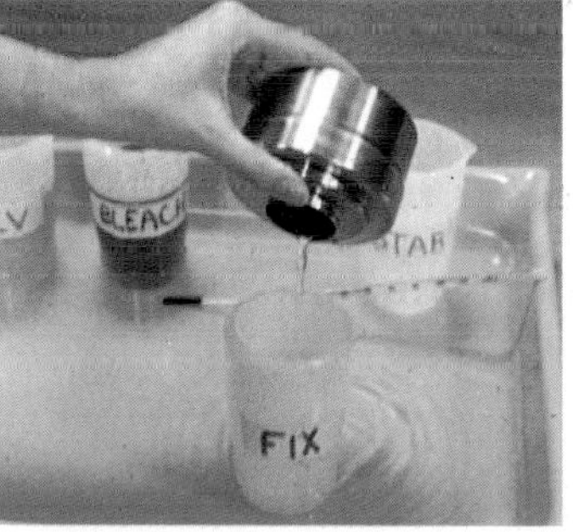

► Drain fixer at correct time.

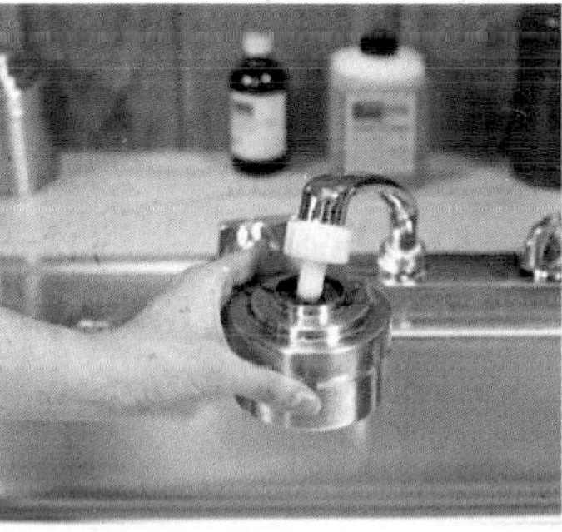
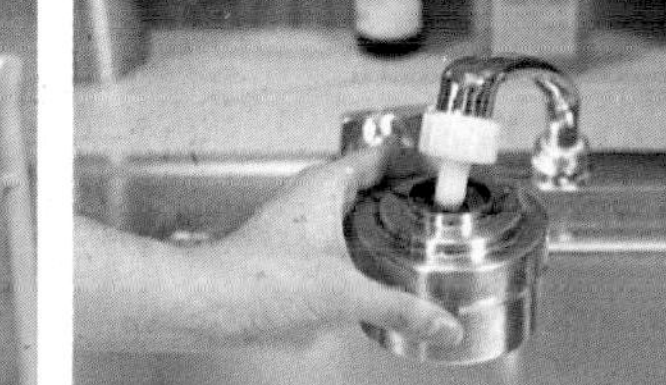
5. Wash film under water again.

► Drain wash water.

6. Add stabilizer, set timer, agitate.

► Drain stabilizer at correct time.

7. Hang film up to dry.

Color Film

Color Slide Film

Tools:
Totally dark room
Film tank and reel for 35 mm film
Thermometer accurate to ½°F (0.3°C)
Timer
Graduated beakers (4)
Chemical solutions
Water-bath tray
Clips
Slide mounts
Hook-type bottle opener
Scissors

Some color slide films can be processed at home, and most of the advice given about negative films applies to transparency film. Temperature is only slightly less critical: The first developer must be accurate to within ½°F (0.3°C). Another difference is that you must wait until after the fourth step, rather than the second, to open the tank and expose the film to room light.

The transparency developing process shown in the table at right below has eight steps. The entire process takes around half an hour, depending on how long you develop your film (see below). If you use a different film or processing kit, check the instructions for the appropriate times, temperatures, and sequence of steps. Once your strip of transparency film is processed and dried, you can cut apart the individual images and seal them in cardboard adhesive mounts or in more expensive plastic or glass mounts. When mounting in glass, make sure to blow away any dust from the transparency with a rubber bulb or compressed air.

A good technique to know about is ***push processing.*** By adjusting the time some films spend in the first developer, you can increase their effective speed by one or more stops. In general, the time should be increased by 30 to 60 percent per stop, but you should check the instructions on the film or processing chemicals for specifics. With this technique, a film rated at ISO 160 can be exposed at ISO 320. You must, however, expose the whole roll this way. (Don't forget to adjust your film speed dial, and set it back again when you're through.) This extra speed can be particularly useful in marginal lighting situations or to permit a faster shutter speed or smaller aperture for better depth of field. EKTACHROME P800/1600 Professional Film is specifically designed for push processing and will minimize the increased contrast and loss of shadow detail that can occur with this technique.

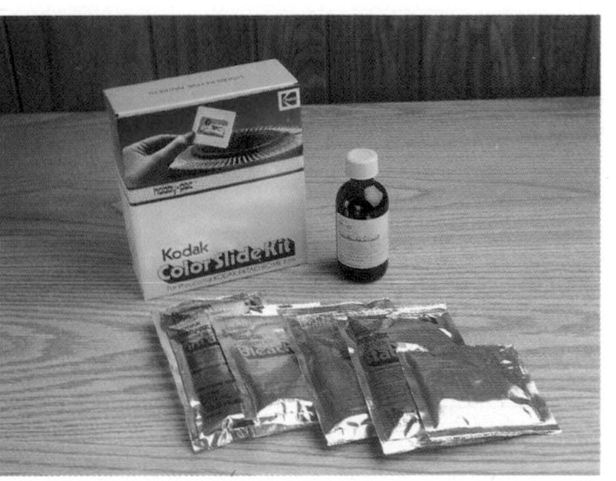

Michele Hallen Infantino

The chemicals for processing color transparency film, which come in concentrated liquid form, can also be purchased separately or in kits. Some of the chemicals are supplied in two parts that must be combined just before processing.

One of the advantages of color slide film is that it can be given extra development to achieve an effective ISO speed higher than its normal rating. In this picture, such push processing allowed the photographer to use a higher shutter speed in low light to freeze the motion of the runners.

Processing KODAK EKTACHROME Films (for Process E-6) in the KODAK HOBBY-PAC Color Slide Kit

Processing				Agitation (seconds)		
Step	Minutes*	°F	°C	Initial	Rest	Agitation
1. First Developer	6½†	100+/−½‡	37.8+/−0.3	15	30	5
2. Wash	1–3	70–110[1]	21–43.5	4 complete rinses		
3. Color Developer	6	100+/−2‡	37.8+/−0.3	15	30	5
4. Wash	1–3	70–110[1]	21–43.5	4 complete rinses		
5. Bleach-Fix	10	70–110[1]	21–43.5	15	30	5
6. Final Wash	4	70–110[1]	21–43.5	6 complete rinses		
7. Stabilizer	1	70–110[1]	21–43.5	15—(initial only)		
8. Drying	10–20	<140	<60			

**Includes 10 seconds for draining in each step.*
†See instructions for using solutions more than once.
‡An extensive range of time/temperature combinations can be used successfully when processing KODAK EKTACHROME Films in the KODAK HOBBY-PAC Color Slide Kit. Refer to the kit instructions.
[1]Although a wide range of temperatures is indicated, it is always wise to keep process temperatures similar to protect the film from extreme changes. ±5°F would be a reasonable operating temperature variance.

Norman Kerr

Making Color Prints

Printing from Color Negatives

Pure white light is composed of red, blue, and green light—the three additive primary colors. (Additive means that, when blended in equal amounts, white light is produced.) Color negative film has layers for recording each of these colors, but images appear in their complementary (opposite) colors. In the red-sensitive layer, red objects appear cyan (blue-green); in the green-sensitive layer, green objects appear magenta (blue-red); and in the blue-sensitive layer, blue objects appear yellow. Most objects are of mixed hue and affect two layers at once. Cyan, magenta, and yellow are called subtractive primary colors, because when combined in equal amounts, neutral density (or the absence of light) is produced.

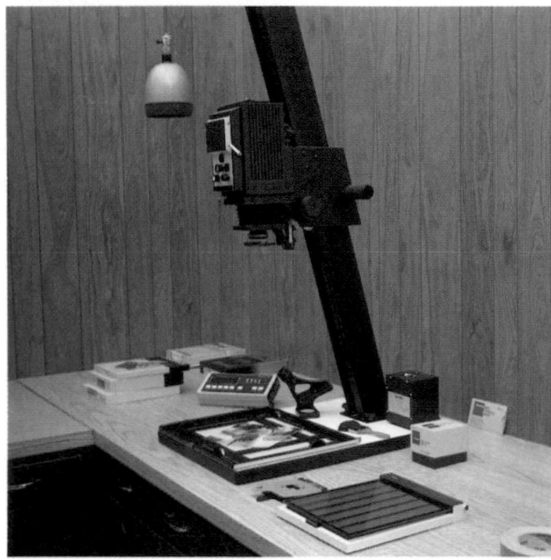

Michele Hallen Infantino

The equipment you need for printing from color negatives is shown in the picture at left. The enlarger here has a color head with built-in dichroic filters, but you can also use a separate set of color filters (page 252). Other materials include an easel, photographic paper, a timer, a camel's-hair brush or compressed air for cleaning negatives, and a safelight with the filter recommended for the paper you are using. The voltage regulator shown here is optional. Equipment for processing is described on page 266.

Making a print from a negative with an enlarger is the reverse of taking a picture with a camera. Light passing through the negative makes a latent image in the silver halide and gelatin emulsion of the printing paper or EKTAFLEX PCT Film. At the same time, the dye layers in the negative bring out their complementary colors in the color-receiving layers of the paper or EKTAFLEX PCT Film. The proportion of these colors is adjusted with color filters in the enlarger head, which also contains the light source, negative, and lens. When the paper is treated with chemicals, a positive image appears.

EKTAFLEX PCT Film is processed in one solution and then laminated to EKTAFLEX PCT Paper. The image transfers from the film to the paper during lamination.

An image can be enlarged or reduced by raising or lowering the enlarger head, which increases or decreases the distance between the negative and the paper. Print exposure is controlled both by an adjustable aperture in the lens marked with the familiar *f*-numbers and by the length of time that the light source projects the image. The aperture is best used for large changes in

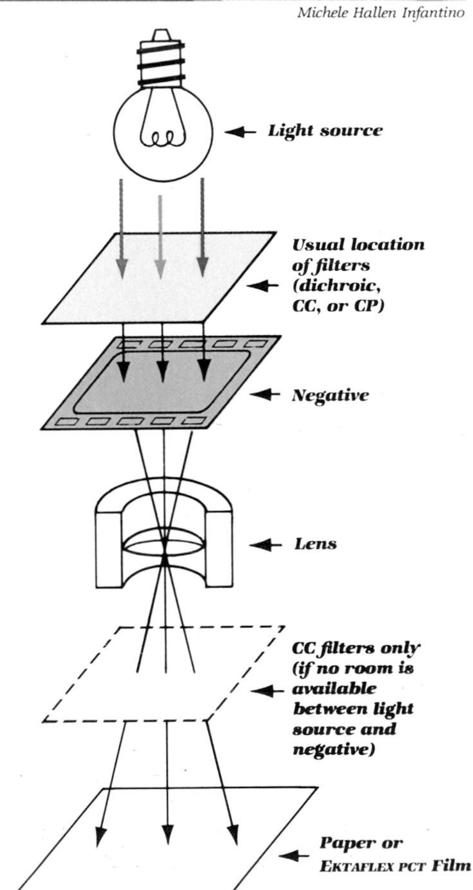

As the schematic diagram of an enlarger at left illustrates, almost any type of filter can be used above the lens—built-in dichroic filters, gelatin color compensating (CC) filters, or acetate color printing (CP) filters. But to avoid distortion, only the gelatin CC filter should be used below the lens.

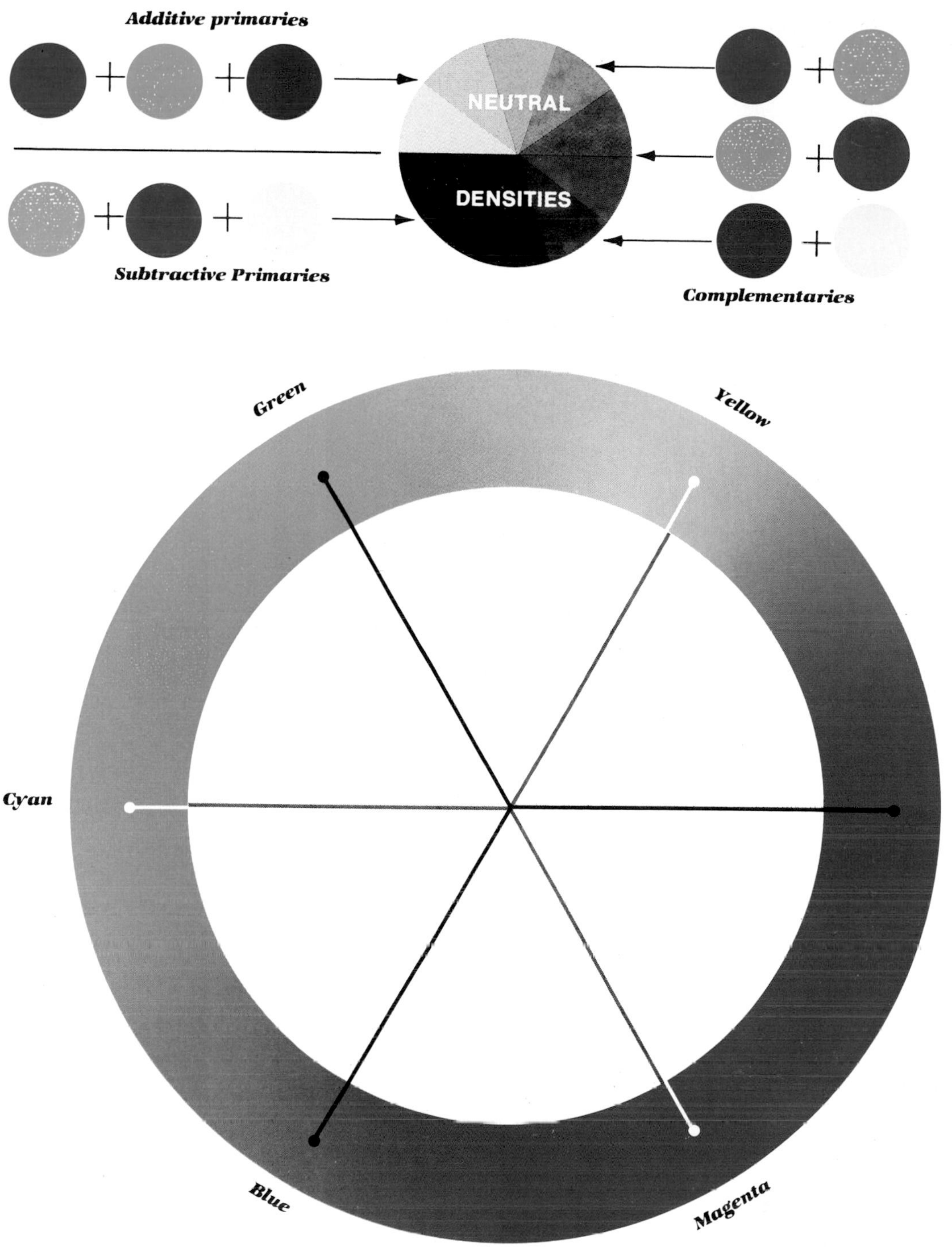

When the visible spectrum is shown as a color wheel, as at left, each of the three additive primaries—red, green, and blue—is directly opposite its complementary—one of the three subtractive primaries, cyan, magenta, and yellow. The interaction of the additive primaries in projected light with the subtractive primaries in filters gives the control needed for color printing. The subtractive primary filters work by blocking, or "subtracting," their complementary additive primaries from the light. Note, as shown at top, that when all three additive primaries, or all three subtractive primaries, or any two complementaries, are added together, the result is white, black, or shades of grey, usually called neutral density.

exposure and adjustments in time for smaller changes. As with a camera, changing one *f*-stop doubles or halves the exposure, the same effect as doubling or halving the exposure time.

A printing mask incorporated in the color negative (for improved color rendition) gives a strong orange cast, but you can also see the subject's complementary colors. The reversal of both colors and tones in the negative makes it hard to tell how the print will look, but with proper exposure and color filtration, it will be a close match for the original scene. For a first attempt at printing, use a negative that was properly exposed in the camera and processed and printed by a photofinisher. The prints will be a good guide for color and exposure.

Color Prints

Printing from Color Negatives

Tools:
Enlarger
Color printing filters
Easel
Color printing paper or EKTAFLEX PCT Negative Film and Paper
Safelight with appropriate filter (see the recommendations for the color material you use)
Camel's-hair brush or compressed air
Timer
Voltage regulator (optional)

For color or black-and-white printing you can use an enlarger equipped with a tungsten or tungsten-halogen lamp and a heat-absorbing glass in the lamphouse. Cover all light leaks in the enlarger head with aluminum foil or an opaque, noncombustible material. For 35 mm negatives, the enlarger lens should have a focal length of 50 mm. Since electrical power drops off at mealtime, when many appliances are in use, a voltage regulator can help maintain constant power to your lamp. If you don't have a regulator, ask your power company when the voltage is at peak.

Keep color paper or EKTAFLEX PCT Film tightly sealed, and refrigerate it according to the instructions, to protect it from heat and humidity. Remove the package from the refrigerator at least two hours before you begin printing to avoid condensation and to let the paper reach its normal sensitivity. Don't open it until you are ready to insert the paper into the enlarging easel.

Use safelights and filters that are correct for the color material you are using, and be certain you have the correct wattage bulb in your safelight. Color paper can start to fog with just a few minutes' exposure to safelights. Let your eyes get accustomed to the safelights so that you can see the paper's emulsion-coated side, which must be facing up when you expose the paper.

The most convenient but expensive method for filtering the enlarger light is a special enlarger head with dial-in dichroic filters, one for each of the subtractive primaries. To adjust the color balance in the print, you just turn the dials in the proportions necessary. The dials are marked in single units of filter density.

Individual colored filters may be used to make color prints with enlargers without dichroic heads, although, with greater incremental steps in density, they are somewhat less precise. When acetate color printing filters are used between the lamp and the negative, they can be scratched or slightly abused with no ill effect. And there's

Light source can be a tungsten bulb

The series of pictures above and at right shows most of the things you will need to equip your enlarger for printing color negatives. The tables at right list the filters required.

Photos by Raymond Miller except where noted.

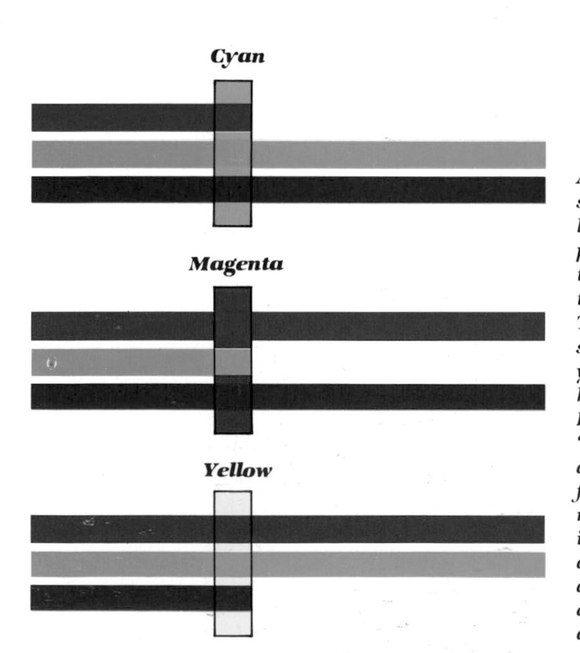

As the diagram at left top shows, red, green, and blue in light are called additive primary colors because when they are mixed, or "added," together, they form white light. The lower three diagrams show why cyan, magenta, and yellow pigments in filters are known as subtractive colors: Each one blocks, or "subtracts," one of the additive primaries. A cyan filter, for example, blocks the red in white light. The amount it blocks depends on the density of the filter. When added together, they block all colors in light, forming neutral density.

. . . or a tungsten-halogen lamp.

Heat-absorbing glass protects film.

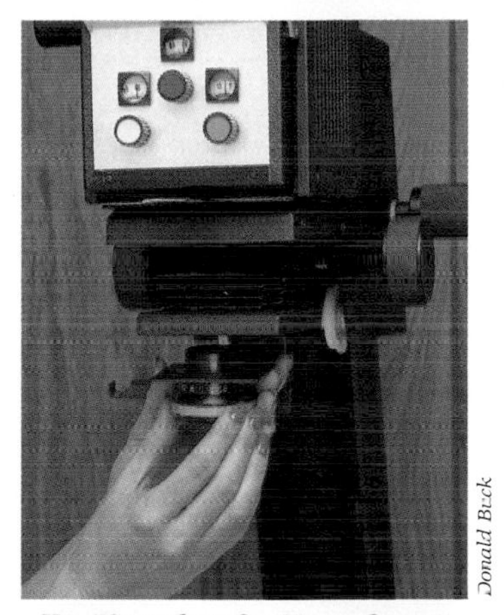

Donald Buck

Use 50 mm lens for 35 mm format.

A UV filter is essential.

Donald Buck

Dial filtration on dichroic head.

CP filters slip in above negative.

no practical limit to the number of filters you can use in this position because you can stack them to change color density and balance without affecting the sharpness of the image. If you have to mount filters under the lens, on the other hand, you must use optically correct (and more expensive) gelatin filters, which don't interfere with the precise light rays projected by the lens. Even so, a maximum of three filters can be used in this position, which means that you'll need more individual filters to create required combinations than if you were using them above the lens. Filters made for use below the lens (or on a camera) are called color compensating (CC) filters; those for use strictly above the lens are known as color printing (CP) filters. Keep filter use in mind when you buy an enlarger.

Filters are designated by a series of letters and numbers that tell you their type, density, and color. For example, a CP20Y filter is an acetate color printing filter with a density of 0.20 (to blue light), and its color is yellow. The one filter you must always use with conventional color printing materials is an ultraviolet filter, No. 2B or CP2B, to block UV radiation. Place this filter permanently above the negative carrier.

Color Printing Filters

If your enlarger accepts filters above the negative, you'll need the following color printing (CP) filters:

CP2B (acetate; always used)

CP05M	CP05Y	CP40R
CP10M	CP10Y	CP80R
CP20M	CP20Y	
CP40M	CP40Y	
	CP80Y	

Color Compensating Filters

If you must place the filters below the lens, you'll need the following color compensating (CC) filters:

Gelatin No. 2B or CP2B (acetate; always used)

CC05M	CC05Y	CC05R
CC10M	CC10Y	CC10R
CC20M	CC20Y	CC20R
CC30M	CC30Y	CC30R
CC40M	CC40Y	CC40R
CC50M	CC50Y	CC509R

Color Prints

Exposing the Color Negative Print

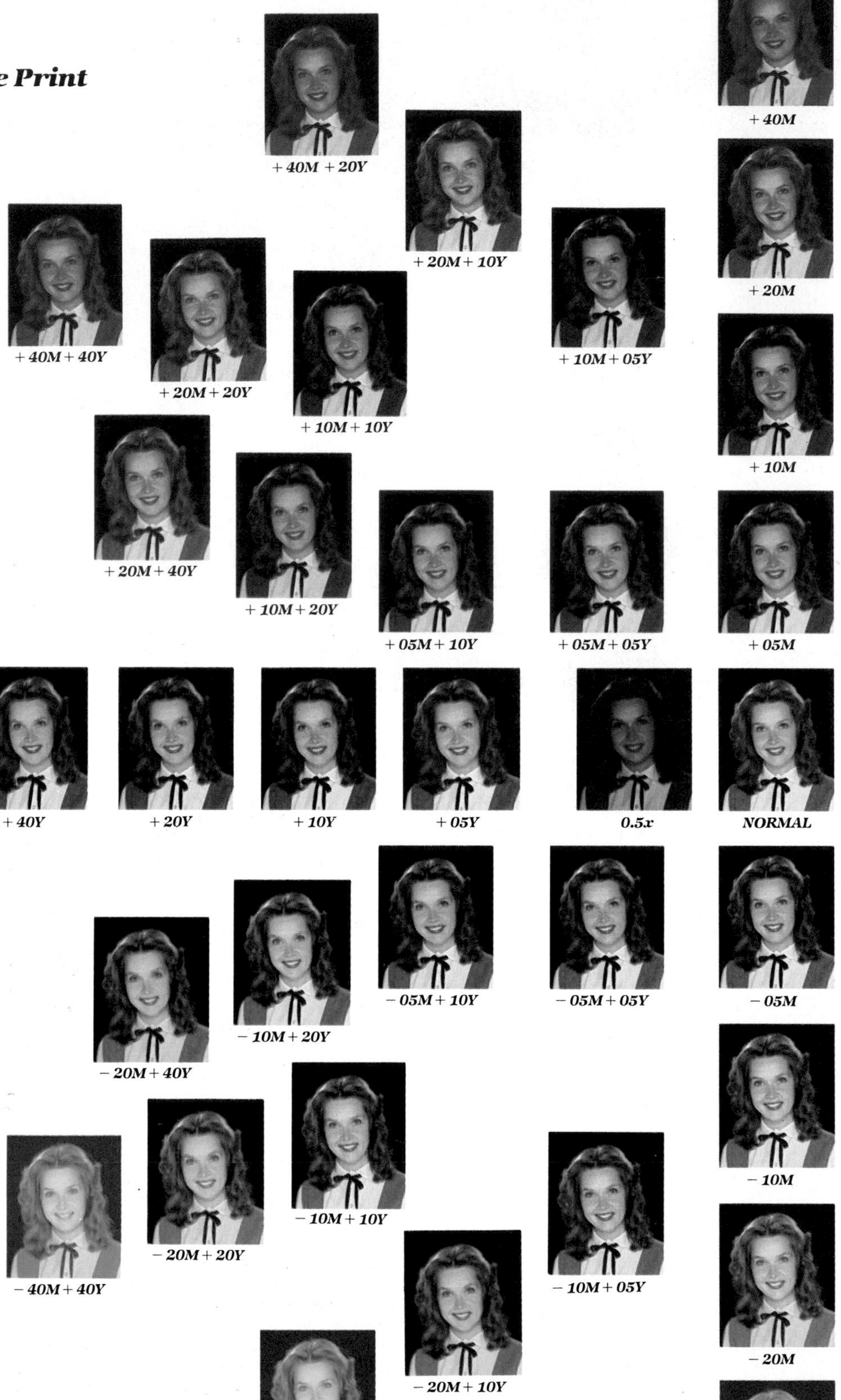

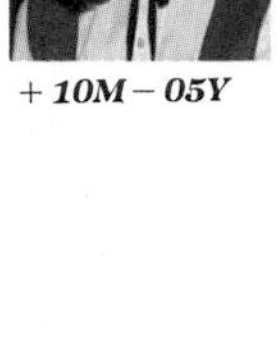

+40M

+40M +20Y

+20M+10Y

+20M

+40M+40Y

+20M+20Y

+10M+10Y

+10M+05Y

+10M

+10M−05Y

+20M+40Y

+10M+20Y

+05M+10Y

+05M+05Y

+05M

+05M−05Y

+40Y

+20Y

+10Y

+05Y

0.5x

NORMAL

2.0x

−05M+10Y

−05M+05Y

−05M

−05M−05Y

−10M+20Y

−20M+40Y

−10M

−10M+10Y

−20M+20Y

−40M+40Y

−10M+05Y

−10M−05Y

−20M

−20M+10Y

−40M+20Y

−40M

+20M – 10Y

+40M – 20Y

+10M – 10Y

+20M – 20Y

+40M – 40Y

+05M – 10Y

+10M – 20Y

+20M – 40Y

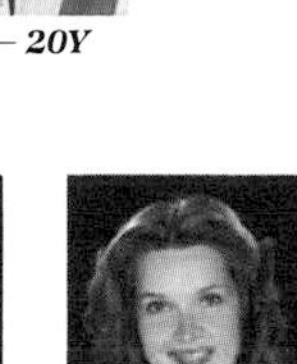

– 05Y

– 10Y

– 20Y

– 40Y

– 05M – 10Y

– 10M – 20Y

– 20M – 40Y

– 10M – 10Y

– 20M – 20Y

– 40M – 40Y

– 20M – 10Y

– 40M – 20Y

Robert Olson

Making a Test Color Print

1. Dust the negative with a camel's-hair brush and place it in the carrier and then in the enlarger, with the emulsion (dull) side down for conventional paper, up for EKTAFLEX *PCT Film. With the enlarging lens at maximum aperture for the brightest image, raise or lower the enlarger head and adjust the easel to size, and compose the image as desired. Focus the image on a sheet of paper the same thickness as your printing material. (If you're using a grain magnifier, you'll get a sharper grain image one stop down from maximum aperture.)*

2. Dial the filtration—or make the filter pack—suggested in the instructions for your paper or EKTAFLEX *PCT Film. If you are using CC or CP filters with* EKTAFLEX *PCT Negative Film, start with 40M and 40Y. Because negatives vary, a starting filter pack is largely guesswork, but your test print will point you in the right direction.*

3. Using a piece of dark cardboard as a mask (with a one-quarter section cut out), place a sheet of your paper or EKTAFLEX *PCT Film in the easel and expose the upper left quarter of the paper for ten seconds at f/5.6.*

4. Flip the card and expose the upper right quarter for ten seconds at f/8.

5. Expose the lower right quarter for ten seconds at f/11.

6. Expose the lower left quarter for ten seconds at f/16. Process your test print.

7. When the print is ready for viewing, decide which exposure is best. (The exposure may fall in between the quarters.) Then, examine the correctly exposed quarter to determine what color, if any, is too strong and by how much. Pay close attention to flesh and neutral tones. Compare your print made with EKTAFLEX *Materials to the examples in the display at left (called a "ringaround"), and then make the filter correction indicated below the example. Conventional color printing paper may require different filtration. Use the* KODAK *Color Print Viewing Filter Kit to assess color balance, and when you change the filtration, adjust the exposure to compensate. With CC or CP filters, see page 264.*

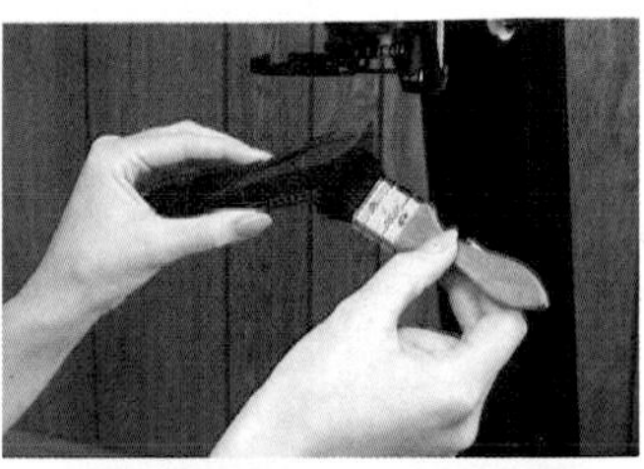

Brush off the negative (1).

Dial the filtration (2).

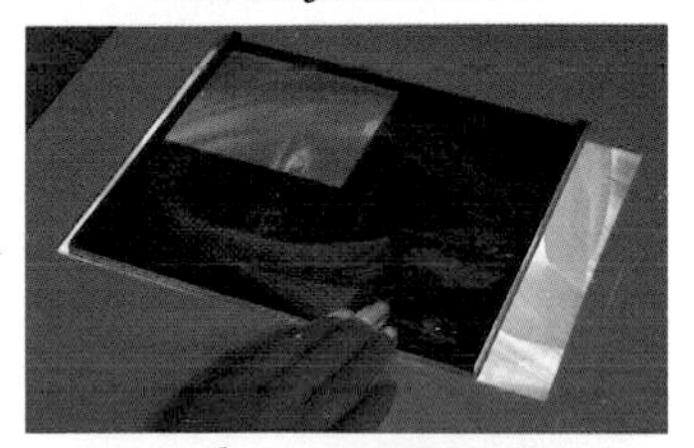

Expose the top quarters (3 & 4)

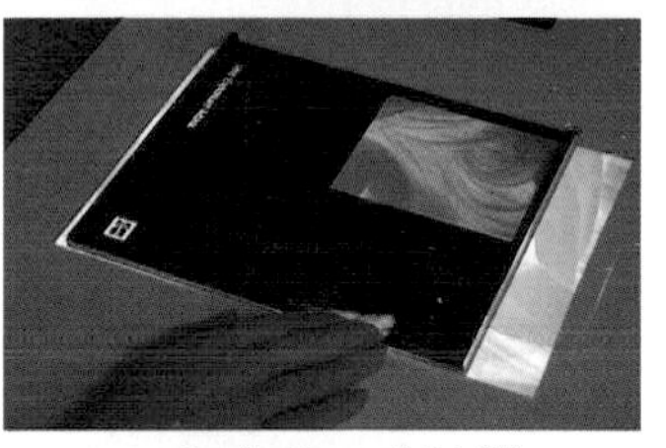

. . . the bottom right (5)

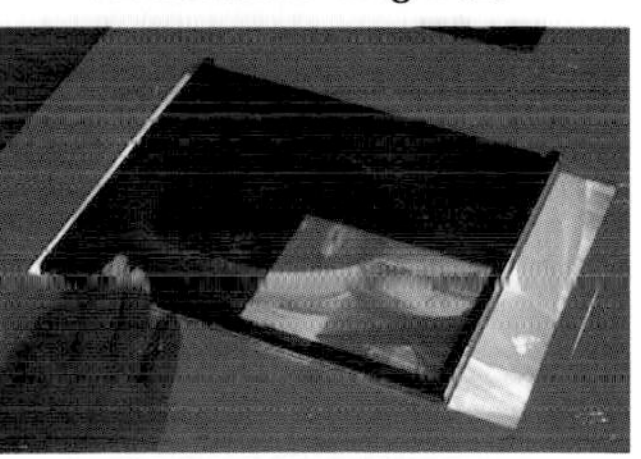

. . . and the bottom left (6).

Tom Beelmann

A test print (7).

Color Prints

Adjusting the Color Negative Print

Like most filters, color printing filters have different densities that transmit light in varying quantities. When you change filters to correct color balance, you have to adjust either the enlarging lens's *f*-stop or the exposure time to be sure the print receives the same amount of light you determined to be correct on the basis of your test print. Keep in mind that significant changes in exposure time may cause colors to shift somewhat, requiring further correction. (Modest adjustments such as those in the chart at right shouldn't have a significant effect on color.) For large exposure changes it's better to use the enlarging lens aperture, although because a slide or negative curls slightly you should avoid opening the lens wider than *f*/5.6, to ensure adequate depth of focus in the negative plane.

The table at top right shows the changes in CP or CC filters you must make to correct color balance when using EKTAFLEX PCT Printmaking Materials. Other negative printing materials may require different filtration changes to produce the same effect. The table also gives you the new exposure times you must use to compensate for the change in filters. The new times are based on ten seconds' exposure for your test print. A second print made with these corrections should be much closer to what you want.

If you need further adjustments, refer to the second table, which indicates filter changes for making more subtle color corrections in your final print. The exposure change required with each filter change is given in the third table and is adjusted for the light loss caused by surface reflection. Divide your exposure time by the factor for each filter you remove and multiply it by the factor for each filter you add. For changing two or more filters, multiply the individual factors together and use the product. Dichroic filters, which are much more efficient than CP or CC filters, require less change. Follow the enlarger manufacturer's suggestions.

KODAK Color Print Viewing Filter Kits are extremely useful for assessing and correcting the color balance of a print. Such judgments must be made when the print is thoroughly dry, though, because it will have a strong bluish cast and seem much darker when it is wet.

As you raise or lower your enlarger to change the image size on the easel, the brightness of the image will also change. As the enlarger goes higher, for example, the projected image gets larger but dimmer because the same amount of light must cover more surface area. To compensate for this change in the amount of light striking the paper, you must also change the exposure settings. If the lens-to-paper distance increases, increase the exposure time or lens aperture size; if it decreases, reduce the exposure time or aperture size. Although a new test print will indicate the needed change more precisely, you can use the following formula to calculate a new exposure for a different enlarger height:

$$\textit{New time} = \textit{Old time} \times \frac{(\textit{New enlarger height})^2}{(\textit{Old enlarger height})^2}$$

For example, the correct exposure on a 4 × 5-inch print is eight seconds at *f*/11, and you now want to make an 8 × 10-inch print from the same negative. The original lens-to-paper distance was ten inches, and after raising the enlarger and focusing the lens to produce an 8 × 10-inch image, you find the new distance is twenty inches. Apply the formula:

$$\textit{New time} = 8 \times \frac{20^2}{10} = 8 \times \frac{400}{100} = 32$$

The new exposure time would be thirty-two seconds. You can shorten the exposure time to keep the color balance consistent with an eight-second exposure by opening the aperture two stops (effectively halving the time twice), to *f*/5.6. If the corners of your image appear to be out of focus at *f*/5.6, you can compromise with a sixteen-second exposure at *f*/8 and adjust color accordingly.

This "do-it-yourself" standard negative can be used to locate the best average point for your equipment. The woman's face and the photographic grey card will help you make subtle adjustments.

Stephen Kelly

Changes in CC or CP Filters and Exposure Time

	Amount of color variation from normal	Change in filter pack	Approximate exposure for new filter pack* (in seconds)
Too red	Slight	Add 10M and 10Y	13
	Moderate	Add 20M and 20Y	15
	Great	Add 40M and 40Y	17
Too green	Slight	Subtract 10M	8
	Moderate	Subtract 20M	7
	Great	Subtract 40M	7
Too blue	Slight	Subtract 10Y	10
	Moderate	Subtract 20Y	9
	Great	Subtract 40Y	9
Too cyan	Slight	Subtract 10M and 10Y	8
	Moderate	Subtract 20M and 20Y	7
	Great	Subtract 40M and 40Y	6
Too magenta	Slight	Add 10M	12
	Moderate	Add 20M	14
	Great	Add 40M	15
Too yellow	Slight	Add 10Y	11
	Moderate	Add 20Y	11
	Great	Add 40Y	11

*Based on an original exposure time of 10 seconds.

The Standard Negative

A standard negative is a useful control when you want to change printing materials or enlarger lamps or to check processing. Select a negative that has been properly exposed under known conditions and processed normally and that you know makes an excellent print. If you've printed it previously, you should have an accurate record of the filter pack (set of filters) it needs with your particular equipment and printing material. When you change any one element of your printing process, print your standard negative first to determine what adjustments, if any, your new setup may require.

Your standard negative should be typical of the majority of negatives you will be printing. It should include a sensitive area—neutral grey or flesh tones, for example—so that any future variation from it can be detected. Avoid negatives that would make pleasing prints over a wide range of color balances. If you take a picture to be used specifically as a standard negative, include a photographic grey card in the original scene for additional control. Once you have determined the exposure and filtration for your standard negative, you can easily correct for slight differences caused by changes in paper or solutions. With practice, you will be able to shorten the time it takes you to analyze and correct a print.

Final Change in Filter Pack (if needed)

Appearance of previous print	Amount of change desired		
	Very slight	Slight	Moderate
Too red	Add 05M and 05Y	Add 10M and 10Y	Add 20M and 20Y
Too green	Subtract 05M	Subtract 10M	Subtract 20M
Too blue	Subtract 05Y	Subtract 10Y	Subtract 20Y
Too cyan	Subtract 05M and 05Y	Subtract 10M and 10Y	Subtract 20M and 20Y
Too magenta	Add 05M	Add 10M	Add 20M
Too yellow	Add 05Y	Add 10Y	Add 20Y

Factors for CC and CP Filters

Filter	Factor	Filter	Factor
05Y	1.1	05R	1.2
10Y	1.1	10R	1.3
20Y	1.1	20R	1.5
30Y	1.1	30R	1.7
40Y	1.1	40R	1.9
50Y	1.1	50R	2.2
05M	1.2	05G	1.1
10M	1.3	10G	1.2
20M	1.5	20G	1.3
30M	1.7	30G	1.4
40M	1.9	40G	1.5
50M	2.1	50G	1.7
05C	1.1	05B	1.1
10C	1.2	10B	1.3
20C	1.3	20B	1.6
30C	1.4	30B	2.0
40C	1.5	40B	2.4
50C	1.6	50B	2.9

Color Prints

Processing the Color Negative Print

Tools:
KODAK EKTAFLEX Printmaker
EKTAFLEX PCT Activator
EKTAFLEX PCT Negative Film
EKTAFLEX PCT Paper
Timer
KODAK 13 Safelight Filter (amber) with 7½-watt bulb
Rubber gloves, eye protection, protective clothing

Once exposed, your print must be processed to yield a recognizable image. With traditional color printing systems, a piece of color printing paper was subjected to a series of time-consuming, temperature-critical chemical baths to bring out color and density. A color printing system has emerged from new technology that avoids the tedium of carefully monitoring a rigid series of critical temperatures and process times. KODAK EKTAFLEX PCT Materials make color processing simple—perhaps simpler than any other darkroom procedure. For this reason, we'll discuss color print processing using EKTAFLEX PCT Materials for illustration. If you already own or have access to another color print processing method, carefully apply the manufacturer's instructions for the apparatus and for the chemicals.

Processing prints from negatives can be done in the dark or under a weak safelight, KODAK 13 Safelight Filter (amber) with a 7½-watt bulb four feet from the working area. Processing prints from slides must be done in complete darkness. With EKTAFLEX PCT Materials, incidentally, the processing for prints from slides is otherwise identical to that for negative printing.

Basically, the ***KODAK EKTAFLEX Printmaker*** is a sophisticated tray with a set of rollers at one end. You operate the printmaker following a continuous series of steps for making your print. This includes submerging the exposed film in activator

Tom Beelmann

and then laminating the processed film with a piece of EKTAFLEX PCT Paper. Before starting a printing session in your darkroom, you must follow these basic preliminary procedures to set up the printmaker.

Your printmaker must be attached to a firm level surface such as a table or bench top with screws or C-clamps. Make sure the drain valve is closed. Then pour EKTAFLEX PCT Activator into the printmaker to the top of the fill posts. After use, drain the activator out of the tray and thoroughly rinse the printmaker with water. Read the label on the activator bottle. It is very caustic and any spills or splashes should be quickly cleaned up. Avoid all contact with skin and eyes.

The ***EKTAFLEX PCT Activator*** solution that starts the processing in the film is used right out of the bottle as long as it is within 3°F(1.7°C) of room temperature. But, because the solution is hightly caustic, you should be careful with it. Wear rubber gloves, protective clothing, and goggles (or some eye protection) when you pour it. If you get splashed, wash with plenty of soap and water. The activator has a working life of about 72 hours when exposed to air in the printmaker. This translates to about 75 8 × 10-inch prints per 3-quart bottle. At the end of each printing session, drain the printmaker and store the activator in a sealed bottle. It will keep like this for up to a year after you first open the bottle.

EKTAFLEX PCT Film is available in 8 × 10-inch (20.3 × 25.4 cm) and 5 × 7-inch (12.7 × 17.8 cm) sizes. If you want to make prints from slides, get the reversal film. For prints from negatives, buy the negative film. The reversal film must be handled in total darkness. The negative film can be handled

To process a print with EKTAFLEX PCT Printmaking Materials:
In white light (room light) before exposing the EKTAFLEX PCT Film:
1. Fill the printmaker with activator solution to the top of the fill posts.
2. Place a sheet of EKTAFLEX PCT Paper emulsion side (white side) down on the paper shelf of the printmaker to cover luminescent number "1." The left side of the paper must be under the tines of the paper rake. Turn off room lights. Use KODAK 13 Safelight Filter (amber) for working with EKTAFLEX PCT Negative Film. Expose the film with your enlarger.
3. After exposure, place the exposed film, emulsion side up on the film ramp to cover luminescent number "2." Immediately turn on the timer, and allow several extra seconds.
4. When the timer reaches the start time, move the ramp slide, number "3," smoothly downward so that the film enters the activator solution. Return the slide to its former position at the top of the ramp.
5. Just before the soak time is over, begin turning the crank, number "4," clockwise at two revolutions per second. When the soak time is over, move the film rake handle, number "5," slowly toward the rollers until you feel the rollers pull the paper and film.
6. Continue turning the crank smoothly and steadily until the laminated film and paper are cranked out of the rollers. Return the film rake handle to its index mark. Uneven cranking causes stripes on the print. Look at your watch or the clock and note the time. Handle the laminate sparingly and carefully by the edges.
7. When the film and paper have been laminated together long enough (see table), peel them apart. The print cannot be washed or ferrotyped.
8. Color and density can be judged as soon as you peel the lamination apart.

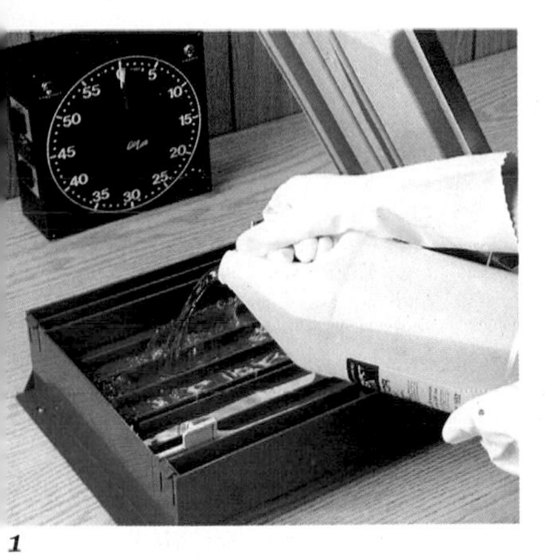

1

2

3

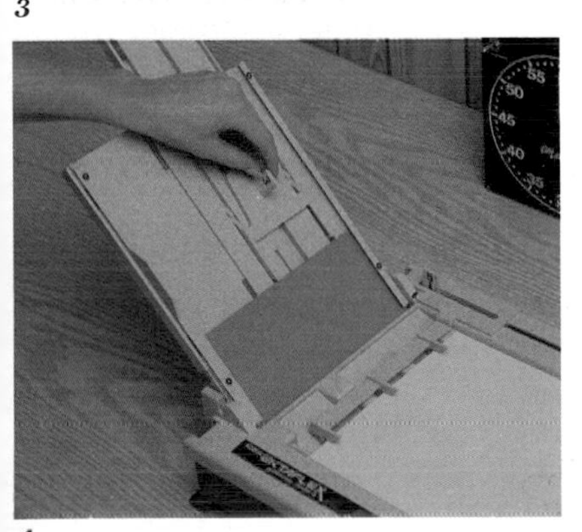

4

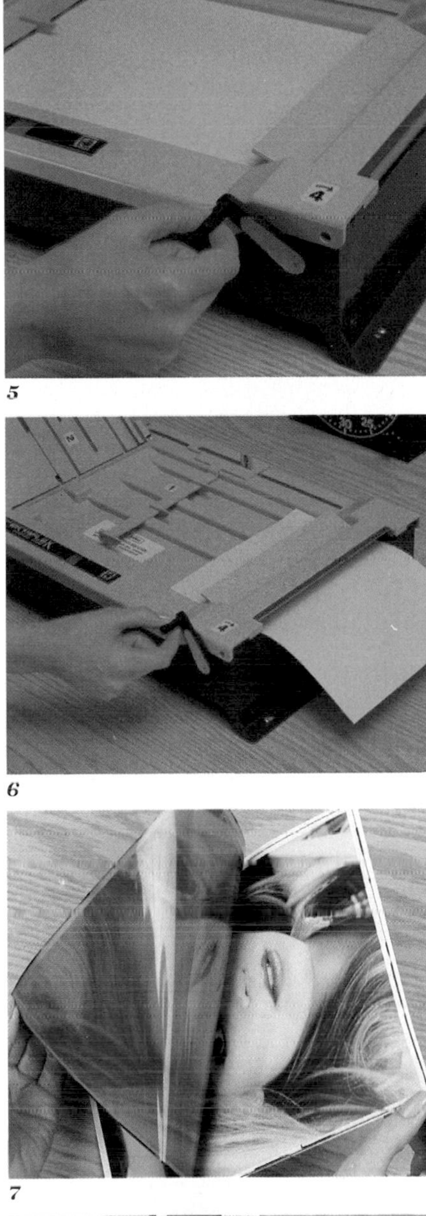

5

6

7

8

Tom Beelmann

under a KODAK 13 Safelight Filter (amber) with a 7½-watt bulb at least four feet (1.2 metres) away. But this safelight is so dim that you're just as well working in the dark. Luminescent labels on the printmaker make it easy to operate in the dark. For ease of handling, the film is notched: when the emulsion side is facing you, the code notch is on the right end at the top edge.

High temperatures and humidity can spoil the film. Store the unexposed sheets in a cool place (55°F [13°C] or lower) in the original packaging. To avoid condensation on unexposed film, allow the film package to warm up to room temperature before opening. Close the foil bag after removing each sheet. If the EKTAFLEX PCT Film is left out of the bag for extended periods, it may change in color balance or curl excessively.

The same ***EKTAFLEX PCT Paper*** is used with negative and reversal film. It makes no difference which film you use. EKTAFLEX PCT Paper is available in sizes corresponding to the film, and in two surface finishes: F (glossy) and N smooth (semi-matt). The paper is *not* sensitive to light and can be handled in room light and stored at room temperature. But, just like the film, the paper must be kept in the original bag until you use it. This prevents the paper from becoming distorted in high or low humidity conditions. Distorted paper may not laminate properly.

Temperature/Processing Time

As with all processing and printing, consistent conditions will give you consistent results. Soak time and lamination time should be determined by room temperature.

Room Tempera-ture		Activator soak time	Lamination time for negative film
°F	°C		
65	18	20 sec	8–15 min
70	21	20	7–12
75	24	20	6–10
80	27	20	6–10

This information is subject to change. Check the instruction sheet packaged with the film for the latest recommendations.

Color Prints

Printing from Color Slides

As the pictures at right show, there are two ways of making prints from a slide. One is to have the transparency copied onto color negative film by a processing lab. This "internegative" can then be printed as described on the previous pages. If you usually print color negatives and occasionally want a print from a slide, this method is fine. But if you shoot mostly color slides, it's easier and less expensive to print directly from the slide.

Since you are printing a positive image instead of a negative one, the chief difference between printing slides and printing negatives is that filtration changes and the exposure time for density corrections are reversed. To print directly from transparencies, you need EKTAFLEX PCT Reversal Film or conventional reversal paper and chemicals. The equipment is almost the same as for color negatives. Be especially sure that your enlarger is equipped with a heat-absorbing glass. You'll need a No. 2B or a CP2B UV filter. Don't bother to get a safelight filter, however, since the paper must be handled in total darkness.

If your enlarger uses CC or CP filters above the negative or CC filters below the lens, you'll need these cyan filters in addition to the ones listed earlier:

CP filters	*CC filters*	
CP05C	*CC05C*	*CC30C*
CP10C	*CC10C*	*CC40C*
CP20C	*CC20C*	*CC50C*
CP40C		

Don't get cyan filters with the suffix "-2." They don't have the right absorbtion characteristics for most slide printing.

The procedures on the following pages are for KODAK EKTAFLEX PCT Materials. Other slide processes may differ significantly. Always follow the manufacturer's directions. The infrared cut-off filter mentioned in some instructions is expensive and not necessary in the home darkroom.

If you use acetate color printing filters above the negative in your enlarger, you need only four additional cyan filters.

If you use gelatin color compensating filters beneath the lens of your enlarger, your will need six more filters—all cyan—than for printing from negatives.

Michele Hallen Infantino

You have to remove a transparency from its mount before putting it into the enlarger. Handle it carefully; fingerprints may damage the film and will show up as blemishes on the final print.

Donald Buck

Print from a negative

Derek Doeffinger

Print from a slide

Original color slide

Derek Doeffinger

Internegative

In addition to the technical differences between a print from a slide and a print from an internegative (or a negative shot in the camera), the two have a different appearance. An image on reversal material tends to be more contrasty than a print from a negative, and its color saturation is higher. Some photographers make the choice between shooting slides or negatives on the basis of this difference.

Exposing the Color Slide Print

Before you start making prints from slides, install a heat-absorbing glass and a UV filter in your enlarger and cover any stray light leaks around the lamp housing. In the following procedure, the exposure and filtration are for EKTAFLEX PCT Reversal Film.

1. Carefully remove the slide from its mount. Dust it gently. Put it into the negative carrier and then into the enlarger with the emulsion (dull) side up. The projected image should look like the reverse of the original scene. Cover any light leaks around the slide with black masking tape, or use a black paper mask.

2. Dial the dichroic filtration suggested in the instructions for EKTAFLEX PCT Reversal Film. If you use filters in a drawer, try a starting pack of OM-OY-OC.

3. Adjust the enlarger and easel to frame the image to your liking, then focus the lens carefully, as described for printing from color negatives (page 263). Focusing is easier with room lights off.

4. In total darkness, insert a sheet of EKTAFLEX PCT Reversal Film in the easel. Using a piece of dark cardboard as a mask (with a quarter section cut out), place a sheet of EKTAFLEX PCT Reversal Film in the easel, and expose the upper left quarter of the film for fifteen seconds at *f*/4. Flip the card, and expose the upper right quarter for fifteen seconds at *f*/5.6. Expose the lower right quarter for fifteen seconds at *f*/8. Expose the lower left quarter fifteen seconds at *f*/11.

5. When the test print is ready to be viewed, determine which aperture produces the best exposure and compare the color balance with the original slide to determine which color, if any, is excessive and by how much.

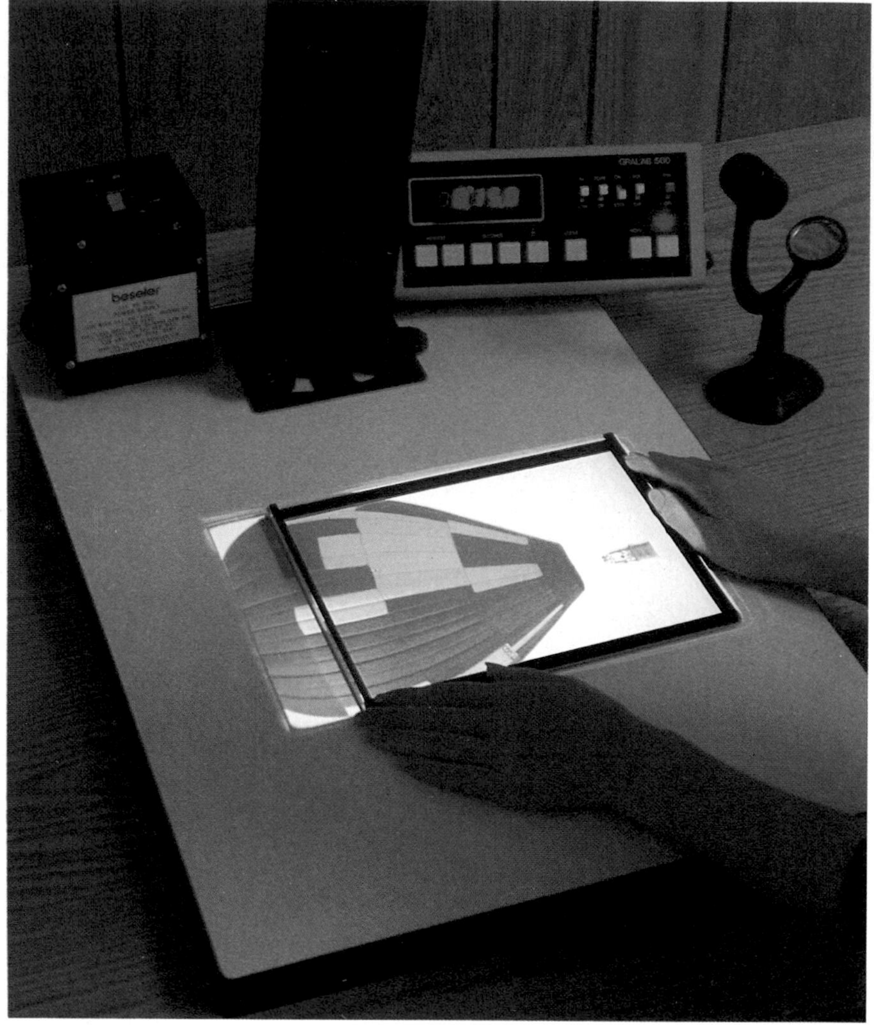

Tom Beelmann

6. Using the guidelines on the next page, adjust the filtration and exposure and make another print. Repeat the process until you get a print that is correct. When you do, note the filter and exposure combination. Using them, you can get good results on all similar slides from the same type of film enlarged to the same degree. These "coordinates" are also a good starting point for correcting other types of slides.

When you print from slides, you see the image—reversed with EKTAFLEX PCT Reversal Film—projected in its original colors, making it much easier to focus, crop, and adjust the filtration.

A cardboard mask was used to give this test print four different exposures. In slide printing, the exposures are reversed—the lightest exposure at top left was with the biggest lens aperture.

Martin L. Taylor

Color Prints

Adjusting the Color Slide Print

In adjusting the color balance of a print made from a slide, your chief guide is the slide itself. You should carefully compare midtone areas for discrepancies. To make noticeable changes in prints from slides, you usually have to make greater jumps in total filter density than with color negatives. On an average, you need a 0.20 density change for a slight hue adjustment. If you keep this in mind, the changes themselves are easy. As the table at bottom shows, if a color is too pronounced, you simply subtract some of it from the filter pack—or if that is not possible, you add a filter of the complementary color to the filter pack. Conventional reversal printing materials may require different filtration to achieve the same results. It's better to take out filters than to put more in. This avoids a long exposure, which might affect the color response of the film or paper. If you do not have a filter for the color that you are supposed to add or subtract, use the two colors that produce it. For example, to correct a greenish cast, remove equal amounts of cyan and yellow.

Never use more than two subtractive colors in your filter pack; all three together create a neutral grey density that blocks light and lengthens the exposure. If you do end up with all three in your pack, remove the color of the lowest density from the pack entirely and then subtract the same density value from the other two colors. For example, if your pack has 20Y, 50M, and 50C, remove 20Y, 20M, and 20C, leaving only 30M and 30C. The color balance will remain the same. Whenever you change filters, you must also adjust the exposure to compensate for the density change and, with CC and CP filters, for the change in the number of filter surfaces. Use the filter-factor table on page 265 when you make a one-filter adjustment. If the change involves more than one filter, use the filter factors as a rough guide and make a new test print—or use the color printing computer in the *KODAK Complete Darkroom Dataguide*. When printing slides, remember that increasing exposure makes the print lighter, while decreasing exposure makes it darker. The formula for adjusting the exposure for enlarger-height differences on page 264 also applies to slide printing.

40R

40M

40B

Processing the Color Slide Print

The most efficient way to process prints made from color slides is with KODAK EKTAFLEX PCT Materials. The procedure is identical to that used for printing from negatives, with the following exceptions:

1. EKTAFLEX PCT Reversal Film must be handled in complete darkness.
2. Because the film is heat sensitive, wait 15 seconds between handling and making the exposure.
3. Keep soak times within 1 second for consistent and predictable color balance.

Follow the instructions for processing the color negative print on pages 266–267.

Room temperature			
°F	***°C***	***Activator soak time***	***Lamination time for reversal film***
65	*18*	*20 sec*	*15–20 min*
70	*21*	*20*	*12–15*
75	*24*	*20*	*9–12*
80	*27*	*20*	*8–10*

This information is subject to change. Check the instruction sheet packaged with the film for the latest recommendations.

Color Corrections

If color balance is	*Subtract these filters*	*Or add these filters*
Yellow	*Yellow*	*Magenta + cyan*
Magenta	*Magenta*	*Yellow + cyan*
Cyan	*Cyan*	*Yellow + magenta*
Blue	*Magenta + cyan*	*Yellow*
Green	*Yellow + cyan*	*Magenta*
Red	*Yellow + magenta*	*Cyan*

20R

1 stop overexposed

20Y

40Y

20M

Normal

20G

40G

20B

20C

40C

Robert Olson

Together with the table at left, the picture series above can be used as a guide for correcting filtration when printing from slides. The numbers under each picture show the amount of excess color that needs to be subtracted.

1 stop underexposed

Processing Black-and-White Film

Tools:
Totally dark room or changing bag
Film tank and reel
Scissors
Hook-type bottle opener
Thermometer accurate to 1°F (0.6°C)
Timer
Graduated beakers (3 or 4)
Premixed chemicals OR
Chemicals
Mixing vessel
Storage bottles
Stirring paddle
Water-bath tray (optional)
Film drying clips
Negative storage envelopes

Although black-and-white film is easier to process than color, black-and-white materials in general offer more potential for technical experimentation than do color materials. For example, in color processes certain films must be treated with specific chemicals for precise amounts of time, whereas the development of black-and-white film can be broadly manipulated to control contrast, which is to a black-and-white print what color balance is to a color print. There are also many different kinds of black-and-white developers that produce negatives with very different characteristics—graininess, sharpness, shadow detail—that result in visibly different prints. Ones such as KODAK HOBBY-PAC Film Developer, on which the table at far right is based, give good overall results. Fine-grain developers, on the other hand, inhibit the formation of clumps of silver but require longer development time, and produce negatives of somewhat lower density. Compensating developers preserve shadow detail while yielding higher effective film speed. Rapid developers are also good for pushing film, but they will increase contrast and grain more visibly. Like developers, black-and-white printing papers vary greatly in their characteristics, as we will see on page 279.

Black-and-white printing and film processing require less equipment than color, and temperature is less critical than with color. You can also use a brighter safelight when printing. And if there is running water in an adjacent room, you can set up a usable darkroom in a closet as small as three feet by four feet. For these reasons, black-and-white processing may offer the beginner an easier introduction to darkroom technique.

Developing Times in a Small Tank* (in minutes)

KODAK Film name and packaged Developer	65°F (18.5°C)	68°F (20°C)	70°F (21°C)	72°F (22°C)	75°F (24°C)
PANATOMIC-X					
HOBBY-PAC	4¾#	4¼#	4#	3¾#	3¼#
D-76	6	5	4½#	4¼#	3¾#
D-76 (1:1)†	8	7	6½	6	5
MICRODOL-X	8	7	6½	6	5
MICRODOL-X (1:3)‡			11	10	8½
PLUS-X Pan					
HOBBY-PAC	6	5	4½#	4#	3½#
D-76	6½	5½	5	4½#	3¾#
D-76 (1:1)†	8	7	6½	6	5
MICRODOL-X	8	7	6½	6	5½
MICRODOL-X (1:3)‡			11	10	9½
TRI-X Pan					
HOBBY-PAC	8½	7½	6½	6	5
D-76	9	8	7½	6½	5½
D-76 (1:1)†	11	10	9½	9	8
MICRODOL-X	11	10	9½	9	8
MICRODOL-X (1:3)‡			15	14	13
DK-50 (1:1)†	7	6	5½	5	4½

**Agitate every 30 seconds throughout development*
#Unsatisfactory uniformity may result with development times shorter than 5 minutes
†Diluted to 1 part developer, 1 part water
‡For greatest sharpness (see developer instructions)

Load black-and-white film into a film tank the same way you load color negative film (see page 252). Like all 35 mm films, it must be loaded in total darkness, but once the film is in a lighttight tank you can work with the room lights on.

The preferred temperature for black-and-white processing is 68°F (20°C). The developer temperature is most crucial, and with black-and-white film it is important to maintain consistent temperatures throughout processing. A sudden drop in temperature, for example, can cause the film emulsion to contract, producing an effect known as reticulation. This effect can be used deliberately, as explained on page 283, but inadvertent minor temperature changes can give the film's grain pattern a pronounced oatmeal-like quality. If your developer is at any temperature other than 68°F (20°C) you must adjust the customary time, increasing it if the temperature is below 68°F (20°C) and decreasing it if it is above. The table at left shows the needed adjustments for some KODAK Films and Developers.

Only three chemicals are necessary for black-and-white processing. Besides the developer, you need a stop bath to halt the action of the developer, and a fixer (also called "hypo") to make the image stable. Some workers also use a short (one minute) plain-water presoak before the developer, to facilitate even penetration of the film by the developer. Two other chemicals are also useful: a hypo clearing agent to remove the fixer and reduce the wash time, and a wetting agent to help prevent water from beading and leaving spots on the drying film. For best results, use the chemicals recommended for your film. Most come with instructions for mixing and storing as well as with details on whether they can be reused and, if so, how many times. However, diluted developer cannot be reused.

The following steps are for processing KODAK PLUS-X Pan Film in a small tank at 68°F (20°C), using the KODAK HOBBY-PAC Black-and-White Film Processing Kit. In the optional steps, times are given for KODAK HYPO Clearing Agent and KODAK PHOTO-FLO Solution (wetting agent). Times may differ with other chemicals. Drain the tank completely before proceeding with the next step.

Processing KODAK PLUS-X Pan Film using the KODAK HOBBY-PAC Black-and-White Film Processing Kit at 68°F (20°C)

Processing step	*Minutes*	*Action*
1. Developer	*5*	*Agitate 5 seconds initially; then for 5 seconds every half minute*
2. Stop bath	*½*	*Agitate moderately the entire time*
3. Fixer	*5–10*	*Agitate 5 seconds initially; then for 5 seconds every half minute*
4. Wash	*20–30*	*Remove tank top; wash under a moderate stream of running water*
OR Rinse	*½*	*Remove tank top; wash under running water*
*Hypo clearing agent**	*1–2*	*Agitate moderately entire time*
Wash	*5*	*Wash under running water*
5. Drying	*As needed*	*Hang film and wipe gently with a damp viscous sponge to remove excess water*
OR Wetting agent	*½*	*Bathe in solution; drain briefly*
Drying	*As needed*	*Hang film; do not wipe*

**If you need to conserve water or shorten wash time.*

Robert Kretzer

Robert Kretzer/Raymond Miller

Black-and-white materials afford you enormous control over the tonal values of the print, as well as its other characteristics. The negative that produced this print is shown above.

Making Black-and-White Prints

Exposing the Black-and-White Print

Tools:
Totally dark room
Enlarger with 50 mm lens and carrier for 35 mm negatives
Easel
Timer
Enlarging paper
Safelight with filter recommended for paper
Camel's-hair brush or compressed air

Before printing pictures from a roll of processed black-and-white film, make a contact print of the negative strips so that you can choose the pictures you want to print. Follow the procedure described on page 251 for exposing the contact print, and then develop it as shown on the facing page.

1. Dust the negative carefully with the brush or compressed air. Put it in the carrier and load the carrier into the enlarger with the negative emulsion (dull) side down.

2. Adjust the enlarger and the easel for the image size you want, keeping the lens at maximum aperture for a bright working image. Focus the image sharply on a scrap of printing paper or paper of similar thickness. Then stop the enlarging lens down to *f*/8 for a negative of normal density and to ensure adequate depth of focus in the negative plane.

3. With the enlarger light off and only the safelights on, insert a sheet of enlarging paper in the easel with the emulsion side up. (On a glossy paper, the emulsion is shiny; a fiber-based paper usually curls toward the emulsion.) You can use a half or a quarter of a sheet for the test to conserve paper, provided it can be secured. Until you get a sense of the way different negatives print, start with a number 2 (normal contrast) paper or filter (see pages 278-279). Cover all but one-sixth of the paper with a piece of dark cardboard, as shown in the picture at right above.

Raymond Miller

Make a test print by turning on the enlarger for thirty seconds and moving a cardboard mask across the paper every five seconds to give the print six different exposure times.

When the test print is processed, you will be able to see the effect of the different exposures and choose the best one for the final print.

4. Set the timer for thirty seconds and turn on the enlarger. Expose the strip of paper for five seconds. Then, every five seconds, move the cardboard to expose an additional one-sixth of the paper. The paper will show exposures of five, ten, fifteen, twenty, twenty-five and thirty seconds. If your test print comes out too dark, you can use smaller increments of time, such as two seconds. You can also vary the number of bands depending on what range you think the negative will fall into.

5. Process the test print as shown on the facing page. Then, in room light, examine the test print to determine the best exposure for making an improved final print. You should also use the test to make an initial assessment of contrast, which is explained more fully on the next two pages. In making a test print, be sure to include an image area that shows a sensitive middle tone, such as skin, since such areas are extremely important to the quality of the final print.

Processing the Black-and-White Print

Tools:

In addition to the equipment you already have for film processing and print exposure, you will also need:

4 or 5 trays (the same size as or one size larger than your paper)
Squeegee or photo sponge
Paper developer
Stop bath
Fixer

The rapid developer used to process paper usually shouldn't be used for film. But you can use the same stop bath and fixer, and in a pinch you can substitute water for the stop bath, although this will reduce the capacity of the fixer. (KODAK HOBBY-PAC Kits for processing black-and-white films and papers differ only in the developer.) If you use fiber-base paper rather than resin-coated paper, you can use the hypo clearing agent described for film to reduce the wash time (see page 275). Arrange your trays side by side for a smooth, sequential work flow. Put about one-half inch of working solution in each tray. If possible, place the wash tray in a sink or under a moderate stream of water, or use a special wash tray designed to attach directly to a faucet, as shown here. If your darkroom has no running water, place fixed prints in a tray of still water, exchanging the water frequently under a tap.

As with film, the standard temperature for the chemicals and wash in processing paper is 68°F (20°C), but temperature is less critical, and the solutions can remain between 65° and 75°F (18 and 24°C). In extreme conditions, you can maintain the developer at the recommended temperature by putting the developer tray into a water bath. Heaters for trays are also available commercially.

In the procedure given here, times are average for a KODAK RC paper at 68°F (20°C), using the KODAK HOBBY-PAC Black-and-White Paper Processing Kit. (The exception is KODAK POLYPRINT RC paper, for which normal development time is one and one-half minutes.) For other available chemicals and temperatures, the procedures and times will vary, as they will for fiber-base papers, so follow their specific instructions.

To develop a print, immerse it in the developer by slipping it in at an angle or by pushing it in facedown to wet the entire emulsion, then flipping it over. Agitate the print by gently rocking the tray, and drain it for a few seconds before putting it into the next tray. As always, work under a safelight. You can turn on the room light to examine the print after it has fixed for about 25–30 seconds. For consistency's sake, don't try to control a print's lightness or darkness in the developing tray; change your enlarging exposure to do so. As with prints from color negatives, a black-and-white print that is too dark has received too much exposure, while a print that is too light has received too little exposure and needs more. If the print is off, discard it and make another with a new exposure.

1. Slip print into developer; agitate.

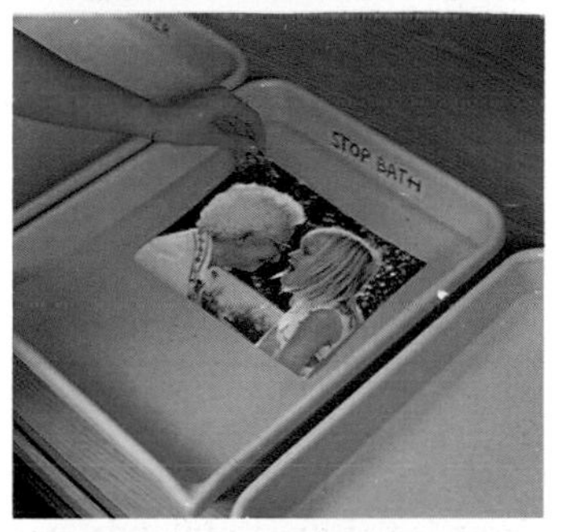

2. Immerse print briefly in stop bath.

3. Put print into fixer and agitate.

4. Wash RC paper for four minutes.

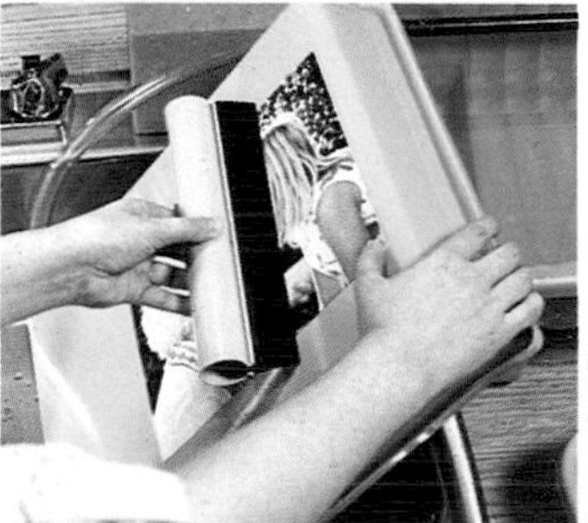

5. Wipe with sponge; air dry.

Raymond Miller

Processing KODAK Black-and-White RC Paper with the KODAK HOBBY-PAC Black-and-White Paper Processing Kit

Processing step	***Minutes****	***Action***
1. Developer	1†	*Be sure print is fully immersed; agitate continuously*
2. Stop bath	►	*Immerse for 5–10 seconds while agitating*
3. Fixer	2	*Agigate frequently*
4. Wash	4	*Use running water and agitate; do not leave print in water*
5. Drying	*As needed*	*Sponge or squeegee both sides of print; dry face up on a towel or hang on a line with spring clothespins*

**Times may vary for other papers and chemical combinations; the long washing times required by fiber-base papers, for example, can be shortened considerably by immersing the print in hypo clearing agent after fixing and before washing—2 minutes for single-weight papers and 3 minutes for double weight.*

†See your paper's instructions for a precise recommendation.

Black-and White Prints

Adjusting the Black-and-White Print

You can create a broad range of effects with your prints by choosing from a wide variety of black-and-white papers. These papers are available in various thicknesses (or weights), surface textures, and surface sheens. The paper itself can be a stark white, a warm white, or a cream white, and the tone of the image that develops can be a neutral black, a warm black, or an even warmer brown-black. Like films, papers also have different speeds, or degrees of sensitivity to light. In general, you'll find that single- or medium-weight papers are economical and thick enough for most uses, although single-weight papers must be handled more carefully than either double-weight fiber or medium-weight RC papers. A smooth surface renders the finest detail, and a glossy sheen yields the richest blacks. A matte (non-glossy) paper is best used for images with primarily light-tone values, such as a bridal portrait.

One of the most important controls in black-and-white printmaking is contrast. Even subtle changes in the range of tones can create striking differences in a monochrome print. An image with deep blacks and bright highlights, and dramatic differences in the steps of grey between them, is said to have high contrast. A print with a softer, subtler range of tones is described as having low or normal contrast. A good negative can produce rich shadows and crisp highlights separated by a full range of grey tones.

There are several ways to control overall contrast in a black-and-white print. When a poorly lighted original scene, incorrect exposure, or processing errors have produced a negative that makes a low- or high-contrast test print, you can improve the contrast of the final print by using a higher- or lower-contrast grade paper. If you are using a variable-contrast paper, you change filters to do this. Within limits, you can also increase development time (or developer concentration) to achieve smaller increases in contrast and reduce development (or dilute the developer) to lower contrast. But you must be consistent if you do this; developing your test print for the same time you intend to process your print, because changing development also changes the overall density of the print and requires exposure adjustments. With graded papers —which are available only in whole-grade increments—this technique can achieve in-between contrast levels.

Black-and-white enlarging papers are available in as many as five contrast grades, numbered 1 to 5. Number 2 is normal. Number 1 is softer—that is, it will reduce the difference between the darkest and lightest areas in relation to a print made on Number 2 paper. Numbers 3 to 5 are progressively harder—they will heighten the differences. Some papers are also simply labeled as soft, medium, hard, extra hard, and ultrahard.

In general, if your negative image is contrasty, with very light and very dark areas, printing it on low-contrast paper will lighten the dark areas and darken the light ones, showing more detail in both. Conversely, if your image is flat and lifeless, with dull highlights and weak, grey shadows, printing it on a higher-contrast paper will brighten the highlights and deepen the shadows. Some subjects (and negatives of them) have inherently high contrast and may look appropriately contrasty even when printed with relatively low contrast; other subjects may still have a good range of grey tones even when printed with substantially higher-than-normal contrast. Although a change in printing contrast can often correct for a less-than-perfect negative, contrast is also an important creative control. For example, a negative that produces a good tonal range on normal-contrast paper may give a more dramatic, abstracting effect with additional contrast.

The display at right shows how changes in printing contrast and exposure can affect the appearance of a print. Making such a "ringaround" can be a valuable tool for evaluating your black-and-white printing efforts. When you get a result you don't like, use the ringaround to determine corrective action. Here, the negative printed best with a No. 2½ variable contrast filter, which, with variable contrast enlarging paper, gives the equivalent of a normal contrast (No. 2) enlarging paper. Prints were also made with density matched filters of much higher (No. 4½) and much lower (No. 0) contrast to show the most dramatic difference. The best exposure time of 8 seconds for the No. 2½ filter became the exposure midpoint for the No. 0 and the No. 2½ exposure series. Even with density-matched filters, filters that give higher contrast (No. 4, 4½, and 5) typically require one stop more exposure. The best exposure time for the No. 4½ series is double that for the other filters.

Filter No. 0

2 seconds

4 seconds

8 seconds

16 seconds

32 seconds

Filter No. 2½

2 seconds

4 seconds

8 seconds

16 seconds

32 seconds

Filter No. 4½

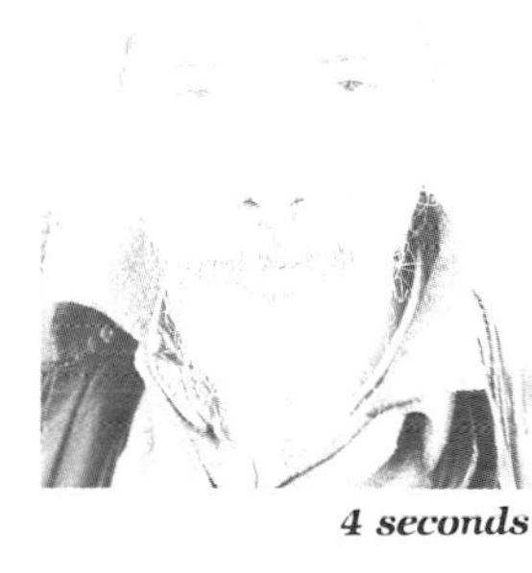

4 seconds

8 seconds

16 seconds

32 seconds

64 seconds

Robert Laster

Keeping a supply of all the contrast grades of a particular paper can be rather expensive. A more economical approach is to use a variable-contrast paper which is available both resin-coated and fiber-base. When used with special filters that fit the enlarger, variable-contrast paper yields, in half-grade increments, contrast grades 0 or 1 through 4 or 5, depending on the manufacturer. Because you can achieve in-between contrast levels without manipulating development, variable-contrast paper offers a more subtle control over contrast than do most graded papers. Some variable-contrast filter systems require that you adjust your exposure to compensate for the differing densities of the filters. Other filter systems have neutral density built into the filters, so that all of them transmit the same amount of light, eliminating the need for significant exposure changes. Improvements in the emulsion and ease of use of variable-contrast papers have made them an attractive choice for all-purpose black-and-white printing, particularly in a convenient RC base.

Basic Printing Controls

When part of a picture is too light, as the little girl in costume is in the top picture here, using a mask to burn-in the area brings it into a more balanced relationship with the rest of the image.

Other darkroom techniques can help you control the appearance of the final print. Although no substitute for careful composition, ***cropping*** can improve some images by cutting out unwanted details or changing their emphasis. To crop a print, raise the enlarger head, refocus, shift the easel around for improved composition, and recalculate the exposure (see page 264). Or, if you're using an easel with adjustable blades (a particularly useful tool for any kind of cropping), you can simply move the blades in and opt for a smaller image size. A 35 mm negative is small to begin with, and if enlarged to a high degree the technical quality of your printed image may suffer.

If an area of a print is too light, ***burning-in*** will give it extra exposure, making it darker while leaving the rest of the print normally exposed. Cut a ragged shape in a piece of cardboard that will let light expose the specific area you wish to burn-in but mask the rest of the print. After giving the print its normal exposure, hold the mask a few inches above the print and expose only the area that is too light. Blur the edges of the area by moving the mask slightly during exposure.

Dodging makes a dark area lighter. Tape a piece of cardboard that is roughly the same shape and size as the area to be dodged to a piece of thin wire and use it as a screen during part of the normal exposure. Keep this dodging tool moving during the exposure to avoid a hard edge between the dodged area and the rest of the picture, and to prevent the wire from leaving a light line in the print. Remember to reverse these procedures when printing from slides. Dodge an area to make it darker, and burn-in an area to make it lighter.

Donald Maggio

Raymond Miller

Donald Maggio

As the sequence above shows, darkroom cropping can increase the impact of a picture by making the subject larger and removing unnecessary foreground or background distractions.

Martin L. Taylor

Taylor/Infantino

Martin L. Taylor

Martin L. Taylor

Taylor/Infantino

Martin L. Taylor

Dodging—holding back light from an area of the print that the overall exposure would otherwise make too dark—is often needed to make important parts of the image more visible. In the series at left, the man's face was lightened while the rest of the print stayed the same.

Tom Beelmann

Beelmann/Infantino

Tom Beelmann

A vignette eliminates distracting backgrounds. The easiest tool for producing one, as shown in the center picture at right, is a piece of cardboard with an oval hole cut in it.

Vignetting is also done with a mask. Cut a centered oval hole in a piece of cardboard to frame your subject. Hold the mask over the paper for the entire exposure, moving it to keep the edges of the vignette soft. With negatives, your border will be white; with slides, the border will be black.

To a certain extent, the keystoning of buildings (see page 220) can be corrected by tilting the easel during enlargement. Be sure, however, to keep the entire image in focus with a small aperture (preferably *f*/16 or *f*/22) on the enlarger lens.

Creative Darkroom Effects

Once you have learned how to make good conventional prints, you may want to try some techniques that alter or distort the image in interesting ways. Although you should use these techniques with discretion, they offer additional possibilities for creative expression.

Most photo dealers sell special ***texture screens***, in both a small size that you can sandwich with the negative in the carrier and in a larger size that can be placed directly on the paper in a printing frame. These screens come in a variety of patterns and in textures ranging from fine to coarse. You can also make your own by shooting an underexposed black-and-white negative of a textured surface, then underdeveloping it and sandwiching it with your working negative when you make the print. For direct contact, try a fine, loosely woven gauze or a sheet of textured glass or plastic.

Other darkroom special effects may require drastic treatment of your film, so you'll probably want to make duplicate negatives or transparencies to protect your originals. One way to do this is by carefully rephotographing good finished prints. For transparencies, you can have a lab make copies, or make them yourself with slide duplicating equipment. You can also contact-print or enlarge black-and-white negatives onto a special sheet film that can be processed like paper, then contact-print or enlarge the resulting positive onto another sheet of film to produce a negative. Slides can be contact-printed or enlarged onto a sheet of transparency duplicating film, then processed to produce a positive by a lab or at home. Sheet films are available in many sizes (4 × 5- and 8 × 10- inch are popular). Black-and-white litho film will yield a high-contrast image, useful for many graphic and linear effects. Slides will produce a good high-contrast negative on it; black-and-white negatives, a high-contrast positive. Color negatives don't work as well,

Donald Maggio

A network of fine lines in a screen placed on the paper during exposure makes this bullfighting scene look as if it was executed in oil. The screen printed alone is at left center.

Donald Maggio

Fabric textures, such as this canvas one, are effective with gentle outdoor shots such as this. A section of the screen is shown at right center.

but can be contact-printed onto special color films that produce positive transparencies that can then be used with any process requiring slides. Many special techniques, such as the ones shown on page 284, require the use of high-contrast images.

Some black-and-white darkroom films, both continuous-tone and litho, allow the use of a red safelight, a real advantage for exacting processes. Since the results of some techniques are unpredictable, it's often wise to make several copy negatives.

The ***Sabattier effect,*** shown at top far right, is more commonly (and mistakenly) known as solarization. Its surreal blend of positive and negative is the result of briefly exposing your film or paper to white light midway through development. The amount of exposure necessary must be determined by tests; and because of the unpredictability of this effect, you should only apply the Sabattier effect to a duplicate negative. With paper, use a very high degree of printing contrast to avoid a muddy image. For a negative, use an image with a lot of shadow values; for a print, select an image with a lot of light tones. These are the areas which contain the most undeveloped silver, and which are thus most affected by reexposure to light. Print development after exposure to light can be controlled with a water bath. The Sabattier effect can also be applied to color transparency film with some interesting results.

Russell Hart

The Sabattier effect results when a photosensitive material is exposed to light during development, causing a partial reversal of the image. It works best with film because images on paper tend to become muddy.

Keith Boas

In reticulation, drastic changes in temperature during processing can create a regular pattern such as this one on a film's emulsion.

Reticulation (lower picture) is a pattern of wrinkles and cracks in a film's emulsion caused by a sudden change in temperature. One way to produce it is to develop the copy negative normally, then rinse it in an acetic acid stop bath at 140°-150°F (60°-66°C) for one minute, immerse it in a cold water bath (below 40°F, 4°C) for one minute; then fix the film in your normal way. Follow your usual cleaning and washing procedures; then air-dry the film quickly with a hair dryer. To intensify the effect, repeat the hot and cold steps with water only, increasing the temperature differences. Freezing the film before you dry it will produce even more dramatic results. Take care in handling the film after hot baths—the emulsion will be very fragile.

Although ***multiple exposures*** can be made effectively in the camera (see pages 242-243), they are different in quality and somewhat less predictable than multiple exposures created in the darkroom. The one of the boy with a kite shown on page 285 was produced by sandwiching two slides, emulsion sides together, in the negative carrier, and printing them as if they were one image. Another approach is to print each image separately on the same piece of paper. This method gives you more control because the images can receive different degrees of enlargement. Remember to reduce the exposure on each to avoid overexposing the print. The third method is to make masks, as described for the technique of burning in on the preceding pages, and to print part of one image with one mask, and part of another image with another mask on the same sheet of paper. Preplanning your composite image by making tissue-paper tracings under the enlarger is a great help.

Creative Effects

Robert Kretzer

Ralph Cowan

The multiple image at right was made by sandwiching the slide of the boy above with an enlarged and cropped transparency of the sunset, then printing them together (see page 283).

To create the high-contrast image at center from the continuous-tone image at top, the photographer printed the original negative on high-contrast film. The resulting film positive was in turn contact-printed with another sheet of high-contrast film to yield a high-contrast negative. Extraneous details were opaqued out on this negative, and the center print made from it. The image at lower left was made by sandwiching a high-contrast film positive and a high-contrast negative with a piece of unexposed high-contrast film. Holding a desk lamp at an angle, the photographer slowly turned the tightly contacted films so that all sides had equal exposure. The resulting film was then contact-printed onto another sheet of high-contrast film, which, after processing, was printed on paper for the final tone-line image.

Ralph Cowan

Michele Hallen Infantino

Part V

The Joy

Caring for Photographs
Displaying Prints
Sharing Photographs
Putting Photographs to Work

Caring for Photographs

Novice and professional photographers alike take pleasure in sharing the results of their photographic efforts with others. Whether you shoot slides or make color or black-and-white prints, you must handle and store your photographs properly for your own and others' long-term enjoyment of them.

In the darkroom or the den, always handle photographic materials by the edges only. Fingerprints and stains are extremely difficult to remove, particularly from slide and negative emulsions. (Solvent film cleaners are available for both color and black-and-white films, but aren't always sufficient.) You should also be sure to place slides, negatives, or prints on surfaces that are clean and dust-free. And don't leave unprotected slides and negatives around your darkroom when you are working.

Processed photographic materials are harmed by a long list of agents, some of which are easily avoided. They should not be subjected to heat, prolonged direct sunlight, high humidity, chemical fumes, or even certain storage materials. Don't keep prints, negatives, or slides in damp basements; in hot, dusty attics; near heat runs or radiators; in chemical-laden wooden furniture drawers; or in a photographic darkroom that may contain airborne chemical dust. The high acidity of conventional paper products can also, over time, damage photographs kept in them. Storage boxes and cases made of acid-free or alkaline-buffered materials—frequently referred to as conservation, archival, or museum-grade—are available from some photographic and art supply houses.

One of the best ways to protect prints that will be viewed frequently is in an album made from materials suitable for long-term keeping. It shields the prints from light and the print surfaces from abrasion or injurious airborne substances. Prints for display can be dry mounted on, or window matted in,

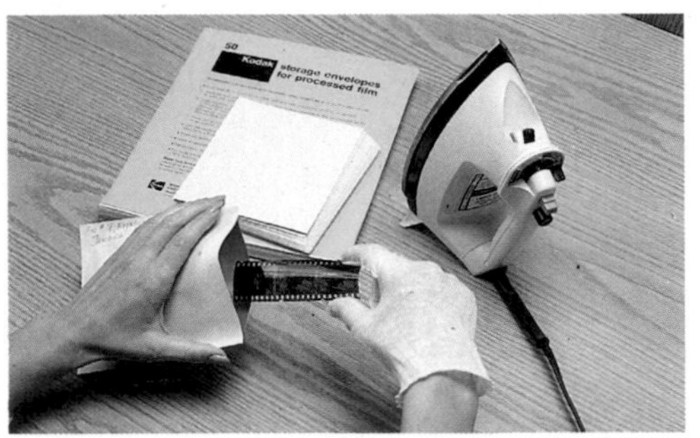

Tom Beelmann

Protect your valuable photographs in envelopes that are suitable for long-term keeping. Identify the contents on the outside of the envelope for easy retrieval.

conservation quality board to diminish the effects of frequent handling. Any print displayed in the open should be placed out of direct sunlight and away from any intense light source. Glass over a photo, as in a frame, will reduce the level of harmful ultraviolet light reaching the print and also protect it from airborne matter. Store loose prints in the dark—ideally in temperatures less than 70°F (21°C) and less than 50% relative humidity (RH)—and protect their surfaces with interleaving paper.

If you store your negatives carefully, you will be able to make another print should you lose or damage one. Neutral-pH envelopes or polyethylene sleeves are most suitable for long-term keeping and will also protect film from scratches and fingerprints. Make sure that the individual negatives or strips are separated so that they won't scratch or nick each other. Wide variations in temperature and humidity can shorten the life of film considerably, so try to maintain both variables at the recommended levels.

Slides, like prints, are meant to be shown. The brief periods of intense light they are occasionally subjected to shouldn't hurt them, if they are stored in a safe, dark place the rest of the time. If you show your slides frequently, though, you might want to have duplicates made for projection, and put the originals away or transfer the originals to special glass mounts. (Glass or PVA slide mounts are less chemically active than

Michele Hallen Infantino

cardboard mounts.) Plastic slide trays are satisfactory for long-term storage, but be sure the cardboard box they're kept in is also safe. Specially designed metal boxes or slide drawers are preferable. As always, avoid heat, humidity, and dust; find a cool, dark place to keep slides.

You can extend the life of important photographs greatly by using KODAK Storage Envelopes for Processed Film, which are made of polyethylene, aluminum foil, and paper that act as a vapor barrier, keeping the moisture level of the photograph constant during storage. In a low-humidity environment, just remove excess air from the envelope after placing your negatives, slides or prints into it; then seal it according to directions. Store the package in a freezer at 0°F (−18°C).

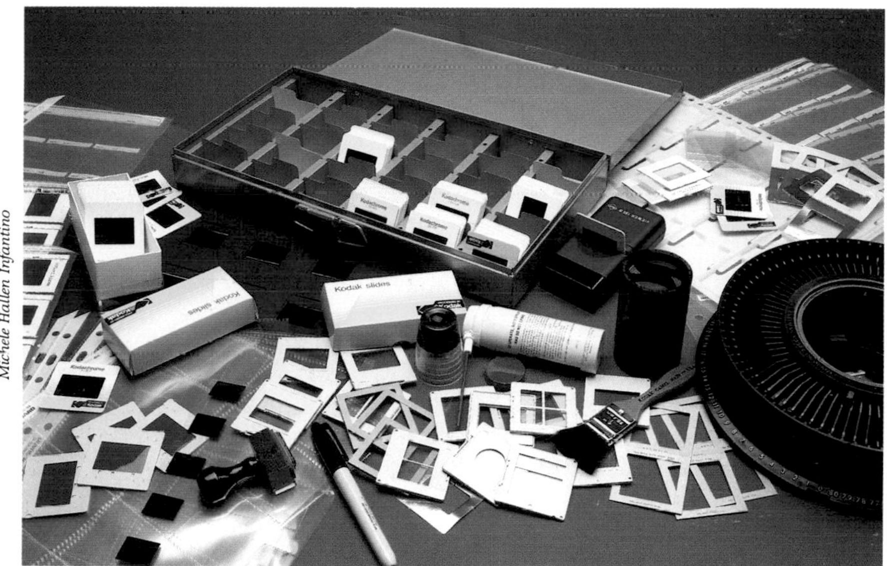

Michele Hallen Infantino

Finally, much of the useful life of a photograph is determined by your darkroom habits. All the storage precautions in the world can't prevent the damage caused by residual chemicals in an inadequately washed print or negative. If long-term keeping is important, publications are available that describe the proper processing procedures for long-term storage of photographic materials, which can include additional clearing steps, and protective treatment with toning solutions to enhance image stability.

There are many ways to store your negatives and prints—from plastic sleeves or envelopes, to binders that hold negatives and contact print sheets, to filing boxes for categorizing prints, negatives, and slides.

Michele Hallen Infantino

Displaying Prints

Although a photo album is the best way to protect your favorite pictures and keep a continuous record of your photographic interests, you also will probably want to highlight your most memorable photos by enlarging or special display. If you don't do your own darkroom work, you can have a commercial photofinisher produce enlargements as big as 16 × 24 inches. These machine-made prints are suitable for most purposes, but unusual negatives or slides or tricky subjects may benefit from the services of a custom photo lab. Because a custom lab hand-enlarges your slide or negative, a print will cost considerably more but it will be made to your exact specifications, including burning in, dodging, and adjusting color balance or contrast. Usually they will redo your print if you aren't satisfied, but don't expect them to work wonders with a bad negative or slide. Many labs are equipped to produce mural-sized prints as well, and some will reproduce photographs on cloth, glass, and other materials, although you can do this much less expensively in your own darkroom. (See page 292.)

The simplest way to display enlargements of a standard size is to use preassembled commercial frames. Such frames come in many forms, from old-fashioned, ornate borders to modern plastic boxes. You can also purchase metal section frames for easy home assembly at most art supply stores. Choose the style according to the feeling of the photograph itself and its compatibility with your decor. For a professional job on a special picture, though, you may want to go to a custom framer, who will offer you an enormous choice of frame styles and matting options. A less expensive alternative is a do-it-yourself framing shop, where the clerks will help you select the materials as well as use the special framing equipment.

Although some commercial preassembled frames come with pre-cut mats, they may not conform to the size of your picture. For this reason you may want to purchase a special tool for cutting a mat's customary beveled edges. With a little practice, this device will let you make professional-style mats, either for framing or for protection and presentation of separate prints. Matboards are available in a variety of weights, colors, and textures, but to avoid discoloration of the board and possible harm to your print, use one described as conservation, museum, or archival quality.

As well as protecting a print, a mat provides an attractive border that isolates and calls attention to the print. In making a mat, think carefully about the size of this border and the color of the board itself. Both will have a powerful effect on the way the print is perceived. There are no established rules about mat size; for example, sometimes the preciousness of a beautiful small print is enhanced by an oversize mat. In other cases a large mat can seem pretentious. If an

Michelle Hallen Infantino

There are many ways to present your photographs, and the choice should be based on which treatment is most suited to the particular image.

Michele Hallen Infantino

As shown below, you can dry mount your print on a larger board or mount it flush with the edges of a thicker board for a simple, bold look. In either case, dry mounting helps to keep the print flat. A professional-looking mat can be cut with a beveling knife or purchased pre-cut for the ultimate in artistic presentation (left). Don't let the mat overpower the image, either in size or color; a showy mat may distract the viewer. If the image is strong, a simple white or off-white mat may often be effective.

Michele Hallen Infantino

Michele Hallen Infantino

image is particularly strong, it is usually best served by a white mat; boards come in all shades of white, from bright white to creamy white.

Although some photographers simply secure their photograph with linen tape to a board that serves as a base beneath the mat itself, others adhere the print to it with dry-mounting tissue. Although you can do this with a household iron, a dry-mounting press requires less practice and poses less risk to your prints. You can find dry-mounting presses in many self-service frame shops, and custom photolabs offer dry-mounting services as well. You can also secure a print with a spray-on photo mounting cement, although this tends to be less permanent. Avoid using rubber cement or paste because it will eventually damage the print.

There are other ways to present your photographs. One popular practice is to mount a picture flush on a rigid material, such as hardboard, lightweight foam board, or even plywood if it is first resurfaced with a thin sheet of mounted board suitable for long-term keeping. Cut the board slightly smaller than the print so that after it is mounted you can trim the edges of the picture flush with the board. The raw edges of the board can be finished using a marking pen. This technique is particularly effective with thick material, since it gives the print a three-dimensional appearance.

Sharing Photographs

Michele Hallen Infantino

Standard 35 mm prints from your photo dealer make perfect postcards or additions to traditional greeting cards. Most dealers can also arrange to turn your favorite photographs into personalized greeting cards, social announcements, or invitations.

In its short history, photography has become a prominent part of our social lives. Prints or slides let us share events or experiences with others who have missed them, or remember them with those who were there. Exchanging photographs with friends and family near and far is one of the special joys of photography.

Many people even personalize their correspondence with postcards made from the standard 3½ × 5-inch print supplied by a photofinisher. Black-and-white photographic paper is manufactured in postcard size, with the back printed like a conventional postcard. Photographs can also serve as social proclamations—a photographic print of a newborn can transform a birth announcement into a very special document; wedding invitations and thank-you cards are also wonderfully enhanced by a commemorative photo. Many photofinishers offer greeting cards that you can slip a print into or will print a holiday greeting together with a negative or slide you supply. Photographs can also make very personal gifts and needn't be limited to the usual framed or mounted print. If you do your own darkroom work, for example, you can purchase a liquid black-and-white emulsion that can be applied to just about any surface, provided it can be safely immersed in the necessary processing chemicals. Bricks can serve as photographic bookends, and many other items can be personalized for a particular recipient. Other processes allow you to produce a photographic image on cloth, which can then be made into a pillow or garment. Check with your photo dealer. Some labs offer these services too.

A very familiar social use of photographs is the slide show. Although homemade slide shows may be greeted initially by good-humored groans, with careful editing and pacing they can provide a genuinely interesting and informative experience. Like a photo essay, a slide show should unfold in a logical way. Some pictures will establish a setting or mood; others will develop your idea or story. Try to make each successive slide relate to the preceding slide in a visual way (with similar or contrasting forms or colors, for instance) as well as in a narrative or thematic way. These considerations will shape your presentation, but be sure each individual image is strong enough to carry the story along. Don't use blurred pictures simply because they make a logical connection, and don't include repetitive pictures just because you like them all and can't choose between them. Avoid jarring changes between light- and darker-toned slides, and try not to jump back and forth between horizontal and vertical formats too often.

To edit your slides, spread them out on a light box or an inexpensive slide sorter, available at most photo dealers. Or you can improvise a light table with a storm window, a sheet of tracing or tissue paper, and a desk lamp. When you have a

Jerry Antos

Light tables for viewing and editing slides come in a variety of styles and a wide range of prices, but you can also use a sheet of rigid, translucent acrylic and a desk lamp or improvise with a storm window (see page 292).

sequence you like, it's helpful to mark the bottom left side of the slide as it faces you (looking like the original scene). When you load the projector tray, the mark should appear on the upper right corner facing away from the screen. It is also useful to insert a 2 × 2-inch piece of thin, opaque cardboard at the end of a tray so that the screen will not turn bright white between slides. Some new projectors have an automatic "dark slide" that darkens the screen after the last slide has been projected. The frequency of slide changes is a personal matter. You should vary the rate to maintain your audience's interest, increasing the speed to create excitement and decreasing it to enforce a more contemplative mood.

The refinements possible in producing a slide show are too numerous to describe here in detail. A dissolve-control unit, which fades the image from one projector as it brightens the image from another, avoiding the normal abrupt change that briefly darkens the screen is just one technique available to improve your presentation. Sound can be added, and the slides changed either manually or with a sound synchronizing device. Some of these devices can be rented for special occasions. If you are considering purchasing equipment, keep in mind that projectors themselves vary in slide capacity, lamp brightness, and the amount of automatic or remote control they allow, all of which will affect the price considerably. Projection lenses vary in aperture (hence brightness) and are available in different focal lengths to accommodate different room sizes. For example, you have to be eighteen feet away to produce an image forty inches wide with a 7-inch lens, whereas you can produce the same-size projection with a 3-inch lens from only eight feet. A zoom lens (usually 4 to 6 inches) lets you vary the image size from a single position. But, as with an enlarger, the bigger the projection is, the dimmer it will be. Like a zoom lens for a camera, a projection zoom has a smaller maximum aperture than lenses of fixed focal length do, and thus a dimmer projected image. Some lenses have a curved field for cardboard-mounted slides that bulge slightly when projected, whereas others have a flat field for rigid, glass-mounted slides. Viewing-screen surfaces also differ. Of the two most common types, a matte screen gives excellent sharpness and a wide angle of view, whereas a beaded glass screen gives substantially brighter images. However, the images on beaded glass screens are slightly softer and the viewing area is much more restricted. Synchronizers and dissolve units also vary greatly in their degree of sophistication.

Finally, one of the most enjoyable social aspects of photography is talking shop with other photographers, amateur or professional. One way to meet them is to take photography courses at local schools, colleges, or community centers. Another is to join a photography club. Some clubs specialize in certain kinds of work—nature, portraiture, etc.—so be sure your interests are compatible with theirs. Clubs often sponsor lectures and organize field trips, competitions, and exhibitions. In the United States, you can find a photo club in your area by writing the Photographic Society of America, 2005 Walnut Street, Philadelphia, Pennsylvania 19103.

Michele Hallen Infantino

An almost professional-level home slide show can be produced with the equipment shown here—two projectors joined by a dissolve unit and controlled by a sound synchronizer and a tape recorder.

Putting Photographs to Work

On a very practical level, a picture can be worth a thousand words. For settling insurance claims or verifying tax deductions after a fire, theft, or natural disaster, for example, it is helpful to have photographs of your valuables and other property to supplement written inventories. Take a complete series of pictures of your home, inside and out; close-ups of antiques, jewelry, electronic, and other small valuables; and detailed shots of large possessions such as cars, boats, or farm equipment. Store the photographs in a protected place, such as a bank safe deposit box. If any of your property is damaged, particularly large items that can't be easily transported, it is useful to photograph details of the damage to help a claims adjuster or even to use as legal evidence.

Greeba Klitgord

Neil Montanus

John Meyers

Whether your valuables are functional or not, photographing them is a way to protect them. If you are a serious collector, it is also a way to show your wares to other collectors without risk. For small shiny objects such as coins, close-up equipment (see page 110) is necessary, as well as polarizing filters for the camera lens and light sources.

Photographs may also help solve consumer complaints. Pictures accompanying a letter about a malfunctioning product can clearly illustrate what is wrong. And photographing different stages in the construction or repair of a house may later help prove a complaint or show the source of difficulty. Even if you are shopping for a home in a new location, pictures of the different houses you are shown will tell your family far more about the options than any verbal description could. Photographs can be a tremendous help in any long-distance sale or negotiation.

A photographic inventory of a collection, such as artwork, stamps, coins, etc., can be particularly important if you are actively involved in buying, selling, and trading. Many collectibles are too large, too valuable, or too fragile to carry around to show other collectors.

Likewise, artists and craftspeople are always in need of photographs of their work to submit for consideration by galleries, organizers of exhibitions, and grants programs. And many galleries and arts agencies keep working files of slides of artists' work for review by prospective clients. Since a poor-quality slide even of excellent work may undermine the artist's efforts, it's important to do a careful job.

A tripod is essential in photographing artwork, as is controlled artificial lighting. Artwork should rarely, if ever, be photographed by window light or in open shade outdoors, common approaches that result in blurred, off-color, and unevenly lighted slides or prints. Unless the artist has

Although we often photograph performances for ourselves, such photographs can be useful to the performers as well, for promotional purposes. Remember that performance lighting is often dramatic, and can throw off your camera's meter.

access to studio-strength flash equipment, it's best to use tungsten-balanced slide film with photoflood lamps. If color prints are needed, color negative film can be filtered accordingly. Because good detail is important, use low-speed, fine-grain films, whether shooting in black-and-white or color.

Two-dimensional artwork should be carefully squared up, using the controls on the tripod head and shifting the tripod and camera around until the edges of the artwork are parallel to the edges of the viewfinder. Leave extra room around the edges if you want a white border on a matted piece. Blank areas can be cropped out on the finished slide with slide-masking tape. If you have to photograph work under glass, the camera and tripod should be baffled against reflections with a generous piece of black paper or cloth, leaving only a hole to poke the lens through.

Flat work should be lighted with two lamps (more for a larger piece)—one on either side, at the same distance and angle (45 degrees or less) from the piece. Meter readings should be taken off a photographic grey card across its surface to make sure the light is even. If it isn't, the lamps should be adjusted and meter readings taken until it is. Watch out for glare on the sides of the image. If reflections on shiny surfaces are a problem, place polarizing filters over the light sources according to instructions and use a polarizing filter over your lens.

Russell Hart

Photography clubs often sponsor workshops and lectures by accomplished photographers, and such events are usually a part of any photography class. Clubs and classes are also a good way to keep tabs on photo contests and exhibition opportunities.

Anthony Ascrizzi

Avoid photographing three-dimensional artwork in a distracting environment. A large sheet of smooth paper will provide a good background; for larger objects, seamless background paper (see page 145) may be needed. Tape or tack the paper against a wall and let it curve gently onto the floor or a table, then place the object to be photographed on its horizontal surface. Choose a paper of neutral color or one that relates to or complements the work. Here, the sculptor/photographer has illuminated the background, allowing the light to drop off toward its top. This treatment emphasizes both the sculpture's shape and the highlights on its arms and head.

John LaPorta

While direct light can be used to photograph two-dimensional artwork, a single, diffused, or bounced light source is best for three-dimensional work. Generally, it should be somewhat to the side and slightly above the piece. Shadows on the surface of the object are important in describing its contours, but if they're too dark, they can be filled in with reflectors. White cards or a diffusing tent should be placed around reflective work such as silver or jewelry. Three-dimensional work should be photographed against a seamless background; it usually only detracts from artwork to include a recognizable background.

Bibliography

Adams, Ansel. ***The Camera.***
New York: New York Graphic Society, 1980.

Angel, Heather. ***The Book of Nature Photography.***
New York: Knopf, 1982.

Callahan, Harry:
Harry Callahan: Color.
Providence, Rhode Island: Matrix, 1980.
Eleanor.
Callaway Editions, 1984.
Water's Edge.
Callaway Editions, 1980.
Harry Callahan.
New York: Museum of Modern Art, 1967.

Cole, Stanley. ***Amphoto Guide to Basic Photography.***
Garden City, New York: Amphoto Books, 1978.

Craven, George M. ***Object and Image: An Introduction to Photography.*** 2nd ed.
Englewood Cliffs, New Jersey: Prentice-Hall, 1982.

Curtin, Dennis, and DeMaio, Joe. ***The Darkroom Handbook.***
New York: Van Nostrand Reinhold, 1979.

Davis, Phil. ***Photography.*** 4th ed.
Dubuque, Iowa: William C. Brown, 1982.

Editors of Eastman Kodak Company, Rochester, New York:
Advanced B/W Photography (KW-19). 1985.
The Art of Seeing (KW-20). 1984.
Basic Developing, Printing, Enlarging in Black-and-White (AJ-2). 1982.
Basic Printing, Developing, Enlarging in Color (AE-13). 1984.
Building a Home Darkroom (KW-14). 1981.
Close-Up Photography (KW-22). 1984.
Color Printing Techniques (KW-16). 1981.
Copying and Duplicating in Black-and-White and Color (M-1). 1984.
Creative Darkroom Techniques (AG-18). 1983.
Darkroom Expression (KW-21). 1984.
Electronic Flash (KW-12). 1985.
Existing-Light Photography (KW-17). 1984.
Kodak Complete Darkroom Dataguide (R-18). 1984.
Kodak Films—Color and Black-and-White (AF-1). 1985.
Kodak Guide to 35 mm Photography (AC-95). 1984.
Kodak Pocket Photoguide (AR-21). 1984.
Lenses for 35 mm Cameras (KW-18). 1984.
Photographing with Automatic Cameras (KW-11). 1984.
Planning and Producing Slide Programs (S-30). 1981.
Quality Enlarging with Kodak B/W Papers (G-1). 1982.
Using Filters (KW-13). 1984.

Kodak Library of Creative Photography, Published by TIME-LIFE Books in association with Kodak:
Take Better Pictures. 1984.
Make Color Work for You. 1984.
Photographing Friends and Family. 1984.
Mastering Composition and Light. 1984.
The Art of Portraits and the Nude. 1984.
How to Catch the Action. 1984.
Take Better Travel Photos. 1985.
Capture the Beauty in Nature. 1985.
Photographing the Drama of Daily Life. 1985.
Photographing Buildings and Cityscapes. 1985.
Print Your Own Pictures. 1985.
Creating Special Effects. 1985.
Set Up Your Home Studio. 1985.
Learning from the Experts. 1985.
Mastering Color. 1985.
Dealing with Difficult Situations. 1985.
The Magic of Black-and-White. 1985.
Extend Your Range. 1985.

Kodak Pocket Guide to 35 mm Photography (AR-22).
New York: Simon & Schuster, 1983.
Kodak Pocket Guide to Sports Photography (AR-23).
New York: Simon & Schuster, 1984.
Kodak Pocket Guide to Great Picture Taking (AR-24).
New York: Simon & Schuster, 1984.
Kodak Pocket Guide to Travel Photography (AR-25).
New York: Simon & Schuster, 1985.
Kodak Pocket Guide to Nature Photography (AR-26).
New York: Simon & Schuster. Forthcoming.

Eisenstadt, Alfred. ***Eisenstadt's Guide to Photography.***
New York: Penguin Books, 1981.

Feininger, Andreas:
The Complete Photographer.
Englewood Cliffs, New Jersey: Prentice-Hall, 1984.
Successful Photography.
Englewood Cliffs, New Jersey, Prentice-Hall, 1982.

Gassman, Arnold. ***Handbook for Contemporary Photography.***
4th ed. Rochester, New York: Light Impressions, 1977.

Goldberg, Vicki. ***Photography in Print: Writings from 1916 to the Present.***
New York: Simon & Schuster, 1981.

Grill, Tom, and Scanlon, Mark:
The Art of Scenic Photography: Technical and Aesthetic Guidelines for the Creative Photographer.
New York: Watson-Guptill, 1982.
The Essential Darkroom Book: A Complete Guide to Black and White Processing.
New York: Watson-Guptill, 1983.

Hedgecoe, John:
The Art of Color Photography.
New York: Simon & Schuster, 1983.
John Hedgecoe's Complete Photography Course.
New York: Simon & Schuster, 1983.

Holloway, Adrian. ***The Handbook of Photographic Equipment.***
New York: Knopf, 1981.

Horenstein, Henry. ***Black and White Photography: A Basic Manual.***
Boston, Massachusetts: Little, Brown, 1977.

Howell-Koehler, Nancy. ***Photo Art Processes.***
New York: Sterling, 1983.

Lahue, Kalton C. ***Petersen's Big Book of Photography.***
Los Angeles, California: Petersen, 1977.

Langford, Michael:
The Darkroom Handbook.
New York: Knopf, 1982.
The Step-by-Step Guide to Photography.
New York: Knopf, 1979.

Leibovitz, Annie. ***Photographs.***
New York: Pantheon, 1983.

Newhall, Beaumont:
The History of Photography: From 1830 to the Present Day. 5th rev. ed.
New York: New York Graphic Society, 1981.
Photography: Essays and Images: Illustrated Readings in the History of Photography.
New York: New York Graphic Society, 1981.

Patterson, Freeman. ***Photography of Natural Things.***
New York: Van Nostrand, Reinhold, 1982.

Porter, Eliot:
In Wildness is the Preservation of the World.
California: Sierra Club Books, 1962.
Intimate Landscapes.
New York: Metropolitan Museum of Art, 1979.

Porter, Eliot, and Porter, Jonathan. ***All Under Heaven: The Chinese World.***
New York: Pantheon Books, 1983.

Rhode, Robert B. ***Introduction to Photography.*** 4th ed.
New York: Macmillan, 1981.

Rosen, Marvin J. ***Introduction to Photography: A Self-Directing Approach.*** 2nd ed.
Boston, Massachusetts: Houghton Mifflin, 1982.

Sacilotto, Deli. ***Photograph and Printmaking Techniques.***
New York: Watson-Guptil, 1982.

Steichen, Edward. ***The Family of Man.***
New York: Simon and Schuster, 1955.

Swedlund, Charles. ***Photography: A Handbook of History, Materials, and Processes.***
New York: Holt, Rinehart, and Winston, 1981.

Szarkowski, John. ***Looking at Photographs: One Hundred Pictures from the Collection of the Museum of Modern Art.***
New York: New York Graphic Society, 1973.

TIME-LIFE Library of Photography, Alexandria, Virginia: TIME-LIFE, Inc.:
The Art of Photography. rev. ed. 1982.
The Camera. rev. ed. 1981.
Caring for Photographs. rev. ed. 1982.
Color. rev. ed. 1981.
Documentary Photography. rev. ed. 1983.
The Great Photographers. rev. ed. 1983.
The Great Themes. rev. ed. 1982.
Photographing Children. rev. ed. 1983.
Photographing Nature. rev. ed. 1981.
Photography as a Tool. rev. ed. 1982.
Photojournalism. rev. ed. 1983.
Special Problems. rev. ed. 1982.
The Studio. rev. ed. 1982.
Travel Photography. rev. ed. 1982.

Tucker, Anne. ***Woman's Eye.***
New York: Knopf, 1973.

Vestal, David. ***The Craft of Photography.*** rev. ed.
New York: Harper & Row, 1978.

White, Minor. ***Mirrors, Messages, Manifestations.***
New York: Aperture, 1969.

White, Minor, and Zakia, Richard. ***The New Zone System Manual.*** rev. ed.
Dobbs Ferry, New York: Morgan & Morgan, 1984.

Index

The New Joy of Photography

was set in the Zapf International family of typefaces
by DEKR Corporation of Woburn, Massachusetts.

The color separations and camera work were supplied by
Color Response, Inc. of Charlotte, North Carolina.

W. A. Krueger Company, of Brookfield, Wisconsin,
printed and bound the book on 70 pound S.D. Warrenfloweb
stock.